# ENGLAND

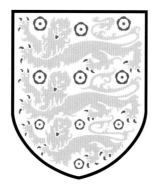

# ENGLAND

## THE
## OFFICIAL
## F.A.
## HISTORY

## NIALL EDWORTHY

*Virgin*

Author Acknowledgements

I would like to thank FA librarian David Barber, a human encyclopaedia
of football, for his saintly patience and anecdotal gems. I'm also indebted
to Bryon Butler of the BBC and Daily Telegraph whose five minutes of advice
saved me several weeks of fruitless labour. My thanks go lastly to Ben Dunn
whose enthusiasm and encouragement have been invaluable.

Publisher Acknowledgements

The publishers would like to thank the following for their help and
enthusiasm: Oliver Frey, Roger Kean and everyone at Prima Creative Services.
Mark Trowbridge and Stephanie May at Allsport, and Philip Burnham-Richards
at Hulton for picture research.

All pictures courtesy of The Football Association and Allsport/Hulton Deutsch.

First published in Great Britain in 1997 by
Virgin Books
an imprint of Virgin Publishing Ltd
332 Ladbroke Grove
London W10 5AH

A catalogue record for this book is available from the British Library.

ISBN 1 85227 699 1

Design and repro by Prima Creative Services

Printed and bound by Amilcare Pizzi in Italy

# CONTENTS

# 1872–1900

# AN ENGLISHMAN'S VISION

*The birth of international football took place in the unlikely setting of a muddy cricket pitch in central Scotland in 1872, but it was conceived several years earlier in the mind of a man with an almost evangelical zeal to see the game take root as a national pastime.*

CW Alcock, one of the founder members of The Football Association in 1863, was one of football's great visionaries. He was the brains behind both the FA Cup and the annual fixture between England and Scotland – two events which, playing on local and national rivalries, sparked an unimaginable interest in the game which spread like wildfire, first through Britain, then Europe and shortly to Africa, South America and beyond. Thanks to Alcock's imagination, football quickly became a national obsession and by the turn of the century a host of clubs had been established in the heart of the country's industrial communities. The England–Scotland fixture drew crowds bordering on 100,000 and there were nationwide debates over selection and tactics long before and long after each fiercely contested encounter.

The original intention of the contest had been to help promote "Association" football as opposed to "Rugby" north of the border where the handling game was relatively well-established. Alcock had witnessed the great interest aroused by rugby's first ever

international between England and Scotland in Edinburgh earlier in 1872 and saw the publicity potential of an Association equivalent. It is worth remembering that at the time, football outside the

*"The dribbling game" quickly caught the public imagination north and south of the border*

**ENGLAND:** The Official F.A. History

cloistered, ordered world of the country's top public schools, was considered in many quarters to be nothing more than a loosely organised riot.

A handful of unofficial internationals had already taken place in London in 1870 and 1871 between the Wanderers, a team largely made up of former public schoolboys, and some London-based "Caledonians" with a few all-comers to make up the numbers (two of the unofficial "Scots" actually went on to play officially for England). The matches were not much more than knockabout affairs between friends, but they had been competitive enough to inspire Alcock to issue a challenge to the Scots for a genuine contest.

If the arrival of international football was meant to be an exciting prospect, little of that thrill comes across in Alcock's official recording of his brainwave. His stark announcement in the FA minutes on 3rd October 1872 reads: "In order to further the interests of the Association in Scotland, it was decided during the current season that a team should be sent to Glasgow to represent England."

Logistical problems almost scuppered the contest, however. First, there was the problem of organisation since the Scottish had no equivalent of the FA. Who did England ask for a game? In the end, Queens Park, Scotland's leading club, picked up the gauntlet thrown down by the English – to the fury of the country's rugby players. In an angry letter to *The Scotsman* newspaper, Scotland's rugby fraternity claimed that football players were not fit to represent the country when national pride was at stake.

There was also the problem of money for both teams. There were no official funds to pay the England party's travelling expenses (although because most of the players were public school and Oxbridge educated, it is hard to imagine them struggling to raise the cash for a return train fare to Scotland). The FA solved the problem by asking the clubs to foot the bill, which they did without hesitation. By contrast, the majority of Scots players had neither private incomes nor an established network of clubs to help them financially.

The original fixture had been scheduled for

*Early international football as explained by "The Graphic" in 1872*

Monday 24th November, but the Scots objected on the grounds that a day away from their businesses would mean lost income and they were only persuaded to play when the match was switched to the following Saturday.

Injury, cruelly, was to rule out Alcock who had picked up a groin strain playing for the Old Etonians in the week before. He had been due to captain the side, but still travelled with the party to the West of Scotland Cricket Club in Partick and played his part in the event he masterminded – as an umpire. Alcock, a future secretary and then vice-president of the FA, picked himself for England's first five internationals, but played in just one – a 2–2 draw at Kennington Oval in 1875. Much admired for the accuracy of his shooting, the great man scored England's first goal and greatly impressed the man from *The Sportsman* who reported: "There it was breasted by the England captain and he pertinaciously adhered to it until he had got it securely over the Scottish goal-line."

A crowd of between three and four thousand (generating gate receipts of £109) turned out for the match on 30th November, more out of curiosity and patriotism than any great interest in the "dribbling" game. It wasn't, after all, every weekend in the mid-19th century that an international sporting contest came to Partick. The reporter from the *Northern British Mail* said the match took place "in the presence of the largest assemblage seen at a football match in Scotland – there being close on 4,000 spectators, including a good number of ladies".

The English had been fully expected to walk away with a handsome victory, the intention of the match being to put on a thrilling exhibition of football skills that would capture the imagination of the Scottish public. But the Scots, despite being smaller and lighter by nearly two stone per player, held their own against their more powerful and accomplished opponents. The match finished goalless but far from disappointed the crowd who, by all accounts, went home in a state of great excitement.

No one, though, could accuse the two teams of adopting defensive tactics with England playing in a 1–1–8 formation and the Scots a slightly more conservative 2–2–6. The Scotland team, who played in dark blue, gave the visitors three hearty cheers as they left the field – a compliment returned by the white-shirted Englishmen. At dinner that evening, the players arranged a re-match in London for the following year.

The dribbling skills of England's first ever captain, CJ Ottoway (Cuthbert to his teammates), were said to be the highlight of the game. Ottoway, who also played cricket for Kent and Middlesex and was an Oxford blue in football, rackets, athletics and real tennis, died six years later at the tragically early age of 28. After a night out dancing, he took an open cab home, caught a chill and passed away a few days later.

The reporter from *Bell's Life* of London sent home a glowing account of what he had seen, describing the match as a "splendid display of football in the really scientific sense of the word... and admired by the crowd who kept the utmost order". The *Northern British Mail* thought the match proved the superiority of Association over Rugby Football. The paper's match report extolled the simplicity of the sport and admired "the skillful and always pleasing dribble... It will readily be admitted that the Association game is one which will commend itself to players who dread the harder work of the rugby mode".

Unfortunately, there is no photographic record of the first ever international as the local photographer did not receive a pre-match guarantee that the players would buy his prints. Fearing he would lose money on the day, he stayed at home. Nor are there any pictures from the return match at Kennington Oval the following year, where the best efforts of the "photograph operator" collapsed amid chaotic scenes because the teams kept pulling faces at the camera.

England won the return match 4–2 at the Oval on 8th March when Old Etonian Alexander Bonsor, a brewer by trade, scored the first goal and had the distinction of being England's top-scorer for all of about ten minutes before he was overhauled by the game's two-goal hero, William Kenyon-Slaney, a Grenadier Guard.

In the immediate years that followed England and Scotland's first encounter, the game boomed north of the border, with a host of clubs springing into existence. And it was an irony not lost on the increasingly frustrated England team that Scotland dominated the first two decades of international football. The aim of establishing a regular annual fixture between the two countries had been for England to teach, and Scotland to learn. But of the first ten matches, England won just twice and were plunged into an early crisis of confidence when they crashed to a 6–1 defeat in 1881 and a 5–1 defeat in 1882.

Though performances began to improve in the second half of the 1880s, England's record against the Scots in the first two decades of competition makes dismal reading. They won just four times in 20 games. (England might have been spared their humiliation

when a feud about whether the ball could be thrown in either direction almost led to the abandonment of the annual fixture in 1882. A delegation from Scotland finally resolved the issue with their English counterparts in a Manchester hotel just days before the match.)

The part played by patriotism in developing the game on either side of Hadrian's Wall cannot be overestimated. Whenever England and Scotland met, it was not just the sporting reputation of the 22 players at stake but the pride of two neighbouring countries with centuries of rivalry, in some form or other, behind them. The foundation in 1882 of the Corinthians, who were to have an immeasurable impact on the development and image of the game, came about as a direct result of England's sequence of ego-bruising defeats to the Scots in those early years.

England were forced to look at ways of improving

*Goalmouth scramble Victorian style: England v. Scotland at the Oval, 1878*

**ENGLAND:** The Official F.A. History

their game as the country's burgeoning band of followers demanded a change in tactics and selection to defeat the Scots. It was this sense of humiliation south of the border which stung a group of largely ex Varsity footballers to assemble a team which would play together on a regular basis. The Corinthian plan was to create a pool of players with a strong understanding of how each other played from which England could draw the bulk of the team.

The England team of the first ten years or so were largely a team of dribblers, but despite their individual crowd-pleasing skills, they rarely beat the Scots, who quickly realised the benefits of a passing game. The Scotland team, whose muddier pitches were less conducive to the dribbling game, were quick to understand that beating three or four players before being shoulder-charged off the ball might well draw a ripple of applause from the crowd but it was not the most effective way of getting from one end of the pitch to the other. (It is almost reassuring to know that over 120 years later, England coach Terry Venables felt the need to remind Paul Gascoigne, his sublimely talented midfielder, of these harsh facts of football life.)

The Scotland team were helped in the early years by the fact that most players were drawn from the Glasgow area, meaning they could train together regularly. The England players, by contrast, were spread all over the country and only met up on the train to Glasgow or at the pre-match dinner in London. NL "Pa" Jackson, the founding father of the Corinthians, pointed out that the Scotland players also had the advantage over their English counterparts of playing all year round as opposed to just in the winter months.

CW Alcock, a man well ahead of his times, was among the first to realise that England needed to develop their passing game. But his wisdom was ignored and the Scottish Football Association secretary, Robert Livingstone, could barely disguise his glee at England's pig-headed refusal to adapt their tactical approach. "They play a selfish game," said Livingstone. "It is a style of play the consequences of which are suicidal."

International football was only in its infancy, but its inventors were already being left behind and it took two decades before they were to catch up. An early history of football, published at the turn of the century, called *Association Football and The Men Who Made It* spelt out England's early failure to make the most of the abundant talent from the country's rapidly-expanding collection of clubs. "While the English were taking their games with due leisure and some ease, the Scotch players went far ahead of them in the sheer mechanical science of the game, in wild enthusiasm and violent paroxysms of club favour," it said.

England's defeats provoked frustration among the public and illustrated the passions that international football were starting to arouse. England were thrashed 7–2 by Scotland in Glasgow in 1878, sparking jubilation among the crowd who reportedly threw their hats and walking sticks into the air at the end of the match. Shortly afterwards, *Bell's Life* published a letter signed by "A Disgusted Englishman" which read: "The England players we had down this time were a splendid lot of players individually, but to my idea they played very selfishly, each one of them appearing to play for himself and not for the success of the side."

The complaints, however, merely testified to the growing importance attached to the international contest. The popularity of the annual fixture, just seven years after the first encounter, is captured by the description of the build-up to the 1878 match which appeared in *Bell's Life*. "All available conveyances were picked up long before two o'clock and a continuous stream of hansoms, dog-carts and buses kept pouring their living freight to the foot of Hampden Hill... every inch of the locality was covered by spectators. In some places, it was packed like herrings in a barrel, but the majority bore it with Christian resignation."

Through the influence of the amateur Corinthians in the South and the professionals in the North and the Midlands, England improved steadily after their disastrous start to the 1880s. But they did not break the Scottish dominance until the 1890s, when professionalism, which was legalised in England

*The English*
*International Football*
*Association Team, 1890*

would field the players who had failed to get into the team to play Scotland. That remained the policy until 1893 when it was decided that England would field one team of professionals and one team of amateurs who would play either the Welsh or the Irish. The matches would take place on the same day or consecutive days and allow the selectors to choose the best team to face Scotland. The system remained well into the next century.

in 1885, prompted a mass exodus south of Scottish players. The Scots who sought employment with English clubs were banned from representing the national side until the embargo was lifted in 1896.

England made the most of the argument raging north of the border and it was not until 1897 that they lost their first match of the decade. The damaging split in the Scottish game, though, only partly explained England's revival.

The competitiveness of the clubs and the tactical influence of the Corinthians was starting to pay off. Even the great Scottish player Walter Arnott was forced to concede: "The Corinthians, who have perfected the tactics of three inside forwards, have created as good and effective a style as I have seen." The England renaissance was greeted with relief at home and welcomed by Alcock, who reflected after England's 4–1 win in Glasgow in 1892 that "a long sequence of victories by Scotland may have had a prejudicial effect on football south of the Tweed".

By then, Wales and Ireland had entered the international fray. England played their first match against the Welsh in 1879 at Kennington Oval, but only managed a narrow 2–1 win over the newcomers. Three years later, they sent a team to Belfast to play Ireland for the first time and rattled up a 13–0 win, which remains their biggest ever victory. In the early matches against the other home countries, England

*G.O. Smith:*
*the Alan Shearer*
*of the 1890s*

**ENGLAND: The Official F.A. History**

Professionalism was the dominant issue of the day. The champions of amateurism were generally to be found among the university-educated or officer-trained classes, who could afford not to be rewarded for their efforts on the football field. They found themselves in conflict with the clubs based in the North and Midlands, who sought to pay their generally working-class players either in the form of "expenses" or "benefits". As competition between the clubs grew more intense, the club owners sought to secure the services of their players with financial rewards. "Shamateurism" was rife by the 1880s and although the FA was opposed to paying players, it realised that the only way to stamp out abuse and irregularities was to accept professionalism as a reality.

Amateurism continued in an uneasy coexistence with the professional code well into the next century and, although England grew less dependent on amateurs, it was not until the 1920s that it became clear that the unpaid part-timers could no longer compete at the highest level. Once again, Alcock had shown himself to be ahead of most of his contemporaries when he argued the case for professionalism, declaring: "Professionals are a necessity to the growth of the game and I object to the idea that they are utter outcasts." But paid footballers remained outcasts to the extent that even though they played side by side with their amateur counterparts in the national side, they ate at separate tables and called the captain of the team "Sir".

By 1899, the entire England team – with the exception of the captain, the great GO Smith – were all paid for playing football. But the attitude of the Birmingham hotel which accommodated the England team in that year illustrated that professionals were still a long way from being respected among the higher echelons of society. The hotel only agreed to put up the team after repeated reassurances from the FA persuaded the hotel that they could bank on the good behaviour of the players.

A year earlier, the two amateurs in the England side, after some painful soul-searching and head-scratching, condescended to take their lunch with the rest of the players for fear of appearing too aloof. The gesture was not exactly socialism on the rampage, but it did show that professionalism was slowly eroding the moral authority of the amateurs.

By the 1890s, international and club football had taken deep root in British life and many of the events and issues of that decade have a strange familiarity to them. Tactics and selection for the national side were hotly contested up and down the country. Hooliganism began to emerge as a serious social problem, with several matches having to be abandoned

## G.O. SMITH

| Position | Centre forward |
| --- | --- |
| Caps/goals | 20/11 |
| Debut | v Ireland (6–1) in Birmingham 23rd February 1893 |
| Last match | v Scotland (2–2) at Crystal Palace 30th March 1901 |
| Club | Oxford University, Old Carthusians, Corinthians |

The greatest centre-forward of his day, despite his refusal to head the ball and despite being a chronic asthmatic and despite being slow and small. CB Fry, the great all-round sportsman and scholar, described why Smith was such an influential player.

"What made him was his skill in elusive movement, his quickness in seeing how best to bestow passes, his accuracy and his remarkable penetrative dribbling. He swung a marvellously heavy foot in shooting – always along the turf and terrifically swift." Smith, England's captain for most of the 1890s, passionately believed a team must be playing wrongly if forwards needed to head. A prep school teacher, he was also an outstanding cricketer, whose century at Lord's won the Varsity match for Oxford in 1896. He was the first England player to be capped 20 times, but never really impressed the Scots who thought him overrated.

ASSOCIATION FOOTBALL

The team who represented England in 1895. The founder of the Corinthians, " Pa " Jackson, is standing on extreme left. Those seated include W. J. Bassett (left), now Chairman of West Bromwich Albion, with Steve Bloomer and J. Goodall, the two famous Derby County players, and R. C. Gosling. Standing at the back is J. W. Sutcliffe, who played both Association and Rugby for England

## BILLY BASSETT

| | |
|---|---|
| Position | Outside-right |
| Caps/goals | 16/7 |
| Debut | v Ireland (5–1) in Belfast |
| | 31st March 1888 |
| Last match | v Scotland (1–2) in Glasgow |
| | 4th April 1896 |
| Club | West Bromwich Albion |

Bassett's reputation as one of the most dangerous players of his generation was such that on an FA tour match in Germany in 1899, he was pursued everywhere he went by a defender who followed his instructions to man-mark the great winger to an extreme. Amused by the attention he was receiving, Bassett walked around the back of goal at one point – only to be followed by his German marker.

Perhaps the greatest player ever produced by West Bromwich Albion, Bassett became the best paid player on £43 a week. He later became a director and then chairman of the club he served so loyally. Bassett cut a slight figure at just 5'5" but he was very quick and terrorised opposition defences with his surging runs and pinpoint accurate crosses. He loved the bigger grounds like Kennington Oval and Crystal Palace, where he would often kick the ball up the touchline and sprint off the pitch to chase it.

His inspirational performance in WBA's 2–1 FA Cup win over Preston North End in 1888 led to his call-up to the England side. He had a long-running contest for his place in the international side with Charlie Athersmith of local rivals Aston Villa. When he died in 1937, the FA asked that, in addition to two minutes' silence before WBA's FA Cup semi-final against Preston, there should also be a rendition of his favourite hymn *Abide With Me*. Albion protested in vain, claiming their players were upset enough and that playing the moving hymn would reduce them to emotional wrecks ahead of the vital match.

as a result of crowd trouble. The FA acted to allay fears of match-fixing by banning betting on matches by players and officials. Lawyers began representing players at disciplinary hearings as they tried to have suspensions and fines for being sent off overturned.

Football was booming. In the 1890 match between England and Scotland the gates at Hampden Park were shut half an hour before kick off with 30,000 (the official figure) crammed inside, before the pressure of those locked out burst down the gates. "The touchline became a scene of surging humanity," reported the *Daily Mail*. In 1895, 30,000 – a record for an international in England – descended on Goodison Park to watch England's 3–0 win over the Scots. A year

later, 300 soldiers and policemen struggled to contain a wild crowd of 60,000 at Celtic Park. The *Daily Mail* was disturbed by the behaviour of the spectators, reporting: "It was an ugly scene while it lasted, however, and the press seats for 200 pressmen from all over the world were threatened with demolition."

In the same year women tried to get in on the act when British Ladies FC played their first match at Crouch End, reputedly wearing night-caps, heavy woollen skirts and shin pads. A crowd of 10,000 turned out, but the match was dismissed by the football authorities as a nonsense.

The 1890s were glorious days for the England team as they put an end to 20 years of Scottish success. Alcock, by now a vice-president of the FA, felt confident enough to announce: "English football would have appeared to reach a high, not far removed from the highest possible standard."

## STEVE BLOOMER

| | |
|---|---|
| Position | Inside-right |
| Caps/goals | 23/28 |
| Debut | v Ireland (9–0) at Derby |
| | 9th March 1895 |
| Last match | v Scotland (1–1) at Newcastle |
| | 6th April 1907 |
| Club | Derby, Middlesbrough |

England's top striker before the Great War, Bloomer scored 19 in his first 14 internationals, including five against Wales in Cardiff in 1896. With his slight build, closely-cropped hair and ghost-white complexion, "Paleface" Bloomer was an unlikely looking athlete. His phenomenal goal tally of 28 goals in 23 internationals made him England's all-time top scorer until Nat Lofthouse finally surpassed him almost 50 years later.

He was the star of his day along with Welshman Billy Meredith, and was said to be able to score from all angles and distances. But there was more to his game than just finishing. "He had the golden gift of splitting the defence with one arrow-like, pinpointed

pass," said Ivan Sharpe, who played with Bloomer at Derby County. Another contemporary writer said: "He is as crafty as an Oriental and as slippery as an eel, and is much given to dealing out electric shocks to goalkeepers at the end of a sinuous run."

He signed for the Rams in 1891 on wages of 7s 6d (37.5p) per week, before moving to Middlesbrough in 1906 for £750. He later returned to Derby and played his last game for the club in 1914, five days before his 40th birthday. Following his retirement he went to Germany to coach, but was interned in Ruhleben at the outbreak of the First World War. He and his fellow inmates began to play football with a ball made from rolled-up paper, socks and twine, before the prisoners (who included a number of other top British sportsmen) were allowed to form a proper Association. Bloomer spent the duration of the war playing football almost every day.

He returned to England as general assistant at Derby in the late 1930s, after a series of coaching jobs abroad. But his health was in decline and, suffering from an alleged drink problem, he was sent on a cruise by the club in 1938, but died three weeks later.

# 1900-1914

# A WORLD OF THEIR OWN

*As the new century dawned,*
*football was well-established as a mass-spectator sport,*
*so much so that crowd enthusiasm led to football's first major tragedy*
*in 1902. Up to the First World War, only Scotland provided England*
*with a serious challenge as fledgling sides from Scandinavia, France,*
*Hungary and Austria were dispatched with ease.*

England entered the 20th century in optimistic mood, but they were given a rude reminder that there were still two major forces in world football when their cousins from north of the Tweed subjected them to a 4–1 defeat. The match, which took place at Parkhead on 7th April 1900, became known as the Rosebery international after the Scottish team were persuaded by racehorse owner Lord Rosebery to take the field wearing his racing colours of salmon pink and primrose. The dashing new look of the Scots, though, may well have been lost on the majority of the jubilant Parkhead crowd, which was reportedly awash with Scotland's national drink. "As soon as the gates were opened the people flocked in and the long wait was enlivened by patriotic songs, not to mention whisky," reported the *Football Sun.*

Two years later, football suffered its first major crowd disaster when a stand at Ibrox collapsed during the England-Scotland match, leaving 25 dead and hundreds injured. One of the strange aspects of that tragic April day was that most of the crowd were unaware of the catastrophe in their midst. Early reports

suggested that there were only a handful of injuries and so it was decided by the authorities to continue with the game in order to avoid widespread panic.

Celtic and Queens Park had also put in a bid to stage the match, but it was awarded to Rangers on the strength of the club's new stand. Ibrox had an official capacity of 80,000 but at least another 20,000 were said to be inside the ground when overcrowding led to the disaster. Unable to get into the Eastern stand, hundreds of fans descended on the new structure, which was made from wooden planks laid out across metal pylons.

Six minutes into the game, part of the stand gave way under the pressure and seven rows of spectators crashed 40 feet to the ground below. One of the few bright features of that dark day was the subsequent strengthening of the bond between the two footballing nations, with the English clubs as well as the FA raising over £4,000 for the Ibrox Disaster Fund.

*Bob Crompton, captain of England,*
*inventor of gadgets and*
*envied owner of a motor car*

## BOB CROMPTON

| | |
|---|---|
| Position | Right-back |
| Caps/goals | 41/0 |
| Debut | v Wales (0–0) at Wrexham |
| | 3rd March 1902 |
| Last match | v Scotland (1–3) at Sheffield |
| | 4th April 1914 |
| Club | Blackburn |

Bob Crompton was a reluctant star who went on to set England records for most caps and length of international career which stood until after the Second World War. Crompton was a very keen swimmer and water polo player, and it took Blackburn Rovers months to drag him away from his preferred sports after they spotted him playing Sunday League football.

He clearly grew to like his "third sport" as he proceeded to serve Rovers in some capacity or another for 40 years. In his playing days for England he formed a famous full-back partnership with Jesse Pennington, and went on to collect 41 caps at a time when international matches were relatively rare. A large, powerful man with a larger-than-life personality, he captained his country with enormous authority.

Crompton was not fast but he once kept pace with the speedy Alec Smith of Rangers in a match between the English and Scottish leagues, later admitting he had been holding the Scotsman's shorts. The more critical Rovers supporters felt he had a tendency to balloon his clearances, get in the way of the goalkeeper and not apply his considerable bulk to the shoulder charge frequently enough.

For all that, Crompton was one of the most famous and accomplished players of his day. After a draw with Scotland in 1911, the *Daily Mail* said: "Crompton, the England captain, rarely plays a poor game. He generally plays grandly. On Saturday he was superb…his kicking and tackling were perfect and the certainty with which he dashed in and robbed his opponents of the ball was uncanny." A plumber by trade as well as a keen inventor of gadgets, Crompton caused a stir in 1907 when he arrived at Ewood Park in a motor car – then a major status symbol.

The original match finished 1–1 but was later downgraded to a "friendly". It was replayed at Birmingham a month later and ended 2–2, with all the proceeds going to the fund.

Between the turn of the century and the First World War, Scotland continued to provide the only serious challenge in international football. England lost just seven of the 53 official internationals in that period, with five of those defeats coming at the hands of the Scots and the other two by Ireland. Wales, who had no league of their own, won the Home Championship for the first time in 1907, but even that was considered by critics of the day as a type of triumph for English football. "Internationals have lost their significance," moaned the *Daily Mail.* "When we oppose Scotland, Wales or Ireland, we are opposing not these countries but English football."

England's tactics in the 1906 contest infuriated the 100,000 Scottish crowd and led to months of debate before the rules of the game were changed. England kept one man at the back and pushed the rest of their defence to within 20 yards of the Scottish goal-line. At the time, there was no rule about offside being restricted to the defender's half and the law insisted on three players being between the attacker and the goal at the moment of the crucial pass. England's tactics were considered to be inside the rules of the game, but outside its spirit.

A nationwide debate followed before the International Board altered its rule book and restricted offside to within a team's own half. Despite England's negative tactics, they still lost 2–1 to the barely contained delight of their outraged Scottish spectators.

England's first encounters with non-British opposition, on a tour to Central Europe in 1908, did little to dim their sense of superiority. Austria were beaten 6–1 and then 11–1 in Vienna, while the Hungarians succumbed 7–0 in Budapest and Bohemia kept the score down to a relatively respectable 4–0 in Prague. England refused to play any of the Axis powers of the First World War until the 1930s, but when they finally emerged from one of their occasional periods of self-imposed isolation, they were to encounter an Austrian side of very different quality.

In 1909 the summer tour was repeated with equally thumping wins over the Austrians and Hungarians. They turned out to be England's last games against foreign opposition until after the War. The embarrassing ease of their seven wins – during which they scored 48 goals – persuaded the authorities that the Amateur team would provide a more equal contest in future. But even they were rarely stretched, winning 21 of their 26 matches and losing just three.

The England Amateur team, representing Great Britain, had proved its quality during the London Olympics of 1908 where they won the gold medal. The events at White City underlined the gulf between Britain and the rest of the Continent on the football pitch. Sweden, inspired by the famous "Clydeside riveters", sent a team more for the experience than in any hope of winning. (The "riveters" were a group of Scottish workmen, who had been employed by the Swedish authorities to carry out a huge boiler-building contract in Gothenburg and who would spend every free hour playing football. Their recreation fired the imagination of the locals and within a few years the game had taken root in the country.)

Sweden were beaten 12–1 by England and only Denmark put up any kind of resistance before losing 2–0 in the final. The French, rather optimistically, had sent over two teams in the expectation of landing a medal. But any hopes of seeing the *tricolore* being raised to the sound of the *Marseillaise* were emphatically dashed when both teams were routed by Denmark, the B team going down a creditable 9–0 compared to the 17–1 suffered by the A team.

The spectacular failure of France's elite team might be partly explained by the distinctly unathletic behaviour of the players, who demanded that they were supplied with strong cigarettes at half-time. England, meanwhile, went on to underline their effortless superiority over continental all-comers at the Gothenburg Olympics four years later. There, they

# VIVIAN WOODWARD

| | |
|---|---|
| Position | Centre-forward |
| Caps/goals | 23/29 |
| Debut | v Ireland (4–0) at Wolverhampton 14th February 1903 |
| Last match | v Wales (3–0) at Millwall 13th March 1911 |
| Club | Tottenham, Chelsea |

Vivian Woodward was England's most celebrated forward in the early years of the new century who, like his hero GO Smith, remained an amateur for his entire career but was considered to be as good as any professional. Despite being a slightly built figure, Woodward was a mesmerising dribbler with a deadly shot capable of holding his own in the roughest of defensive company.

Perhaps it should be said that he only scored once against Scotland – England's only serious rivals at the time – and a hatful of his goals came against European sides who had only recently discovered the game. Rated by the famous referee JT Holcroft as the finest forward he had ever seen, Woodward helped England, representing Great Britain, win the Olympic gold medal in 1908. Two years earlier he scored eight goals against France, and in 1909 he hit ten against Holland in amateur internationals.

Woodward was equally comfortable with either foot and could play inside, outside or centre-forward. "Rarely have I seen a forward do so much with so little apparent effort," wrote Charlie Buchan. Woodward was captain of the Footballers' Battalion team in the Great War and said to be an enthusiastic pigeon-keeper in later life.

*No Donkey: Vivian Woodward, the greatest goalscorer of his generation*

crushed Hungary and Austria en route to the final where they again beat Denmark 2–0.

The 1909 Home Championship came within a few days of being cancelled, as football got caught up in the industrial unrest sweeping the country. The Players' Union had been established a few years earlier and had affiliated itself to the General Federation of Trade Unions. Strike action in support of the miners threatened to bring the country to a standstill, but just days before the first Home International, the Players' Union said the matches would go ahead so as not to disappoint the public. But that was not to be the end of the matter as an unfortunately worded statement by the Union announcing the intention to play led to another national uproar.

The statement had said England would play and

*England players confer during a match in 1911*

"do their utmost to win" – a turn of phrase which convinced the press and public that the team had contemplated deliberately losing. In one of the more bizarre episodes of England's history, the FA made the players sign a statement declaring their determination to win. England won the Championship by beating Ireland, Wales and Scotland without conceding a goal, but it can only be imagined what the response of the nation might have been had England lost.

The relatively small crowd of 35,000 that turned out for England's 2–0 win over Scotland at Crystal Palace that year was attributed to the Oxford and Cambridge Boat Race taking place a few miles away.

England lost to Ireland for the first time in 1913

**ENGLAND:** The Official F.A. History

## SAM HARDY

| | |
|---|---|
| Position | Goalkeeper |
| Caps/goals | 21/0 |
| Debut | v Ireland (1–0) at Everton 16th February 1907 |
| Last match | v Scotland (5–4) at Sheffield 10th April 1920 |
| Club | Liverpool, Aston Villa, Nottingham Forest |

Born in Chesterfield like so many other great goalkeepers (Gordon Banks, Bob Wilson, Alan Stevenson and John Osborne), Hardy set all standards for his position in a long career (1902–25) interrupted by the First World War. Although he was unusually small for a goalkeeper, his positional sense – like Banks's – was so good that Charlie Buchan swore he never saw him make a full-length dive. But playing at a time when Scotland were the only serious challenge to England, Hardy, who converted from a forward at an early age, was never really tested at international level.

despite dispatching what was described as the strongest team "ever to cross the Irish Sea". The home side were leading 2–1 with three minutes to go when the referee blew for a free kick. The Belfast crowd thought the official had blown for the end of the match and ran on to the pitch to carry off the players amid scenes of wild celebrations. Charlie Buchan, one of the great forwards of his generation, made his England debut that day and scored the opening goal after just ten minutes. But with the First World War just over a year away, the Sunderland striker would have to wait over seven years to win his second cap.

*Fans use their imagination to get a glimpse of the action at Crystal Palace in 1914*

# 1919–1939

## RISING TO THE EUROPEAN CHALLENGE

*The period between the two World Wars*
*was characterised by England's aloofness towards the rest*
*of the football world.*
*But shaken by a handful of close encounters,*
*England rose to the challenge of their nearest rivals, confirming their*
*supremacy with a shattering defeat of Nazi Germany.*

The 1920s were as unsuccessful and unhappy as any period in England's history. At a meeting in Brussels in 1919 England, together with other Allied associations, announced that they would not play Germany, Austria or Hungary. She also refused to play against any neutral countries who were prepared to meet her former enemies in the European War. The hard-line stance was moderated two years later when it was realised that there was no reasonable opposition outside Britain to play against. But despite the change of heart, England's only foreign opponents over the next ten years were Belgium, France, Sweden and Luxembourg.

The 1920s were a time of rapid development in international football – for everyone apart from England. When football's mother country finally

*October 1919: Meredith (right) and Knight*
*tossing before England v Wales*

emerged from her shell at the start of the next decade, she was unpleasantly surprised to discover that the rest of the world were quickly catching up. England re-established her supremacy during the 1930s but she was forced to acknowledge that the continental sides were no longer the pushovers they once had been – by any stretch of even the most jingoistic imagination.

In April 1920, England formally withdrew from FIFA, the governing body of world football, thus leaving Scotland as their only tough challenge over the next ten years. (England had never taken FIFA all that seriously and barely acknowledged its existence when it was founded in 1904.)

England rejoined FIFA in 1924 despite a row over "broken time payments" for amateurs, which the British Associations objected to. But they pulled out for a second time in the build-up to the 1928 Olympic Games in Amsterdam, when the smouldering disagreement over the definition of amateurism erupted onto the agenda again.

Despite the turmoil that was to follow, the decade had begun promisingly enough for England when they recorded one of their most famous triumphs in the Victory International over Scotland at Sheffield in 1920. It was a match played in such appalling conditions that by the end of the match, the mud-drenched players were completely unrecognisable.

The England team, nine of whom had seen service during the war, found themselves 4–2 down at the turnaround. But in the second period they defied the downpour to run out 5–4 winners, inspired by the dazzling skills of Burnley's Robert Kelly and the tireless running of Aston Villa's Andrew Ducat and Tottenham's Arthur Grimsdell. (Ducat was also a talented cricketer for Surrey and played in one Test match. He died while batting at Lord's during the Second World War.)

Writing many years later, left-back Jesse Pennington, who would have at least doubled his 25 caps but for the intervention of the war, described the match as the highlight of his playing career. "I am often asked what was the greatest match I ever played in and there is no doubt that it was the 1920 international at Sheffield. It rained throughout the game, we could hardly keep our feet, especially in the first half when we so faced the wind and the rain. This was to be my last international, but it left a lasting impression not for that fact, but because of the craftsmanship of both sets of forwards."

*Above: England v Scotland at Glasgow, April 1923*

*Below: an FA team leave Euston Hotel
before a tour of Canada in 1926*

The Victory International, however, proved to be a rare triumph over the Scots during the inter-war years. England won just six of their encounters to Scotland's 11 over that period and they had to wait until 1930 to win their first Home Championship since 1913.

England's chaotic selection arrangements gave the Scots an advantage before a ball was even kicked. This was the era of the one-cap wonders when you could barely walk down a town high street without bumping into someone who hadn't played football for England at some point. The selectors were hopelessly amateur in their approach to picking the side, with individual preferences and club prejudices taking precedence over the national cause. In the first 33 internationals after the war, England used 145 players, a great many of whom were never to pull on the famous white shirt again.

During an 11-year period, England tried eight different goalkeepers and seven centre-forwards in teams showing an average of five changes per game. Sixty years later Sir Alf Ramsey, by contrast, would average just over one change per game for his first highly successful years in charge.

The impression that English football was slipping from its lofty pedestal was reinforced by the poor performances of its leading club sides on summer tours to the continent.

Foreign associations and fledgling clubs were eager to invite English teams who, they believed, would provide them with a lesson in the finer arts of the game. Too often, though, and with unhelpful diplomatic consequences, the English teams would treat the tour as nothing more than a holiday. Several continental clubs lodged protests after welcoming and then thrashing teams that were appreciably inferior to what they had been expecting.

In England, there were calls for only the very best sides to be chosen to play abroad and for those teams to take their contests seriously. Newcastle United, the 1927 English champions, were one of several leading sides to come in for heavy criticism after their tour to Central Europe in 1929 resulted in a string of humiliating defeats. The attitude of the Newcastle team sparked anger in Hungary where it was felt they had not received value for money from their

*Everton's Dixie Dean, pictured in 1928, scored 12 goals in his first five England games*

## DIXIE DEAN

| Position | Forward |
|---|---|
| Caps/goals | 16/18 |
| Debut | v Wales (3–3) at Wrexham |
| | 12th February 1927 |
| Last match | v Ireland (1–0) at Blackpool |
| | 17th October 1932 |
| Club | Tranmere, Everton, |
| | Notts County |

There is a story that such was Dixie Dean's reputation as a formidable header of the ball that when he met Liverpool goalkeeper Elisha Scott on a railway platform Dean nodded hello and Scott instinctively threw himself to the ground to save. Dean, who actually hated the nickname "Dixie" and preferred to be called Bill, was a goalscoring phenomenon for both Everton and England. In the 1927/28 season he scored an astonishing 60 league condescending visitors. An FA inquiry into the matter concluded: "We are of the opinion from the indifferent displays given by the Newcastle United players during the tour that the Hungarian Football Association were justified in endeavouring to cancel the contract."

But Newcastle were not the only offenders, with Bolton Wanderers, Everton and Huddersfield Town among others who came in for some angry reviews. Newspapers of the day slammed the performances of the "holiday" teams who they insisted were bringing shame to the country. Headlines of the day captured the angry mood back home: OUR DEGRADING FOOTBALL!.... ENGLAND'S LOST PRESTIGE!..... HOW OUR CRACK TEAMS LET DOWN BRITAIN!....

In 1927, England's first win over Scotland since the Victory International seven years earlier generated a sense of national optimism that would be cruelly exploded by the arrival at Wembley the following year of The Wee Blue Devils.

The Scots of 1928 – described by one observer as looking "undernourished" on their arrival at the Twin

*Scotland's "Wembley Wizards" take the field in 1928. Described as looking "undernourished", they went on to destroy England 5–1*

goals, including three in the last match of the season against Arsenal, to clinch the record which still stands today and is unlikely ever to be broken.

The start to his international career was no less spectacular, with 12 goals in his first five games. He scored both goals on his debut in a 2–1 win over Scotland, two more against Wales, then on tour, he hit hat-tricks against Belgium and Luxembourg and two against France. His prodigious goalscoring talents ensured his playing career started in painful fashion. As a 17-year-old he was told by a defender that if he dared to score another goal he would personally make sure it would be his last. Dean found the target for a second time and shortly afterwards his opponent kicked him so hard in the groin that he later had to have a testicle removed.

Dean, who was born and died on Merseyside, was not especially tall at 5'10" but he was exceptionally powerful, very quick and a mighty

header of the ball. He scored 379 goals in 437 league matches, but his England career went into decline when he was just 25 years old. The goals began to dry up at the same time that "stopper" centre-halves began to emerge in the late 1920s, and he scored just six times in his other 11 internationals.

But Dean, who was also injured in a motorbike accident when he was 26, had the misfortune to be playing at a time when chaos governed the selection policy of the national side. His fellow players, though, were in no doubt about his ability. Both Charlie Buchan and Eddie Hapgood, the England captain of the 1930s, both chose Dean in their teams of all-time greats.

Dean later ran a Liverpool pub, called the Dublin Packet, for 15 years before working as a security man for Littlewoods Pools. He died at Goodison Park in 1980 shortly after the final whistle had blown on a Merseyside derby.

Towers – showed their enormous appetite for beating England by subjecting their hosts to a 5–1 thrashing. It was one of Scotland's greatest ever performances, and their mesmerising ball skills and slick passing bewildered their more heavy-footed opponents, and were all the more impressive for the fact that heavy morning rain had sodden the Wembley turf.

The 1920s were a disappointing decade for England. The mother country of football, whose club sides, grounds and crowds were the envy of the world, retreated in on itself at a time when it could have been helping to shape football's new world order. It was perhaps fitting that the decade should draw to a close on a disappointing note, with England being beaten by foreign opposition for the first time in their 57-year history. The honour of ending their proud record fell to Spain, who were coached by former Middlesbrough and England winger Fred Pentland. Spain beat their illustrious visitors by the odd goal in seven in the searing afternoon heat of Madrid in mid-May.

Those who jumped to England's defence pointed out that the defeat had come at the end of a gruelling tour to France and Belgium and was played in temperatures that England's pale-skinned players had never experienced. Several players emerged in the second half with bandages soaked in icy water wrapped around their heads, and England did well to hang on to their lead until Spain struck twice in the dying moments of the game to the delight of the raucous 30,000-strong Madrid crowd.

By the early 1930s Englishmen were forced to accept that the game established by their grandfathers was now being played to the very highest standards on the continent. Any residue arrogance towards foreign teams was smartly dispatched by the Austrian Wunderteam who came to England in 1932 amid great excitement in the rest of Europe. The match was seen as a showdown between the world's two most powerful football nations. But the feverish anticipation never really took hold in an England where a victory for the home side was taken for granted by all but a few (the few being those who had actually seen Hugo Meisl's Austrian team play).

England's implacable sense of superiority should have been given a severe jolt the year before when they were beaten 5–2 by France in Paris, despite fielding a full complement of professionals. The defeat was described by German football journal *Der Kicker* as "a bombshell over Europe", but at home it was seen as nothing more than a passing aberration which would be put right the next time the two sides met.

On their return home, the England camp rolled out some rather lame excuses which would spark howls of tabloid derision if they had been offered by a modern day England manager. The French were in much better physical condition because they had been training intensively for two weeks before, it was claimed. French officials were almost embarrassed by their success and politely pointed out that the team had only assembled on the eve of the match. England had beaten France 6–0, 5–1 and 4–1 on their previous three encounters and the Frenchmen had been hoping that, once again, England would put on a masterful exhibition of skill from which they could learn something.

*England take the field to face Hugo Meisl's Austrian "wunderteam" for the "match of the century"*

## SAMMY CROOKS

| | |
|---|---|
| Position | Outside-right |
| Caps/goals | 26/7 |
| Debut | v Scotland (5–2) at Wembley |
| | 5th April 1930 |
| Last match | v Hungary (6–2) at Highbury |
| | 2nd December 1936 |
| Club | Derby |

Originally a miner who played for his colliery in the North East, Crooks became one of England's most dangerous forwards of the 1930s. He switched from inside-forward to wing when he turned professional with Durham City and made himself a regular on England's right flank and even kept the precocious young Stanley Matthews out of the side. Small, quick, blond and with an eye for goal, Crooks became known as the "human torpedo" after his habit of hurtling himself full-length to head the ball at any height.

He seemed to lose his way to goal at the end of his international career, as he failed to find the net in his last 11 games.

As for Austria, it was widely thought they would go the same way as the last foreigners to visit England. Spain had been thrashed 7–1 a year earlier as England took revenge for their watershed defeat in Madrid in 1929. But the Austrians, coached by Briton Jimmy Hogan but guided by the great Hugo Meisl, were a different proposition altogether. They arrived in London with the formidable record of 11 wins and two draws in their previous 13 matches, which included a 5–0 demolition of Scotland. Two years earlier Meisl's side had fired more than a shot across England's bows in a goalless draw in Vienna. But brought up to believe in British invincibility on the football field as well as the battlefield, the crowd who crammed into Stamford Bridge that December day were expecting nothing less than a thumping England win.

The few siren voices advising respect for the Austrians were drowned out by the patriotic boom

*Sammy Crooks exercises*
*on the eve of England's match v Hungary*
*at Highbury in 1936*

of a nation yet to experience defeat to a foreign side on their own soil. One of the few to fear an upset was Ivan Sharpe, a member of Britain's 1912 Olympic gold medal team, who had seen Austria dismantle the Scots in Vienna six months earlier. "We have had quite enough shattering of our sporting prestige, for the foreigner is so apt glibly and falsely to say from these things 'Great Britain is decadent'. Our stronghold has ever been soccer. So let us realise the worldwide importance of this match," warned Sharpe.

Captain AJ Prince-Cox, who had refereed several of Austria's matches, felt that only the heavier English pitch would save the home side from defeat. "The Austrians are the best footballing nation on the continent and they will make England go all the way. How can one expect the Austrians to produce their best form in a country where, very often, local fire brigades have to be called in to pump surface water off grounds?"

The match sparked a frenzy of public interest on the continent, where tour operators arranged for parties to travel to London. Associates of a number of Dutch, French and Belgian football clubs all made the trip. A group of unemployed Austrians even made the arduous journey from Central Europe only to be refused entry by customs officials on their arrival at Newhaven for not having the correct paperwork.

Restaurants and cafes all over Europe employed interpreters to listen to the match on the wireless and provide running updates for the diners and dancers. The importance of the game was reflected in the presence in the stands of HRH Prince George and the Austrian ambassador.

The Austrians took the field in their red shirts, prompting cheers of "Up the Arsenal" from the 42,000-strong crowd. England scored after just three minutes and added a second just before the half-hour mark. By then, though, the visitors had overcome their nerves and were starting to draw gasps of admiration and ripples of applause from around the ground as they strung together a series of slick passing movements. The tactical adventure and accomplished

## CLIFF BASTIN

| | |
|---|---|
| Position | Inside/outside-right |
| Caps/goals | 21/12 |
| Debut | v Wales (3–1) at Liverpool 18th November 1931 |
| Last match | v France (4–2) in Paris 26th May 1938 |
| Clubs | Exeter, Arsenal |

Bastin joined Herbert Chapman's Arsenal for £2,000 in 1929 and went on to establish one of English football's most successful striking partnerships with the great Scot Alex James. Bastin, a shy character nicknamed "Boy" on his arrival at Highbury from his native Devon, was a genuine prodigy. He made his debut for Exeter at 15,

**ENGLAND: The Official F.A. History**

Arsenal at 17, England at 19 and had won every major honour in the game by 21.

Blessed with a powerful left foot, keen positional sense and a bewildering body swerve, Bastin scored a remarkable 33 league goals from the right wing during the 1931/32 season. A forward of great versatility who could play either inside- or outside-right as well as right-half, Bastin was also a very "modern" winger in that he would position himself ten yards in from the touchline.

He scored England's goal in the 1–1 draw with Italy in 1933, prompting the Turin crowd to chant "Basta Bastin" ("Enough Bastin"). He was a central figure in Arsenal's all-conquering side of the 1930s, winning five championship medals and two FA Cups. "Though neither fast nor exceptionally clever, Bastin was one of the greatest forwards of his generation," said former Arsenal, Sunderland and England striker Charlie Buchan, who took up writing at the end of his playing career. "He had an ice-cool brain and always seemed to be in the right place at the right time." He had trouble with his hearing which affected him later in his playing career. He retired to Exeter where he owned a pub before dying after a stroke in 1991.

*9th April 1938: two Scottish supporters shake hands with Bastin prior to the England team's departure from the Euston Hotel, for the Wembley match against Scotland*

*Carter demonstrates
the correct way
to head the ball*

ball control rewarded Meisl's side with a goal
on the stroke of half-time.

In an end-to-end second half,
England stretched their lead 13
minutes from time, were pegged
back to 3–2 within seconds, and
went further in front two minutes later before the
Austrians set up a nerve-jangling final five minutes
with their third goal. England hung on for victory,
but nobody who filed out of Stamford Bridge after the
game was in any doubt that they had seen a team who
were at least the equal of England and whose scientific
passing game was clearly superior.

At the post-match dinner FA Treasurer
AH Kingscott saluted the "moral victory Austria had
gained that afternoon". The match had fired the
imagination of the football public and prompted a
string of challenges to both England and Austria from
all over the world.

Admiration for the English game remained
undiminished after the narrow victory over the
Austrians. Writing a year later, Meisl hailed the
inspiration to continental teams of England and the
other Home Countries. "Any football nation that puts
up a good game against England, Scotland, Ireland or
Wales has every reason to be proud. Take no notice
of those who argue that Britain is decadent in sport."

A Hungarian football writer managed to ruffle
a few English feathers in 1933 with the
publication of football's first world rankings, in which
he placed England third behind Scotland and top
nation Austria with the Italians in fourth. Even if his
gradings were a little off the mark, they did at least
show the belief abroad that the continental teams were
fast catching up. Just as the absence of English clubs
from Europe in the late 1980s was to have a damaging

## RAICH CARTER

| | |
|---|---|
| Position | Inside–right |
| Caps/goals | 13/7 |
| Debut | v Scotland (3–0) at Wembley 14th April 1934 |
| Last match | v Switzerland (0–1) in Zurich 18th May 1947 |
| Clubs | Sunderland, Derby, Hull |

Raich Carter (real name Horatio) was considered
by many to be the best forward of his generation,
but he was denied the chance to prove it by the
outbreak of war in 1939. Carter, already a
formidable force in English football, was 25 at the
time and the best days of his playing career were
about to be lost. He was said to have played his
best football in the unofficial internationals of the
war years when he featured in an England line-up
which included the illustrious names of Stanley
Matthews, Tommy Lawton, Jimmy Hogan and
Denis Compton.

When he returned to the England side after the
war, it had been over nine years since his last cap.
(He scored in the first minute of the first post-war

**ENGLAND:** The Official F.A. History

effect, so too did England's disdainful attitude to the rest of Europe seem to restrict the development of their game in the 1920s.

The first World Cup took place in Uruguay in 1930, but England were not to grace the competition with their presence until Brazil 1950. Defeats to Czechoslovakia, Austria (in 1936), Belgium, Switzerland, Yugoslavia, Wales (twice) and Scotland (five times) between 1933 and the outbreak of the Second World War appeared to confirm the doom merchants' views that England had stood still while the rest of the world had moved forward.

England, though, had a habit of stepping up their game for the matches which were seen to really matter – that is, where the opposition had started to make noises about being the best in the world. The matches against Italy in 1934 and Germany in 1938 are

match v Northern Ireland) but was finally edged out of the side by Stan Mortensen after playing his 13th and final game against Switzerland in 1947. A powerful inside-forward with a good awareness of the game, an accurate pass and a fierce shot, Carter was a fine all-round sportsman who also played cricket for Derbyshire and his native Durham.

Carter's talent was obvious from an early age and, although he was rejected by Leicester because he was thought to be too small, he represented England at schoolboy level. A few years later at the age of 23, he was inspiring Sunderland to the 1936 league title. Carter, a difficult, thorny character, was easily distinguishable on the pitch by his hair, which turned silver at an early age. He took over as player-manager of Hull City before steering them to promotion from Division Three North in 1948.

He retired from English club football in 1952 having scored 216 in 451 outings, and joined Cork City in 1953 before returning to manage Leeds United in 1956. He suffered a stroke in 1987 and died seven years later.

outstanding examples of England rising to the challenge. Both countries were under fascist governments who saw football as a means of furthering an impression of their country's supremacy, and both well understood the propaganda value of beating the mother country of football at her own game. The match against Italy in 1934 – dubbed the Battle of Highbury – was so violent that the FA seriously considered ending its participation in all international matches. There had been much at stake, with the recently-crowned world champions Italy determined to underline their pre-eminence over the unofficial champions. The match was billed in one Italian newspaper as "The most important football match that has been played anywhere in the world since the Great War".

There was no disguising the political importance of the match which was arranged at the initiative of Benito Mussolini's government who wanted a victory for fascism. The Italian team of the day was even known as Mussolini's Azzurri, with the authorities quick to understand the political benefits to be reaped from associating themselves with a muscular, all-conquering national football team. Pride in Italy's football team meant pride in Italy.

Mussolini, who offered the players a bonus of 150 pounds – a massive sum in the 1930s – and an Alfa Romeo sports car if they beat the English, took his football seriously. In a match in Rome the following year, Italy were trailing at half-time. Il Duce promptly dispatched a message to the dressing room informing the players they would be called up for national service unless they won. Italy won the match.

The political dimension to the Battle of Highbury was given dramatic expression when the many Italian expatriates in the Highbury crowd gave the fascist salute during the rendition of the national anthems.

Italy were managed by the great Vittorio Pozzo, the father of Italian football, who was under no illusions about the sheer physical presence of his opponents. Pozzo had been at Stamford Bridge to witness the famous clash with the Austrians after which he sung

the praises of England's awesome strength in the tackle and the shoulder charge. "The formidable violence of the charge takes the breath away," he said.

Pozzo, however, thought England could be outwitted tactically, and they may well have been had not a foot injury to Italy's Argentinian-born centre-half Monti after just three minutes sparked a match of unrelenting violence. Monti was said to have been in such pain that a cloth was pushed in his mouth to stop his screaming as he was taken off to hospital. The Italians were convinced the injury to their star player had been deliberate and they responded with a wave of ugly challenges.

Centre-forward Ted Drake, one of seven Arsenal players in the England line-up, was punched on the chin early on. But Drake, never a player to shy away from the rougher aspects of the game, said national pride lay behind England's determination to soak up the Italian violence. "We were playing for England. We had no choice but take what they threw at us."

A year earlier, England's captain Eddie Hapgood made his international bow during England's 1–1 draw

*"The Battle of Highbury" in 1934 was one of the most violent matches in England's history*

with Italy in Rome, and caused a certain amount of amusement when he struck Il Duce himself with a no-nonsense clearance into the stands. But there was nothing amusing about the elbow that flattened his nose and forced him to leave the Highbury pitch. Hapgood said one of the Italians had casually sauntered over to him and "carefully smashed his elbow into my face". The England captain was also to reveal that at the extremely subdued banquet which followed the match, his assailant had simply laughed in his face.

While Italy set about trying to inflict as much physical damage as possible, England swept into a 3–0 lead, with two goals from Eric Brook and one from Drake, after utterly dominating the opening quarter of the match. (England even had a penalty saved inside the first minute). "The Italians simply went berserk and were kicking everybody and everything in sight," recalled Hapgood.

The one England player who really enjoyed his afternoon was Arsenal's Wilf Copping, arguably the hardest man ever to pull on an England shirt. In his element when the rough stuff started, Copping, whose speciality was the then legal two-footed lunge, shoulder-charged and tackled with ferocious enthusiasm for the full 90 minutes. He, more than any other player, saved the day for England when their goal was under siege for much of the second period. The visitors hit back with two goals after the turnaround before England hung on for a famous if ugly victory. With the exception of goalkeeper Frank Moss, the entire England team had some form of a physical trophy to boast for their bloody efforts.

The ferocity of the contest caused an uproar. An FA councillor summed up the official post-match mood: "It is quite impossible, if we are to conserve all that is good in the game, that we should continue to play matches against the players of nations, who either because of temperament or lack of knowledge of the rules, are unable to distinguish between that which is right and that which is wrong."

*The London Evening Standard* was even more critical of the Italians' behaviour. "Italy remain the football champions of the world. If, in order to win such a title, it is necessary to acquire an outlook revealed by the Italians, I prefer that we shall remain among the less exalted football people."

The match was also a depressing experience for a young Stanley Matthews, who did not regain his place in the national side for 12 months. "It was the roughest match I ever played in," said Matthews years later. "It cost me my place in the England team." One newspaper reporter was so disturbed by what he had seen that he signed his report "By Our War Correspondent".

***England captain Eddie Hapgood (right) wasn't smiling when an Italian elbow flattened his nose***

Germany came to North London a year after the Italians, but they brought with them little of the type of political tension which had attended the visit of Mussolini's Azzurri. The German team, by all accounts, were immaculately behaved on and off the Tottenham pitch and even had the good grace to lose by three goals to nil.

Three years on, and with Hitler's fascist regime heading inexorably for a military showdown with Britain and her Allies, the mood was very different when England faced the Germans in Berlin's Olympic stadium. The match became famous for two reasons. First, because the England players were obliged to give the raised arm salute and second, because England destroyed German hopes of proving their Aryan supremacy by thrashing their hosts 6–3.

A sense of hostility between Britain and Germany was growing by the day in the tense build-up to the Second World War and, like Mussolini, the Nazi regime understood the symbolic power of sport. Two years earlier, Hitler and the champions of Aryanism were embarrassed by the black American sprinter Jesse Owens, who exploded the Nazi myth of racial

inferiority by sprinting and jumping to four gold medals at the Berlin Olympics.

The football match against England provided the Germans with another chance of a propaganda coup. Like the Italian fascists, the Nazis saw the political dividends to be had from a German victory over the inventors and unofficial world champions of football. The Germans had been spirited away to the depths of the Black Forest, where they trained intensively for two weeks. By contrast, England arrived at the end of a gruelling season without having trained for the match. "We must have appeared a pretty washed-up bunch of athletes when we met the German team on the eve of the match," recalled Stanley Matthews. "They were as bronzed as Greek statues."

The teams ran out to a deafening roar from the 110,000-strong crowd bellowing "Sieg Heil!" amid a swirling mass of red swastika flags with just the odd Union Jack to give the England players encouragement. The importance that the Nazis attached to the match was reflected in the leading figures who attended the match: Goebbels, Hess, Ribbentrop and Goering were all in the Olympic

*15th May, 1938: England v Germany.*
*Taking the field in front of*
*a crowd of 110,000 which included*
*Goebbels and Goering*

*Hitler was desperate*
*for a symbolic win*
*over the mother country of football.*
*But the hosts were no match*
*for Matthews and Co*

Stadium to cheer what they expected to be an emphatic German win.

At the Berlin Olympics, Great Britain had sparked a row by not giving the raised arm salute. Anxious not to cause a diplomatic incident during a delicate stage of Anglo-German negotiations, it was agreed between the FA and British ambassador Sir Neville Henderson that the England players should give the salute. Some accounts suggest that the players were furious that they were pressurised into making the gesture, while others suggest it did not become an issue until later.

What is certain is that England's raised arms caused a storm in the press back home, but that no one seemed too upset when the England team repeated the salute in Milan the following year (and to all four sides of the ground).

Captain Eddie Hapgood reflected towards the end of his life: "I've been in a shipwreck, a train crash, and inches short of a plane crash but the worst of my life was giving the Nazi salute in Berlin."

A stunned silence, though, quickly descended on the fervently partisan crowd as England raced into an early lead.

The final blow to Nazi pride was struck moments from the end of a match England totally dominated, when Len Goulden ripped the net from the crossbar with a ferocious volley to seal the 6–3 win.

# 1946–1963

## NEW WORLD ORDER

*England entered into the new spirit of internationalism
that followed the end of the Second World War by emerging from
its self-imposed isolationism and rejoining FIFA.
The national team had learnt from the mistakes of the 1920s,
when continental teams were treated with barely concealed disdain.
Gone was the condescending attitude towards
'Johnny Foreigner' and there was even the odd expression of hope
– whispered of course – that England could actually
learn something from abroad.*

The results of the first few post-war years, however, did little to undermine the widely held view that England were still the best in the world. In 19 games played between September 1946 and April 1949 England lost just once and found the net a remarkable 72 times. The team-sheets of the day glowed with the illustrious names of Tom Finney, Stanley Matthews, Wilf Mannion, Stan Mortensen, Tommy Lawton, Billy Wright and Frank Swift.

A rude shock was just around the corner, but for the time being England could luxuriate in a mini-Golden Age during which Italy were beaten 4–0 in Turin. Even the one blip on the record –

a 1–0 defeat to Switzerland in Zurich in 1947 – was avenged in an emphatic 6–0 rout at Highbury the following year. That defeat prompted FA secretary Stanley Rous to appoint Walter Winterbottom

***England training at Brighton and Hove ground,
10th April 1947, before meeting Scotland***

# FRANK SWIFT

| | |
|---|---|
| Position | Goalkeeper |
| Caps/goals | 19/0 |
| Debut | v Northern Ireland (7–2) in Belfast 28th September 1946 |
| Last match | v Norway (4–1) in Oslo 18th May 1949 |
| Club | Manchester City |

Frank Swift was the first goalkeeper to captain England and almost certainly the first licensed comedian to achieve the honour. Swift cut an imposing figure for opposition forwards with his huge frame under a peaked cap and his enormous hands which spanned 11 inches and prompted his England teammate Stan Mortensen to call him "frying pans". There was said to be never a dull moment off the pitch when Swift was around, but he was always immaculately professional on it – even if he couldn't resist the odd bit of showmanship.

Swift, who was famed for his one-handed saves, produced one of the greatest ever performances by an England goalkeeper in the first 45 minutes of the

*England goalie Frank Swift, a genial character but an imposing opponent*

4–0 win over Italy in Turin in 1948, when England were being totally overrun. Although he was born into a fishing family, Swift worked at Blackpool gasworks before making it as a footballer. His brother Fred Swift played in goal for Oldham and together, for a number of years, they ran a pleasure boat on Blackpool's seafront during the summer months. He would undoubtedly have won many more than his 19 caps but for the Second World War, when he played for the unofficial England team.

He fainted at the end of Manchester City's 2–1 FA Cup final win over Portsmouth in 1934 after the photographers behind the goal supposedly built him up into a state of giddy excitement. King George V later sent a telegram to Manchester to discover if the giant young goalkeeper had recovered. He had the courage to admit later that not wearing gloves had cost City a goal. He died in the Munich air disaster of 1958 after travelling to Belgrade with the Manchester United team as a journalist for the *News of the World*.

as England's director of coaching, although it was some years before Winterbottom was named manager with the power to suggest his own team. Until then, the constituent parts of the England team, as well as any hope of establishing continuity, lay at the mercy of the FA's international selection committee.

England, who had just lost to the Swiss, arrived in Portugal in May 1947 with their hosts quietly optimistic of victory in the first ever encounter between the two nations. But if ever confidence had been misplaced before a football match, it was in the build-up to this extraordinary encounter in Lisbon. England romped to a 10–0 victory, with Matthews on the right and Finney on the left – playing together for the first time – in irresistible form. Mortensen, on his debut, and Lawton both scored four. "It seemed as if we could see into each other's minds," said Finney.

The match had been preceded by a row over the size of the ball before England were finally granted the bigger version they preferred. Lawton found the net after just 17 seconds and the Portuguese camp threw on a smaller ball, but it made no difference as England proceeded to steamroller their hosts (who also made two illegal substitutions). The 62,000 who saw the

## TOMMY LAWTON

| | |
|---|---|
| Position | Centre-forward |
| Caps/goals | 23/22 |
| Debut | v Wales (2–4) in Cardiff 22nd October 1938 |
| Last match | v Denmark (0–0) in Copenhagen 26th September 1948 |
| Clubs | Burnley, Everton, Chelsea, Notts County, Brentford, Arsenal |

Tommy Lawton would probably be England's top goalscorer but for the interruption of the Second World War. With his almost supernatural ability to hover in the air, he was regarded by many as the finest header of the ball who ever lived. Against Holland in 1946 he became the first player to score four goals for England – a feat he repeated in the 10–0 demolition of Portugal the following year, when he also hit the fastest ever England goal after just 17 seconds. Lawton, they said, had everything: pace, strength, good technique and, of course, a great head. His strike rate of 16 goals in 15 games remains a post-war record. He worked as a tanner in his hometown of Bolton but was leading the Burnley attack at just 16 and England's at 19.

As a member of England's great war-time team alongside Stanley Matthews and Raich Carter, he scored four times in an 8–0 rout of Scotland at Maine Road, including one with an overhead kick while sitting on the ground. He succeeded the legendary Dixie Dean as Everton's centre-forward after transferring from Burnley for a record £6,500. He later joined Notts County for a new record of £20,000 when the club were in Division Three South and where his reputation added thousands to the home gate. He worked as a publican and journalist before his death in 1996.

*18th May, 1948: England v Italy, Turin. Tommy Lawton tackles Italian goalkeeper Bagigalupo*

match went home disappointed, but were not as upset as the Portuguese team itself, which failed to show for the post-match banquet.

A year later England flew to Italy where, in the heat and hostile atmosphere of the Comunale Stadium in Turin, they achieved one of their most famous victories. For much of the first half it had looked as if it would be the visitors and not the hosts who would be swept aside. Only the athleticism and bravery of goalkeeper Frank Swift kept England in the game as the Azzurri, inspired by the great Mazzola, laid siege to the English goal. The 90,000 supporters packed into the stadium bayed for a rout – and they got one.

England broke out of defence with a devastating move started by Matthews, who skipped past a couple of Italians and released his club colleague Stan "the electric eel" Mortensen. The Blackpool forward raced towards the by-line just outside the penalty box and from the sharpest imaginable angle, and with a defender closing him down, he fired the ball inside the near post to the astonishment of all who saw it.

Finney added a second and then a stunning third after a sweeping move which had started with goalkeeper Swift – before Mortensen completed an extraordinary reversal of fortunes with a fourth. England had given Italy a lesson in composure under pressure and in deadly finishing, and had every right to feel on top of the world. "The Turin game was the sweetest of victories. It was the best England team I ever played in and Italy were the best team I'd ever played against," said Matthews. Little can Matthews or anyone have guessed on that triumphant day that within just a couple of years, England's deep-rooted belief in their infallibility would be dramatically shattered.

*Stan Mortensen scores England's first of four goals against Italy*

England's proud 77-year record of never having lost to non-British opposition on home soil came to an end at Goodison Park in 1949 when they were beaten 2–0 by Eire. The trusty excuses of travel fatigue, strange food, blistering heat, end-of-season weariness, hostile crowds and biased refereeing were often trotted out when the national team lost abroad. England's true strength could only be tested at home, ran the general public view. The Goodison defeat, though, was brushed aside on the argument that nine of the Irish team played football in the English league, and therefore England had lost to a team of quasi-Englishmen.

*Mortensen in action during the England–Italy match in Turin, 18th May 1948*

that year he hit a hat-trick against Sweden, turning possible defeat into a 4–2 win. His goal in England's 4–0 win over Italy in Turin in 1948 is still remembered by those who saw it, Mortensen firing the ball from the goal-line into the far top corner from the most oblique of angles.

He was originally considered too slow to make a great forward, but after intensive training he soon became feared throughout the game for his great acceleration. His speed and a powerful, accurate right-foot shot made him a deadly goal poacher who thrived off the service from the flanks provided by Matthews and Tom Finney.

He suffered serious head injuries when during the war his Wellington bomber crashed in a fir plantation, killing his colleagues. (The trauma left him suffering from insomnia for many years after). He played for Blackpool in three FA Cup finals, scoring the first ever hat-trick at Wembley in 1953, although even then the other Stan stole the glory in what became known as the "Matthews final". Long before he pulled on an England shirt, Mortensen played for Wales in an unofficial international during the war when the Welsh lost a player through injury.

## STAN MORTENSEN

| | |
|---|---|
| Position | Forward |
| Caps/goals | 25/23 |
| Debut | v Portugal (10–0) in Lisbon 25th May 1947 |
| Last match | v Hungary (3–6) at Wembley 25th November 1953 |
| Club | Blackpool |

Playing much of his career alongside Stanley Matthews for both club and country, Stan Mortensen often had to put up with being referred to as "the other Stan". But although overshadowed by his illustrious contemporary on occasion, Mortensen was a major figure in English football and a regular fixture in the England team in the immediate post-war years. He made a spectacular impact on his England debut when he hit four goals in the 10–0 rout of Portugal in Lisbon in 1947. Later

# Walter Winterbottom (1946–1962)

The scholarly, bespectacled figure of Walter Winterbottom was given a frosty reception by his players after being appointed England's first ever manager after the Second World War. Stanley Matthews even went into print to say that the country's best footballers needed no lessons in how to play football – especially from someone who had a short, undistinguished career as an amateur with Manchester United. But when Winterbottom retired 16 years later he left behind not just a lasting legacy in the form of a nationwide coaching network, but also the affection of all those who played under him.

Winterbottom, a qualified PE teacher and RAF wing commander in the war, was named team manager as well as director of coaching with responsibility for the development of the game at all levels and he made no secret that he saw the latter as the more important of his two jobs. Under Winterbottom greater continuity was also established at the highest level with the introduction of the England Under-23s and Youth teams.

He was at the mercy of the FA international selection committee throughout his time in charge and he showed his tact and patience in coping with the amateur ramblings and prejudices of some of its members. Fortunately for Winterbottom and England, there could be little argument about selection in the immediate post-war years when he took charge of one of the greatest teams of all time, which included Stanley Matthews, Tom Finney, Raich Carter, Tommy Lawton, Wilf Mannion, Billy Wright, George Hardwick, Neil Franklin and Frank Swift.

Winterbottom, who did not have an assistant until he was joined by Burnley's Jimmy Adamson in 1962, had to do everything as England manager. At the 1958 World Cup in Sweden he had to organise food, accommodation, travel and financial matters as well as try and find time for training. He once had to cancel a trip to watch Sweden – England's likely opponents in the quarter-finals – because he had to organise medical treatment for an England selector who had come down with an attack of shingles. Eight years earlier at the World Cup in Brazil he even had to do the team's cooking.

Winterbottom presided over three of the lowest moments in England's history when they lost to the USA in 1950 and the Hungarians in 1953 and 1954. England also had a poor World Cup record under Winterbottom, winning just three out of 14 games in four finals. But he was among the first to understand the need for a radical shake-up in the whole structure of English football, although he would not be in charge to reap the benefits of his reforms.

He resigned after England's poor showing in the 1962 World Cup in Chile to become General Secretary of the Central Council of Physical Recreation, even though he was under no pressure from the FA, who were happy for him to build the team for 1966. It was widely thought at the time that he left in the hope of taking over as FA secretary from Sir Stanley Rous, who had recently been named president of FIFA, but the post was given to Denis Follows.

Winterbottom never established a rapport with the England squad as Ramsey would and many of his players openly admitted to not understanding a word of his often cerebral team-talks. But it is difficult to find a former England player with a nasty word to say about a man who tackled two newly-created posts with bottomless enthusiasm and good humour.

**England record P139 W78 D33 L28 F383 A196**

*The scholarly Winterbottom in earnest discussion with Billy Wright*

Six months later England won a match which from hindsight they might have wished they had lost. It came in front of a crowd of 134,000 at Hampden Park in April of 1950 and ensured England's participation in their first ever World Cup. FIFA had decreed that the Home Championship could double up as a qualifying group for the finals, generously stipulating that both the winners and the runners-up of the annual tournament would go through. But the match became a winner-takes-all decider for the Scots, who stubbornly refused to travel to Brazil as anything but British champions.

England's pride was burdened by no such qualifications and they were happy to get on the boat for Rio de Janeiro whatever the outcome. England wanted the Scots, as fellow Britons, to join them in the finals and after the match captain Billy Wright begged George Young, his Scottish counterpart, to put pressure on the Scottish FA to reconsider their position, but to no avail. A draw would have been enough for both teams, but there was never any question of a fix. The ancient rivalry between the two countries ensured the annual encounter was fought out with its customary ferocity. England booked their passage with a goal from Roy Bentley of Chelsea as the Scots were left counting the cost of their masters' high-mindedness.

## WILF MANNION

| Position | Forward |
|---|---|
| Caps/goals | 26/11 |
| Debut | v N Ireland (7–2) in Belfast 28th September 1946 |
| Last match | v France (2–2) at Highbury 3rd October 1951 |
| Clubs | Middlesbrough, Hull |

Dubbed as the "golden boy" of English football owing to his thick crop of blond hair and precocious talent as a youngster, Wilf Mannion played a major part in the all-conquering England

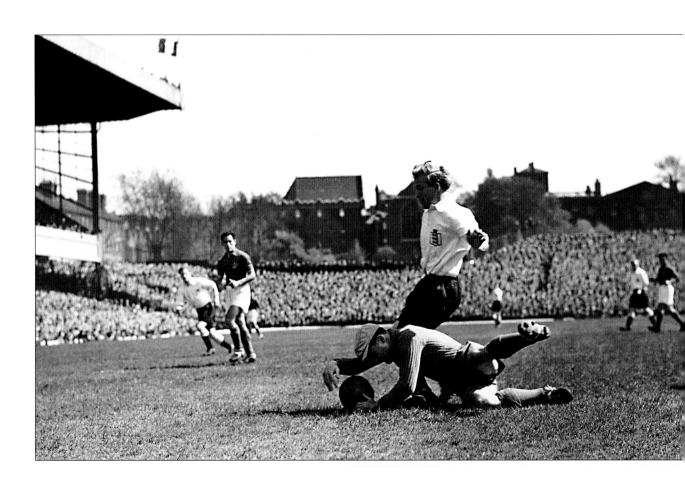

The fourth World Cup, the first since 1938, was a travesty of organisation, a logistical nightmare for everyone involved. For England, it will always be remembered as providing the lowest point in their history, the time when a huge hole was blown in their conviction that they were the untouchables of world

side of the immediate post-war years. Mannion's was another great career cruelly interrupted by the Second World War. He was one of the game's great schemers and contemporary descriptions of him are littered with the word "clever".

A flair player with great acceleration, Mannion provided the perfect link between forwards and halves with his constant efforts to bring others into the game. Mannion was a crowd-pleaser who could score spectacular individual goals, but his main strength was as a creator. He played for England in the early years of the war before he was posted to the Middle East, where he served with the Green Howards regiment. He hit a hat-trick on his debut against Northern Ireland in 1946 and scored two more for Great Britain in the win over the Rest of the World shortly afterwards at Hampden.

He worked at Vauxhall Motors in Luton for a time and, after his career came to a controversial end, he worked on a building site for a period. He did not play for Middlesbrough for six months and was made unavailable for England after a wages dispute led to a confrontation with the Football League when he refused to disclose details of alleged illegal payments. He is Middlesbrough's most capped player and was a member of the infamous England team that crashed to a shock 1–0 defeat to the United States in the 1950 World Cup. "Bloody ridiculous, can't we play them again?" he said as he left the pitch.

*"Golden Boy" Mannion denied by French goalie Da Rui at Highbury in 1947*

football. The tournament was preceded by a series of acrimonious rows and withdrawals. There would be just 13 teams in the finals and, for reasons unknown to logic, they would be divided into two groups of four with a third group featuring just three countries and a fourth, incredibly, just two. The organisers even forgot to schedule a final and were only saved permanent embarrassment by the lucky outcome of the final match of the final league. (Uruguay's dramatic 2–1 victory over their Brazilian hosts was later recognised as the official final). The travel arrangements were equally chaotic with teams forced to cover thousands of miles between matches.

If the administrators and travel agents had surpassed even the wildest expectations of their incompetence, the builders of the now magnificent Maracana stadium were not much better. When 200,000 crammed into the arena for the final, they entered one of the world's largest building sites.

The trophy for the winners had been named after Frenchman Jules Rimet, one of the founders of the competition who hid the 12lb solid gold figure under his bed during the German occupation of France in the war.

For England, the country that had given football to the world, the chance had arrived to prove they were the best. They edged Brazil as favourites and confidence was understandably high in a team that had beaten virtually everyone since the war and could boast the names of Matthews, Finney, Wright, Mortensen, Mannion and Milburn. They arrived just four days before their first match, and without a doctor or a cook (Winterbottom did much of the cooking).

In their opening game, goals from Mortensen and Mannion gave England a 2–0 win over Chile at the Maracana, while the United States showed they had not come to Brazil to be a laughing stock by restricting Spain to a 1–0 win. But England still had every reason to look upon their next game, against the Americans, as nothing more than a practice match. Their opponents were a team of unknowns captained by a Glaswegian, Eddie McIlvenney, who had been given a free transfer by Wrexham in 1947.

## STANLEY MATTHEWS

| | |
|---|---|
| Position | Outside-right |
| Caps/goals | 54/11 |
| Debut | v Wales (4–0) at Cardiff |
| | 29th September 1934 |
| Last match | v Denmark (4–1) in Copenhagen |
| | 15th May 1957 |
| Clubs | Stoke (twice), Blackpool |

*The great Stanley Matthews torments another defender*

Even 30 years after he finally hung up his boots at the age of 50, Stanley Matthews needs no introduction to football fans around the world. He was quite simply one of the greatest players the game has ever seen. When a match programme in the 1954 World Cup in Switzerland listed him as St Matthews, there were some who said it was not a typographical error.

The idol of several generations of schoolboys, the "Wizard of Dribble" was an unlikely-looking sporting hero with his skinny legs and frail frame. But with his devastating acceleration, perfect sense of balance and superb close control, he terrorised defences for 33 years. Like maverick talents before and after him, Matthews often found himself excluded by England selectors who fretted over how to accommodate his genius. He was given just

54 England caps but would have had 119 if he had played every match from his first cap to his last. (There were 22 years between his first and last England goal).

His critics said he was too individual and that Tom Finney was a better team player to have on the right flank, but when Finney switched to the left and with Matthews on the other side, England produced some of their best performances of the period.

The son of a boxer known as The Fighting Barber of Hanley, Matthews inherited his father's obsession with fitness. A strict regime of early nights, breathing exercises in his bedroom, long walks and a lifelong abstinence from cigarettes and alcohol were the key to his longevity as a player.

He played his first match for Stoke at 17 and for England at 19, when he played poorly against Wales. In the following match he looked completely out of his depth in the ferocious so-called Battle of Highbury against Italy. The early doubts about his stomach for the big occasion were later raised

England arrived in the team bus already dressed in their unfamiliar blue kit as there were no changing rooms at the ground in the mining town of Belo Horizonte. England dropped Matthews to the bench, seeing no reason to risk injury to their most dangerous player on the uneven surface. The match

began as everyone expected; England pouring forward, creating chances at will but somehow failing to hit the target. Lulled into a state of complacency by the ease of their early efforts – not to mention 80 years of thinking they were indomitable – England found themselves a goal behind eight minutes from the interval when Haiti-born Larry Gaetjens headed the Americans into the lead. England threw themselves forward with increasing desperation. They hit the woodwork five times, had a "goal" scooped from a yard behind the line and allegedly had two good penalties turned down.

But it finished 1–0 and England trooped from the field in a state of disbelief, Mannion muttering "Bloody ridiculous. Can't we play them again?" The defeat of football's mother country by a motley team of part-timers (most of whom had been at a party until the small hours of the night before) sparked wild celebrations among the 10,000 strong crowd. The Americans were carried from the field on the shoulders of the locals and bonfires were lit on the terraces. When the result arrived on the wires in England, one newspaper thought it was a mistake and changed it to 10–1. Another paper was quick to understand the fatal blow that had been struck to England's self-esteem and bordered their match report in black. "It was just one of those freak results you get in football – a bit like North Korea beating Italy in 1966," reflected Finney years later.

at various points in his illustrious career as England's selectors sought excuses to omit him. But Matthews produced many great performances on the big stage. He single-handedly rescued England from a humiliating first home defeat to foreign opposition with three goals with his left foot (his "wrong" one) in a 5–4 win over Czechoslovakia at Tottenham in 1937. The following year he ran the German defence ragged as England swept to a 6–3 win in front of a 100,000 Swastika-waving fans in the Berlin Stadium. His outstanding display in Blackpool's 4–3 1953 FA Cup final win over Bolton led to the match being dubbed the "Matthews final". He was given one of his many recalls at the age of 41, when he achieved the near impossible task of making Brazilian left-back Nilton Santos look out of his depth in a 4–2 win at Wembley.

He was the first ever European Footballer of the Year, was said to put at least 10,000 on an average gate when he played and was once declared King of Soccer in Ghana. He was knighted a month before his 50th birthday in 1965, and remains the only footballer to earn the distinction solely for his contributions as a player. A few weeks later people came from all over the world to see his final game for Stoke, although he did make a brief comeback with Hibernians of Malta at the age of 55. Even then, Matthews admitted he still suffered from nerves before a game.

Matthews was also a model of modesty and once declared: "I'm no hero. Doctors and nurses are heroes. Surgeons and people like that. We had a real hero born right here in Stoke-on-Trent, Reginald Mitchell, who designed the Spitfire. He saved Britain. Now that's my idea of a hero."

England could still qualify by beating Spain, advance to the final stages and show the American experience had simply been a stroke of the most horrible misfortune by going on to win the trophy. Matthews was restored to the right wing with Finney switching to left, and Newcastle hero Jackie Milburn was chosen to bring extra pace up front. England lost 1–0 after Milburn had a goal controversially disallowed for offside. The team the whole world had expected to reach the final were thus out of the World Cup, their reputation in tatters. England's fallen heroes quickly flew back across the Atlantic after changing their departure bookings which had been scheduled for after the final.

The Brazil fiasco ushered in an unhappy period for the national team in which the need to adapt to the demands of the modern game was made obvious. England had not so much fallen behind as the rest of the world had caught up, and in a number of cases, overtaken them at speed. The United States had destroyed a huge psychological barrier for teams playing England and Yugoslavia were the first to enjoy it, becoming the first non-British side to draw in England later in the year. In May 1951, England almost surrendered their unbeaten home record before two goals in the last ten minutes from Mortensen and Milburn salvaged a 2–1 win over Argentina.

The following year England travelled to Vienna to face Austria in a match billed as "the match of the century" (just as it was when England played Hugo Meisl's Wunderteam exactly 20 years earlier). The Austrians were regarded as the best team in Europe and had recently scored eight against Belgium, seven against Yugoslavia, six against the Republic of Ireland

*Walter Winterbottom with the England Team, 21st November 1951*

*25th November 1953: Wright and Hungary's Puskas lead the teams out at Wembley before the match which rocked English football*

**ENGLAND:** The Official F.A. History

and twice beaten Scotland in the year before. England, who had drawn 2–2 with Austria at Wembley six months earlier, took the match so seriously that they even had a full training session before setting off.

Vienna was still under Allied occupation and 2,000 British soldiers amid the 60,000 crowd made themselves heard as England, all speed, power and quick passing, launched themselves at the more patient and technical Austrians. England won 3–2 thanks largely to Nat Lofthouse who was later dubbed "The Lion of Vienna" for his heroics. The mighty Bolton centre-forward scored twice and was unconscious when his second crossed the line after he collided with the Austrian goalkeeper at the end of a 50-yard sprint from the centre circle. The British soldiers carried the England players from the pitch

*England under siege as Wright (left) and Ramsey (in net) look on helplessly*

*Hungarian centre-forward Hidegkuti heads the ball past England goalie Gil Merrick to score his team's sixth goal. Hungary won 6-3*

after an heroic performance which restored much of the gloss to England's reputation.

The view of the "flat-earthers" that England were still the best in the world was dramatically exploded by Hungary in November 1953. England were beaten 6–3 before an astonished full-house at Wembley and no one who witnessed the massacre dared offer any excuses. It was not just that England had lost at Wembley for the first time, but it was the manner of the defeat which shook the game to its roots. England did not even play badly but they were no match for the "Mighty Magyars", the 1952 Olympic champions and one of the greatest teams of all time. Hidegkuti gave the visitors the lead inside 60 seconds as the Hungarians, who lost just once between 1950 and 1956, motored to an emphatic win and were even said to have relaxed towards the end. The English conviction that foreigners could not shoot was buried for all time.

"The Hungarians played some of the most brilliant football it has ever been my pleasure to see," said England captain Billy Wright. The watershed defeat effectively ended the career of six England players, and the team found itself in a state of shock and disarray just six months before the World Cup finals. But that was not the end of England's painful awakening. They travelled to Budapest for a final warm-up game before the World Cup with a team described by some sections of the press as the worst ever after an unconvincing display in the Home Championship. Hungary fielded ten of their victorious Wembley team while England showed seven changes but little improvement. They were beaten 7–1 and the defeat remains their heaviest to this day.

Nobody apart from the Swiss seemed to be happy with the choice of Switzerland as a venue for the 1954 World Cup. Switzerland, like Sweden in 1958, was not considered a major footballing nation capable of creating enough interest to fill grounds for all the matches. Even the ambassadorial Finney felt moved to comment: "The locals appear to be considerably more interested in climbing up and down their

mountains, explaining why their clocks are so much better than any other in the world."

England, though, arrived in sheepish mood after the shredding of their self-esteem at the hands of Hungary. They brought a relatively old squad with an average age of 29, which included the evergreen Matthews, 39, back in the side by popular demand. Lofthouse, England's battering ram of a centre-forward, who was averaging a goal a game at the time, was their best hope of finding the net. England were clear favourites going into their opening match against Belgium in Basle, which was televised back home, but after opening up a comfortable 3–1 lead, they let the Belgians back into the game with some poor

*27th June 1954: England are beaten by four goals to two – by Uruguay – in the World Cup match in Basle*

defending. The match went into extra-time and finished a memorable 4–4. The game also proved a turning point for Billy Wright, who moved to centre-half after an injury to Luton's Sid Owen and stayed there for the rest of his career.

England's next game was against the hosts, who needed just a draw in Berne's Wankdorf stadium to send them through. England, without the injured Matthews or Lofthouse, needed a win, which they got courtesy of goals from the Wolves pair Jimmy Mullen and Dennis Wilshaw. England were into the quarter-finals against the holders Uruguay, who had just beaten Scotland 7–0. The match was one of the best of the tournament and England were unlucky to lose 4–2. England defended resolutely and were always a threat coming forward when Matthews had the ball, but they were let down by Gil Merrick's poor goalkeeping. Still in a state of shock after his Hungarian experiences, Merrick's mistakes led to three of the Uruguayan goals. England were out, but they went home with their heads a few inches higher than when they had returned from South America four years earlier.

## NAT LOFTHOUSE

| | |
|---|---|
| Position | Forward |
| Caps/goals | 33/30 |
| Debut | v Yugoslavia (2–2) at Highbury 22nd November 1950 |
| Last match | v Wales (2–2) at Villa Park 26th November 1958 |
| Club | Bolton |

*Lofthouse shows his aerial power with a goal against Russia at Wembley in 1958*

Like fellow Bolton-born Tommy Lawton before him, Nat Lofthouse was the outstanding centre-forward of his generation. He bagged two goals on his debut against Yugoslavia and two in England's 3–2 win over Austria in 1952 which earned him the nickname "Lion of Vienna". He may just as well have been dubbed the Lion of Highbury, Villa Park, Zürich, Wembley, New York, Cardiff, Basle, Copenhagen and Helsinki as Lofthouse scored twice for England on 12 occasions. But it was the bravery and whole-heartedness of his performance in Vienna which were remarkable. (He was

unconscious when his second goal crossed the line after a heavy collision with the Austrian goalkeeper).

Although not tall, Lofthouse was a classic powerhouse centre-forward relying on brute strength and speed. But he is remembered none too fondly by Manchester United fans after barging goalkeeper Harry Gregg into the net for one of his two goals in Bolton's 2–0 FA Cup triumph of 1958. He was named Footballer of the Year in 1953 and scored three times in the 1954 World Cup in Switzerland, but was surprisingly left out of the 1958 squad for Sweden. His prodigious goalscoring, though, forced an England recall for a brief period in 1959. Lofthouse, who made his debut for Bolton at 15, has remained loyal to the club all his life serving them as player, reserves coach, manager, scout and president.

After the traumatic defeats to the Hungarians and the poor showings in the World Cups of 1950 and 1954, England enjoyed a period of steady success in the four years before the next World Cup in Sweden. They lost just six of their 31 matches in that time, twice beating world champions West Germany

(the surprise conquerors of mighty Hungary in the 1954 final) as well as Brazil and Yugoslavia. The international committee received some rare credit for their vision in introducing a radical shake-up of how the game was developed at all levels. Greater emphasis was placed on the development of technical skills from an early age and more importance was attached to junior international teams.

The Under-23 side was launched with great success and established continuity with the senior side. Six players in the team that beat France in late 1957 had graduated from the Under-23s. The players coming through were quicker to settle down as they had some idea of what to expect at the highest level and had already developed an understanding with some of their colleagues.

One player who needed no lessons in technique was the 40-year-old Stanley Matthews, who continued to bewitch opposition defences 20 years after his international debut. In April 1955 The Wizard of Dribble was outstanding as England hammered Scotland, who thought they were the best team in Britain because they had only lost to Hungary 4–2. England beat them 7–2, their biggest defeat of the Auld Enemy since 1878, but Matthews created so many chances that the score could have been 14–2. Matthews received an ovation and he was again the star when England beat Brazil 4–2 a year later. He set up three goals, and England could even afford the luxury of missing two penalties. After one of the spot-kicks was awarded, Wembley was treated to one of the more bizarre spectacles in its history when a Brazilian player walked away with the ball in disgust at the decision. He was pursued by the referee, who was pursued by the rest of the Brazil team, who were pursued by England captain Billy Wright as a giant human snake weaved its way around the pitch.

England were undoubtedly re-emerging as a major force, but their well-settled side and best laid plans for Sweden suffered a heavy blow with the tragedy of the Munich air disaster on 6th February 1958. Among the 23 who met their death on the snowbound runway were eight of Manchester United's brightest stars, three of whom were key figures in the England team. Duncan Edwards, just 21 but already a veteran of 18 caps, Tommy Taylor, a prodigiously talented centre-forward and Roger Byrne who had won 33 consecutive caps at left-back, all lost their lives.

England only booked their passage to Sweden with a last-ditch equaliser in Dublin against the Republic of Ireland who needed to win to qualify. A dramatic encounter appeared to be heading for an upset after an early Irish goal, but with the crowd howling for the referee to blow the final whistle, Tom Finney skipped down the wing and delivered a perfect cross for the airborne John Atyeo to head into the net. England were through but the press, among others, were not amused.

The composition of the final squad was also a source of contention with the names of Matthews and Lofthouse conspicuous by their absence. The inclusion of Johnny Haynes, yet to prove himself at international level, was widely questioned as was the omission of Brian Clough who had scored 42 goals for Middlesbrough that season. The much maligned Derek Kevan of West Bromwich Albion and his tough, no-nonsense understudy Bobby Smith of Spurs went instead. Winterbottom had assembled a young 20-man squad of whom only four had reached double figures in caps.

Despite the tragedy in Munich and despite a morale-sapping 5–0 defeat to Yugoslavia in Belgrade a month earlier, it was a confident group of Englishmen who flew into Sweden. Ever sensitive to the problems caused by wrenching players away from their families for long periods, Winterbottom made sure England were the last team to arrive just as they were in 1950 and 1954. Sweden 1958 is now regarded as the first real World Cup. There were no political tantrums, no travel difficulties and no high-minded sniffiness towards the competition. Twenty-eight years after the inaugural event in Uruguay, the winners of the World Cup would for the first time have every right to consider themselves the best in the world.

One anomaly in the organisation of the tournament was the seeding which was based on geography and not on form. The system left England in the toughest group after they were drawn alongside Russia, the best team in Eastern Europe, Austria, the best team in central Europe and Brazil, the best team in South America and soon to prove the best in the world.

*Continues on page 54*

**ENGLAND: The Official F.A. History**

## DUNCAN EDWARDS

| | |
|---|---|
| Position | Left-half |
| Caps/goals | 18/5 |
| Debut | v Scotland (7–2) at Wembley |
| | 2nd April 1955 |
| Last match | v France (4–0) at Wembley |
| | 27th November 1957 |
| Club | Manchester United |

When the aeroplane carrying Manchester United back from Belgrade crashed into a building on a snowbound runway at Munich airport in 1958, 23 people died including eight of "Busby's Babes". Among the dead was one of the most outstanding talents English football has ever produced. Duncan Edwards, a 21-year-old already regarded as the most complete player of his generation, was the last to die. Had he survived, they say, it would have been Edwards, and not Bobby Moore, climbing the steps at Wembley to receive the Jules Rimet trophy from Queen Elizabeth II in 1966.

His immense strength almost saw him make a remarkable recovery, but after three weeks he died after suffering terrible injuries to his kidneys, lungs, thigh and pelvis. (He regained consciousness at one point and briefly talked to his parents before

*All-time greats Matthews, Edwards and Wright train at Highbury*

relapsing into a coma.) Edwards' reputation as a footballer was not one artificially dressed up by retrospective sympathy after his tragically premature death. No one who saw him in action disputes that he was a genuinely magnificent player.

## TOM FINNEY

| | |
|---|---|
| Position | Outside-right |
| Caps/goals | 76/30 |
| Debut | v Northern Ireland (7–2) in Belfast |
| | 28th September 1946 |
| Last match | v USSR (5–0) at Wembley |
| | 22nd October 1958 |
| Club | Preston |

Tom Finney was one of the greatest wingers of all time and perhaps the greatest all-round forward ever produced by England. Although he was naturally a left-footed player, Finney preferred to play on the right wing – an unfortunate choice for an Englishman with international ambitions living at the same time as Stanley Matthews. Finney was seven years the great man's junior, but the ageless talent of his rival meant that their England careers more or less coincided. Finney, though, was a far more versatile player than Matthews and was happy to play on the left or down the middle.

England often exploited this flexibility of the man they still call the "Preston plumber" to devastating effect. Against Portugal in Lisbon in 1947 Finney switched to the left wing and with Matthews installed on the right, the two of them tore the home defence to ribbons to set up a crushing 10–0 win. The following year, England employed the same strategy against a powerful Italian side in Turin – and won 4–0. He spent much of the war years in

His formidable talent had been spotted by a United scout while Edwards played for Dudley Town Boys at the age of 11, when the average age of the team was 15. Not long after, Old Trafford manager Matt Busby drove south and woke the Edwards' household at midnight before getting young Duncan out of bed at 2 o'clock to sign a contract. Before arriving at Old Trafford Edwards worked on his weaker left foot to make sure it was as good as his right.

Powerfully built, quick, strong in the tackle, good in the air and blessed with two good feet and great skill for a big man, Edwards was good enough to win the first of his 18 England caps at just 18 years and 183 days, having played for the Under-23s at the age of 16.

He scored a goal in England's 3–1 win over West Germany in 1956, after a surging run and a shot of such power that the Berlin crowd spent the rest of the match chanting "Boom Boom" each time he touched the ball.

"If I had to play for my life and take one person with me, it would be Duncan Edwards," said another United legend, Bobby Charlton. Stained glass windows dedicated to one of the lost treasures of English football adorn St Francis church in his home town of Dudley.

*Tom Finney*

the Middle East where he played for the British Services XI while serving with the Tank Corps, but he walked straight into a brilliant England team in the first post-war international in 1946. He went on to win 76 caps, the last one at the age of 36, and undoubtedly would have won many more but for Matthews and the war.

Finney's outstanding qualities were his balletic balance and his speed off the mark to round defenders and get in crosses. Although he was a slight figure, he was tough and capable of absorbing the most violent attentions of humiliated full-backs. Like Matthews, he was never happier than when dancing around defenders, but unlike Matthews he could also score goals and by the end of his England career he had 30 to his name. For one of the most remarkable players of all time, Finney had little by way of silverware to boast at the end of his magnificent career. He never won a League or FA Cup winners' medal but his individual talent was recognised in 1954 and in 1957 when he won the Footballer of the Year award.

## JACKIE MILBURN

| | |
|---|---|
| Position | Forward |
| Caps/goals | 13/10 |
| Debut | v Northern Ireland (6–2) in Belfast 9th October 1948 |
| Last match | v Denmark (5–1) in Copenhagen 2nd October 1955 |
| Club | Newcastle |

*Jackie Milburn:*

*England hero, Newcastle legend*

A bronze statue in the heart of the city stands as a tribute to a man whose name still inspires awe in Newcastle. Many felt Jackie Milburn deserved more than his 13 international caps, but he had the misfortune to be playing at a time when brilliant England forwards were thick on the ground. "Wor Jackie", uncle to the Charlton brothers, was never a great header of the ball but he had great pace and was a lethal finisher with both feet. He featured in Newcastle's three FA Cup triumphs of the early 1950s and set the record for the fastest goal in an FA Cup final this century after just 45 seconds in 1955 against Manchester City. (Chelsea's Roberto di Matteo shaved two seconds off the record in 1997.)

One of the two goals he scored in the 2–0 win over Blackpool was hailed as the greatest goal seen at Wembley after he hit the back of the net with a ferocious 25-yard volley. He had a perfectly good goal disallowed against Spain in the 1950 World Cup, which cost England a place in the next stage and with it a chance to make up for the humiliating defeat to the United States in the previous match. He spent his entire playing career at Newcastle and was later made a Freeman of the city. When he died in 1988, thousands poured onto the streets of Newcastle to pay their final respects.

England's first opponents were the mighty Soviets, the Olympic champions, who trained intensively in the build-up to Sweden and whose political masters back home were keen that they should put on a show of strength for the non-Communist world. The USSR had emerged as a major force in world football since the Second World War. Dynamo Moscow had won the affection of the English football public when they toured in 1945, delighting everyone with their neat, scientific football and their eccentric behaviour. (They ran out of the tunnel at Stamford Bridge with great bouquets of flowers which they presented to the Chelsea players before the match).

The Soviets' 10–0 win over Finland in the qualifiers underlined their superpower status, but England had reasons of their own to be confident after forcing a draw in Moscow shortly before the finals. Anatole Granatkin, chief of football in the Soviet ministry for sport, was one of many who made England favourites in Sweden. But given the integrity of information emanating from Soviet ministries during the Cold War, England had good reason to decode his comments as no more than a bluff.

The Soviets were certainly not frightened to impose

themselves by fair means or foul, conceding a remarkable 33 free-kicks by half-time. They went 2–0 up but England fought back in the second half and equalised five minutes from time with a penalty from Finney, the awarding of which led to the great goalkeeper Lev Yashin throwing his flat cap at the referee.

England had escaped after keeping their heads while the brutal Russians set about kicking their opponents. "Just when they should have been making the match an exhibition of scientific soccer, they turned it into a rough house. They tripped, they pushed, they kicked," reflected Finney, his legs a black and blue testament to the close attentions of his Russian markers. The match-saving penalty was virtually Finney's last kick of the competition. He was ruled out with a knee injury after reporting that it took

*The England team manager talks tactics at Stamford Bridge before a trial match against Chelsea in 1955. The team was practising for the upcoming match against Spain*

him five minutes to walk the eight yards to his bathroom the next morning.

Next up for England were Brazil whose extravagantly talented squad could boast the names of Garrincha, Didi, Pele, Nilton Santos and Vava. Brazil were so "modern" they even had their own psychiatrist although, according to some reports, the good brain doctor did little more than choose the best rumba records to be aired while the players trained. The contest was the first ever goalless draw in the World Cup finals and proved to be one of the most entertaining matches of the series. It was dominated by Brazil in the first half and England in the second. England, roared on by the Anglophile crowd and 200 Royal Navy sailors whose ship had docked in Gothenburg, were the only team to stop the eventual champions from scoring.

The match was described in one newspaper as a "feast for the gourmet", and England were looking well-placed after taking two points from the toughest two sides in the competition. With only an off-colour

*England keeper McDonald denies Vava during England's 0–0 draw with Brazil in the 1958 World Cup*

Austrian side standing in their way, England were confident of reaching the quarter-finals.

England travelled to the small inland town of Boras for a match they needed to win to be sure of qualification. Winterbottom fielded an unchanged side against a supposedly demoralised Austrian team who had been beaten by the USSR and Brazil without scoring. But they were held to a 2–2 draw after Bobby

## BILLY WRIGHT

| | |
|---|---|
| Position | Defender |
| Caps/goals | 105/3 |
| Debut | v Northern Ireland (7–2) in Belfast 28th September 1946 |
| Last match | v USA (8–1) in Los Angeles 28th May 1959 |
| Club | Wolves |

Billy Wright's career reads like one long triumph against the odds. After being written off as too small when he was a youngster and having recovered from an early broken ankle, Wright went on to prove that sheer enthusiasm and bloody-minded determination can go a long way in football – even at international level. By almost every contemporary account, he was not the most naturally gifted of players, but he made the most of what he had and by the end of his career he could boast being the only player in the world to be capped 100 times or more.

He was not an ambitious distributor of the ball but he read the game well and timed his tackles and interceptions to perfection. He converted to centre-half from right-half almost by mistake after a last-minute injury to a colleague, and quickly showed that he was good in the air despite his lack of inches. Wright had a schoolboy's uncomplicated relish for the game and went about his job with an undemonstrative and unflappable efficiency. He became the bedrock of the England team in the 1950s and was to Walter Winterbottom what Bobby Moore was to Alf Ramsey in the 1960s and Bryan Robson was to Bobby Robson in the 1980s.

Like another England captain, Gary Lineker, Wright was never booked throughout his long career with Wolves and England. He captained England 90 times – a total second only to Moore's 91 – and had the difficult job of lifting the team's morale after three of the lowest moments in England's history; the 1–0 defeat to the United States in 1950 and the 6–3 and 7–1 defeats to the mighty Hungarians in 1953 and 1954. He married Joy from the Beverley Sisters, managed Arsenal for four years in the 1960s and was later in charge of the England Youth team.

*Billy Wright:*
*captain of England 90 times*

Robson had his second goal of the finals controversially disallowed for hands. (Robson insists to this day that the ball hit his side and the official Istvan Zsolt who disallowed both his goals was scratched from the list by the World Cup organisers.) In the other match of Pool IV Brazil beat the USSR 2–0 with a breathtaking performance – literally in the case of Vava who, after his second goal, was mobbed by his colleagues. When the scrum of celebrants finally cleared, Vava lay unconscious and had to be carried from the field for medical attention.

The arcane logic of the qualification system meant that England now had to face the USSR for a second time in a play-off match to decide who would advance to the last eight. England had never played the Russians before 1958, but now they were to meet them for the third time in a month. As so often in this tournament, England were poor in the first half, but they besieged Yashin's goal in the second with some attacking football of the highest quality, roared on by a Swedish crowd with an understandable fear and loathing of all things Soviet.

The USSR, however, hit England with a goal against the run of play and hung on for an unpopular victory. England lost a match they had manifestly

## JIMMY DICKINSON

| | |
|---|---|
| Position | Left-half |
| Caps/goals | 48/0 |
| Debut | v Norway (4–1) in Oslo 18th May 1949 |
| Last match | v Denmark (5–2) at Wolverhampton 5th December 1956 |
| Club | Portsmouth |

Jimmy Dickinson, who was capped 48 times by England and was a veteran of the World Cup campaigns of 1950 (Brazil) and 1954 (Switzerland), must be a candidate for the least flamboyant player ever to pull on an England shirt. His conspicuous absence from the football dispatches of the day testify to the quiet, dependable efficiency with which he went about his duties as England's left-half for seven years.

### Jimmy Dickinson:
### Mr Dependable

One of football's "gentlemen", Dickinson was the ultimate club man, playing 764 league games for his beloved Portsmouth between World War Two and 1965. Dickinson's talent was spotted in the playground by schoolteacher Eddie Lever, who went on to manage Pompey. He made his debut for the South Coast club in 1943 while serving with the Royal Navy. Six years later he established himself in the England team, but lost his place after he was forced to switch to centre-half at Portsmouth.

Dickinson, who was awarded the MBE, scored just one goal in his England career – an own goal which saw Belgium draw level at 4–4 in the 1954 World Cup. A model professional who was never booked, Dickinson was also a great tennis player. His devotion to Pompey later saw him employed as a press officer, scout and briefly as manager. After three heart attacks, he died in 1982 at the relatively early age of 57.

deserved to win. They arrived home to be met by a hostile press who called for the resignation of virtually anyone with the remotest connection to the team. The criticism in the papers raged for days, overshadowing the superb performances of Wales and Northern Ireland who were both finally knocked out at the quarter-final stage. But proof of England's superiority over the Soviets was underlined a few months later when they beat them 5–0 at Wembley.

The brilliance of the champions Brazil, playing with the so-called "fourth back style" similar to Hungary earlier in the decade, had raised the tide mark of quality in world football leaving England and the other Home nations flapping around in a sea of uncertainty about the future. "Tactics" was still a dirty word in England, but Brazil prompted a minor awakening. There were calls for the establishment of colleges to train managers as well as for the redefinition of Winterbottom's job. (The England boss had to do everything in Sweden including book the air tickets.) England, though, took heed of the Brazilian lesson and when they appeared in Chile four years later, they lined up in 4–2–4 instead of the traditional 2–3–5 of British teams.

The national team was not exempt from the massive changes that swept through English football in the late 1950s and early 1960s. The very image of the footballer provided evidence of the transformation; baggy shorts had been replaced by a shorter version, collared shirts by V-necks and heavy

*England skipper Johnny Haynes and Bobby Charlton in practice before a World Cup qualifier against Portugal in 1961*

boots discarded in favour of a lighter below-the-ankle model. There was a whiff of Brylcreem in the air. The abolition of the maximum wage in 1961 ushered in a new era and a new breed of footballer. By then the princely figures of Finney and Wright had already given way to a new generation as England underwent significant alterations in terms of personnel and tactics. The flashy, dashing Johnny Haynes of Fulham was now the captain and Bobby Charlton, a member of the 1958 World Cup squad, had finally established himself in the team. In the artful Jimmy Greaves England had discovered a goalscorer of rare talent.

*26th October 1959:*
*England manager Winterbottom*
*with team at Highbury before a game*
*against Sweden at Wembley*

Critics of the national team were provided with plenty of material in the year following the 1958 World Cup, especially on England's disastrous summer tour of South America when they lost to Brazil, Peru and even Mexico. The tour did at least end on a high note with an 8–1 demolition of the United States, which allowed Wright the satisfaction of avenging the humiliation of 1950 in his 105th and last game for England. The new decade started no better with England losing 3–0 to Spain in Madrid and 2–0 to Hungary in Budapest.

In the new season, however, England were a team transformed as Winterbottom implemented the 4–2–4 formation so brilliantly deployed by the Brazilians. The next six matches brought a remarkable 40 goals, during which Spain were beaten 4–2 in October with a confidence and style which convinced many that

England were again a major force in world football. Spain, with Real Madrid in their heyday, had world-class stars like Di Stefano, Suarez, Gento and Santamaria – names well known to even the notoriously insular English football public.

There was a certain amount of nerves among both players and public in the build-up to the game with fears that the Spanish might do to England what Hungary had done seven years earlier. England, though, were magnificent, the new 4–2–4 formation introduced in the 5–2 win over Northern Ireland three weeks earlier yielding impressive results with Bobby

*Ronnie Clayton in action for England*

## RONNIE CLAYTON

| | |
|---|---|
| Position | Right-half |
| Caps/goals | 35/0 |
| Debut | v Northern Ireland (3–0) in Belfast 2nd November 1955 |
| Last match | v Yugoslavia (3–3) at Wembley 11th May 1960 |
| Club | Blackburn |

Like his contemporary, Jimmy Dickinson at Portsmouth, Ronnie Clayton was a devoted one-club man whose fanatical commitment to Blackburn Rovers continues to this day. Thirty years after hanging up his boots, Clayton, one of the club's most consistent performers and loyal servants, is still to be found at almost every Rovers home game. With a display of loyalty to his club that would be sensational in a modern player, Clayton put Blackburn's cause before the livelihood of his family when he opted to stay with the then unfashionable North West outfit after the abolition of the maximum wage in the early 1960s.

As a right-half he was neat and efficient rather than spectacular and inspirational. Always composed, Clayton was strong in the tackle, commanding in the air and loved to come forward. Blessed with natural leadership qualities and regarded as a model of sportsmanship, he captained England in the last five of his 35 internationals before a temporary loss of form cost him his place. He arrived at Ewood Park with his younger brother Ken and made his debut in the senior side when he was just 16 years old. His rise to the top of his sport was rapid and in 1955 he enjoyed a remarkable year when he was called into the England Under-23 side – then the "B" team – before being given a full cap against Northern Ireland in November. Clayton established a regular place in the side for the next five years, playing for England in the 1958 World Cup in Sweden. Since retiring he has worked as a newsagent and at a tyre company.

Robson and Johnny Haynes – the "2" in the system – providing a smooth link between backs and forwards. Such was England's domination that by the end of the match Spain were hardly given a touch to the delight of the crowd who greeted the landmark win with a hail of newspapers, umbrellas and hats. The victory, and the imperious manner of its achievement, acted like a shot in the arm for the England players who swept all before them in the next few matches. Wales were beaten 5–1, Scotland 9–3 and Mexico 8–0. The exotic new formation pioneered by Brazil and adopted by some of the best teams on the continent, and recently by Ron Greenwood's West Ham, had worked a miracle.

The following April, Haynes was carried off the Wembley pitch on the shoulders of his teammates after England had put nine goals past a Scotland side which could boast Denis Law, Dave Mackay, Billy McNeil and Ian St John in its ranks. The unfortunate goalkeeper Frank Haffey would never play for Scotland again. The English press, so harsh on England in recent years, were now in raptures and the purple patch continued with an 8–0 defeat of Mexico in May which was achieved even without the goalscoring prodigy Greaves. Winterbottom had hit upon not just the right system but also the right team. He used just 13 players during England's six straight wins and was helped to some extent by the clubs who had agreed to the earlier release of their star players in the build-up to matches.

*Wembley 15th April 1961: HM The Queen presents the British International Championship Trophy to Johnny Haynes, after the Scottish defeat*

## RON FLOWERS

| | |
|---|---|
| Position | Left-half |
| Caps/goals | 49/10 |
| Debut | v France (0–1) in Paris |
| | 15th May 1955 |
| Last match | v Norway (6–1) in Oslo |
| | 29th June 1966 |
| Club | Wolverhampton |

Like his contemporaries, Jimmy Dickinson of Portsmouth and Ronnie Clayton of Blackburn, Ron Flowers is one of England's unsung heroes. He was a hard-working, energetic, undemonstrative player with great reserves of stamina. He was a tall, elegant figure on the pitch who loved to come forward and have a go at goal from long range. He made his debut against France in 1955 but was not chosen again for another three years. He played regularly up until England's warm-up tour of Europe before the 1966 World Cup. Four years earlier in Chile he was England's top-scorer with two penalties. A product of the Wolverhampton Wanderers nursery, he was seen as a successor to club colleague and England captain Billy Wright. Now runs a sports shop in the town where he spent his whole playing career.

England thus set out in confident mood on a summer tour of Portugal, Austria and Italy. Portugal, who with Luxembourg provided England's opponents in their World Cup qualifying group, had improved beyond all recognition from the immediate post-war years when England put 20 goals past them in three matches. In 1955 they beat England 3–1 in Oporto and in 1958 they lost just 2–1 at Wembley with a side built on the superb Benfica team of the time.

Mindful of the 5–0 defeat to Yugoslavia in 1958

*Goalscoring sensation Jimmy Greaves*
*goes close at Hampden Park, 1961*

when England had wilted in the blazing Belgrade sun, Winterbottom put the players through an intensive midday training session. The heat treatment seemed to pay off as England fought back from a goal down to secure a creditable draw with a goal from Ron Flowers seven minutes from time. England proceeded to Rome

**ENGLAND:** The Official F.A. History

where they maintained their unbeaten record against Italy with a 3–2 victory before a run of seven wins and one draw came to an end in Vienna where, unable to break down a tightly-packed and well-organised defence, they lost 3–1 to Austria. Winterbottom, though, had good reason to be optimistic about England's chances in Chile the following summer after watching his side score 45 goals and concede 14 in nine matches while growing in understanding with each match. In Greaves and Charlton he had potential match-winners, in Haynes and Robson a strong link between backs and forwards, in wing-half Flowers and centre-half Swan two rock-solid dependables, in Jimmy Armfield one of the best full-backs in the world and in Ron Springett a brave, athletic goalkeeper.

However, England began the 1961/62 season unimpressively and the departures of Greaves to AC Milan and Gerry Hitchens to Inter were certainly a factor in England's slump in form. The Italian clubs would not agree to the players' release until just a few weeks before the World Cup finals and the subsequent reshuffling of the forward line clearly unsettled a side which had developed such a good understanding the year before.

England beat Luxembourg 4–1 in late September but played so poorly that they were booed off. The first goal by Burnley's Ray Pointer, the new centre-forward, sparked ironic cheers from an uncharitable Highbury crowd who switched their allegiance in the second half, cheering Luxembourg's every move and jeering England's. Portugal came to Wembley a month later for the group decider, with England needing only a draw to reach Chile after Luxembourg had astonishingly condemned Portugal to a 4–2 defeat. England triumphed 2–0, with both goals coming inside ten minutes, but it was by no means convincing and captain Haynes again found himself in the stocks of public and press opinion. In April England went to Glasgow to face Scotland, but the same five forwards who scored nine goals a year earlier could not find the net even once as England slid to a 2–0 defeat. After all the euphoria of the year before, the morale of everyone associated with the England team, from the players to the people, was back in the doldrums.

*Bobby Charlton and Bobby Robson in practice at Roehampton before leaving for Gothenburg for the World Cup*

*England manager Walter Winterbottom talks to players during the half-time interval of a practice game against Fulham*

The surprise setting for the 1962 World Cup was Chile, a country of undistinguished football pedigree with a rickety infrastructure and barely any stadia worthy of staging world football's premier event. The country had been ravaged by a series of earthquakes at the time of its bid to host the event. "We must have the World Cup, because we have nothing else," the President of the Chilean Football Association had argued with curious logic. FIFA, perhaps more out of compassion than confidence, granted his wish and most sceptics had been won over by the end of the tournament (with the exception of a handful of Italian journalists whose comments about the host country were said to have been a major factor behind the notorious "Battle of Santiago" between Chile and Italy).

England, the only Home Nation to qualify, disappeared high into the Andes where they were installed as the guests of an American copper company. Although they still felt no need for a doctor, they did at least have a cook this time – an old

Englishwoman called Bertha who helped soften the culture shock with some traditional English dishes. To help them relax and take their minds off the football, there was a cinema, a ten-pin bowling alley and a stunning golf course carved out of the mountain side. England had brought a well-experienced squad with 11 out of the 20 players capped ten times or more. The focus of the team was the captain Haynes, an immensely talented player with a devastating pass. But he was by no means everybody's favourite and was considered by many to be arrogant and intolerant of the mistakes of the lesser mortals in his midst.

In the end, England's tactical reliance on their captain and the poverty of their attacking ideas proved to be their undoing. When Haynes failed, England failed. Asked how his team would cope if they came up against England, a Yugoslav coach said he would simply extinguish Haynes's influence. "Number 10 takes the corners, number 10 takes the throw-ins. So what do we do? We put a man on number 10. Goodbye England," he said. Either

*Mid-air collision between England's Jerry Hitchins and Hungarian goalkeeper during England's disappointing 1962 World Cup campaign*

Hungary had been eavesdropping or they had done their own homework, because that is exactly what they did in England's opening match.

All England's group matches were staged at the revamped Rancagua stadium, a picturesque ground set in the foothills of the Andes, on a lush pitch, bordered by colourful flowerbeds. The word "Hungary" still sent a shiver down English spines even though the team of 1962 was nothing like as strong as the "Mighty Magyars" of the early 1950s. Although there was no Puskas, Hidegkuti or Kocsis to spark a panic attack

among England's defenders, Hungary could boast world-class players in forwards Florian Albert and Lajos Tichy. England went into the match as favourites and came out deserved 2–1 losers after a flat, unimaginative performance which led, inevitably, to some less than complimentary reviews in the press. But their hopes of reaching the quarter-finals were restored with an imperious display against a rough Argentinian side in their next match.

England were unrecognisable from the side that had struggled so wretchedly against the Hungarians

## JOHNNY HAYNES

| | |
|---|---|
| Position | Midfield/forward |
| Caps/goals | 56/18 |
| Debut | v Northern Ireland (2–0) in Belfast 2nd October 1954 |
| Last match | v Brazil (1–3) in Vina del Mar 10th June 1962 |
| Club | Fulham |

Johnny Haynes was English football's first £100-per-week player who opposition fans loved to hate – especially in the North where he was never acknowledged, as he was elsewhere, as one of the

great attacking midfielders of his generation. A Fulham player for all his 18-year career (he never won a club honour), Haynes was often accused of conceit, surliness and intolerance of less gifted players' mistakes. His technical skills and ball control were the equal of any player in his day, but it was as a passer of the ball that Haynes stood apart. His through balls, long or short, were the main weapon in his creative armoury and it is a matter of regret that he was not at his best during the World Cup finals of 1958 and 1962. He shouldered much of the blame for England's lacklustre display in Chile where the twin burdens

*Johnny Haynes in aerial combat with Russian goalkeeper Lev Yashin in the 1958 World Cup play-off*

of captaincy and providing England's creative impetus seemed to take their toll. It was not his fault that his outstanding ability made him the focal point of England's attacking, but when Haynes failed, England failed.

Two years earlier, Haynes, who caught the eye as a brilliant schoolboy international, captained England during one of the team's most impressive streaks when England scored 40 goals in six games including nine against Scotland. He skippered England 22 times in all but never played for his country again after he was injured in a car crash later in 1962. He remained loyal to Fulham even when his England prospects were jeopardised by the club's long spell in the second division. Haynes moved to South Africa in 1970 where he played for and then coached Durban City. He now lives in Edinburgh where he runs a dry cleaning business.

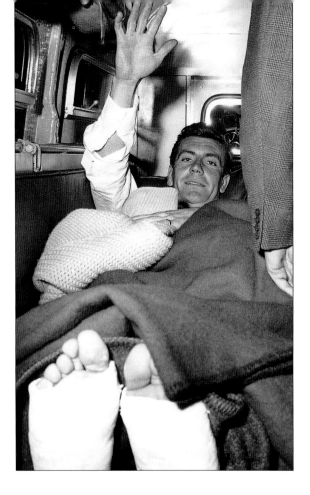

and they swept to a 3–1 win playing some first-rate football. The full-backs Jimmy Armfield and Ray Wilson, both converted forwards, were outstanding on the flanks, the new boy Bobby Moore was coolness itself and Haynes and Charlton were a constant threat coming forward.

Next up were the unknown Bulgarians, playing in their first World Cup, but who would not record their first World Cup win until 1994 in the United States. Just as they would 32 years later, they had qualified by knocking out highly-fancied France, who had finished third in 1958. The East Europeans, though, appeared to be suffering from vertigo now that they had climbed through the foothills of qualification and reached the lofty heights of the finals themselves. In losing 1–0 to Argentina and 6–1 to Hungary, they had quickly earned a reputation as the poorest team in the tournament and even the most pessimistic of Englishmen had little reason to worry.

The England players, though, looked tired and could only manage a goalless draw. After the match there were suggestions that the Bulgars, who had nothing to lose, had let England go through at the expense of an Argentinian team who had hacked the East Europeans black and blue a few days earlier. The fact that Bulgaria had seemed perfectly content just to pass the ball around at the back towards the end of the match was seized upon by the South American conspiracy theorists. Kostov's glaring headed miss in front of goal was also seen as evidence of a European plot, but the English press were far more worried by what they saw as England's chronic inability to break down well-marshalled defences.

England set off for the picturesque coastal town of Vina del Mar to face the mighty Brazilians in the quarter-finals. It was the third consecutive World Cup

that England had come up against the defending champions or competition favourites at an early stage of the series. In Switzerland they had met holders Uruguay in the quarter-finals and in Sweden they were drawn in the same group as favourites Brazil and Russia. Now it was to be the runaway winners of 1958 and the clear favourites back in their own continent four years on. Brazil were without the injured Pele, just 21 but already seen as the world's outstanding footballer, but they could call upon nine of the 1958 winning squad including Garrincha – the star of the tournament – Didi, Gilmar and Nilton and Djalma Santos.

England were a revelation, matching their lustrous opponents attack for attack until the final quarter of the game. Had the off-colour Greaves rediscovered his precocious goalscoring talent, England may well have celebrated a famous win. (One newspaper commented that Greaves's most significant contribution to the match had been when he crawled on all fours towards a dog which had strayed onto the pitch before removing it to the touchline).

The South Americans gained the ascendancy in the latter stages of the match and to the raucous

**ENGLAND:** The Official F.A. History

accompaniment of samba bands finished the best of the 1962 quarter-finals as 3–1 victors. But England had rescued some pride for themselves as well as for a tournament which had been marred by several violent group matches. They played their part in an open, attacking game before Garrincha sealed victory with a dipping, swerving shot from 25 yards which the Brazilian journalists had christened his "autumn leaf shot" – a description which belied the speed and power propelling the ball.

But their efforts failed to earn them a last-minute reprieve from the national press and the painful truth was that after four World Cup finals, England had won just three games out of 14. Inevitably, Haynes, who had looked tired and uninspired for the most part, was the lightning rod for much of the criticism and only right-back Jimmy Armfield and Bobby Charlton emerged with their reputations enhanced. Weeks of soul-searching followed as the press wondered aloud

*Winterbottom gets a retirement gift, subscribed for by 131 of the Internationals who'd played under him*

how a team which had promised so much two years earlier, had delivered so little. The disruptive departures of Greaves and Hitchens could only partly explain England's loss of rhythm.

Stories began to emerge claiming the squad that had set up camp in the Andes was an unhappy one riven by cliques, homesickness and boredom. There were accusations from several quarters that many of the players lacked mental toughness and there were even suggestions that the recent abolition of the maximum wage had led some to think that playing for England was no longer that important. One paper accused many of the players of wearing the white shirt of England like a flag of surrender. The *Daily Mail* believed the whole structure of English football needed an overhaul, declaring: "If England are ever to approach the standard of the magnificent Brazilians it is vital that our whole way of soccer life, from the players and club angle, must change."

Winterbottom was treated a little more deferentially, but it was not long before he resigned after 17 years in charge, during which England had won 78, drawn 32 and lost 27 of their 137 matches.

# 1964-1966

## ON TOP OF THE WORLD

*After England's disappointing 1962 World Cup effort, the press
were crying out for a change in "our whole way of soccer life".
In 1964 they got their wish with the appointment of Alf Ramsey as the new
manager, a man who would foster a new team spirit, reward players' skills
and lead England to World Cup glory.*

Shortly after his appointment as England manager Alf Ramsey announced that England would win the 1966 World Cup. It is difficult to imagine a modern manager making so bold a declaration of intent, but Ramsey was not being reckless or arrogant. He may have been a little naive in handing the executioners on Fleet Street all the rope they needed to hang him if he failed, but he spoke with the quiet certainty of a man who seemed to know something the rest of the world didn't. His comments were immediately relayed around the globe and acted like a challenge not just to his rivals but to those England players who would be charged with the heavy responsibility of delivering his promise. Ramsey had raised the stakes, as well as the expectations of a nation, and in doing so had increased the pressure on himself and his players. But his confidence had the virtue of creating a sense of self-belief as English football focussed on the task ahead. His remarkable success at Ipswich, whom he had taken from the backwaters of English football to the championship title, was another cause for quiet optimism.

Ramsey was only appointed after the post had been turned down by Jimmy Adamson of Burnley, Winterbottom's assistant in Chile, who did not want to spend long periods away from his native north of England. His arrival created a new atmosphere in the England camp. Whereas Winterbottom, the scholarly former RAF Wing Commander, had preserved the gentleman-player, officer-troops divide during his reign, Ramsey was one of the boys. "Just call me Alf" was his message to the players. He was no soft touch, but as a highly successful full-back with Tottenham and England, he had come to understand the benefits of team solidarity. He surrounded himself with players he trusted and who would not stir up dissension in the camp. He would achieve the Holy Grail of international management: fostering a club spirit within the national squad.

Ramsey's reign got off to a poor start in February 1963 with a 5–2 hammering by France in Paris which eliminated England from the 1964 European Championship (then known as the Nations Cup). Defeat to Scotland followed, but it should be noted that his official tenure did not start until May and the teams against the French and the Scots had partly been selected for him. England drew 1–1 with Brazil at Wembley in his first real game in charge, the start of a bewildering series of matches which Ramsey saw as vital to England's hopes of lifting the Jules Rimet trophy. In the first 13 months of his reign England played 11 matches, losing just once to Scotland.

A tour to South America in the summer of 1964 was less heartening. After a quick stop-over in New York to beat the United States 10–0, England flew to Brazil for a four-nation competition and lost 5–1 to their hosts the world champions, drew 1–1 with Portugal and lost 1–0 to Argentina. It was to be the start of a poor run. The reviews in the press grew increasingly hostile, but Ramsey would not be

## JIMMY GREAVES

| | |
|---|---|
| Position | Striker |
| Caps/goals | 57/44 |
| Debut | v Peru (1–4) in Lima |
| | 17th May 1959 |
| Last match | v Australia (1–0) in Vienna |
| | 27th May 1967 |
| Clubs | Chelsea, AC Milan, Tottenham, |
| | West Ham |

A stocky Londoner blessed with an instinctive positional sense common to all the great goalmouth predators, Jimmy Greaves is England's third highest goalscorer with a remarkable strike rate of 44 goals in 57 games. His speed of thought allowed him to read the game better than most and his ability to lose defenders, to disappear from the game only to re-emerge for a vital goal, made him the most feared striker of his day.

Greaves rarely hesitated to serve notice of his talents and can boast the distinction of scoring on his debuts with England, England Under-23s, Chelsea, AC Milan, Spurs and West Ham. He scored a record six hat-tricks for England but his critics (who did not count many defenders in their number) point out that the majority of his international goals came against weak opposition. It is true that he only scored one goal in seven World Cup games, but in Chile 1962 the England team as a whole failed to perform while in the group round of 1966 Greaves, who had just recovered from jaundice, found himself up against teams with nine, even ten, men behind the ball. (By then his overall strike rate, like that of all goalscorers, had slowed down significantly following the arrival of the 4–2–4 system).

He was famously left out of the 1966 final and was so upset he didn't go to the post-match party. His England career petered out after 1966, but he did pit his talents against the world's best in Mexico four years later – as a driver in the World Rally Championship in which he finished sixth in a Ford Escort. He was one of the first English players to be lured by a move to Italy, but he had a terrible time at AC Milan even though he still managed to score nine goals in ten games. He found the tough discipline intolerable and finally demanded a transfer after the club punished him by refusing to release him for England. His dry wit helped him find success as a TV pundit after he won widespread admiration for overcoming a serious drink problem.

*Greaves displays his predatory instincts*

## Sir Alf Ramsey
## (1963–74)

When Alf Ramsey took over the England job in 1963, none of his players could accuse him of not knowing what he was talking about. He was one of them.

He had gone into management after an outstanding career as full-back with Tottenham and England in the 1950s. He had been capped 32 times and had experienced the bitterness of England's watershed defeats to the USA in 1950 and to Hungary at Wembley in 1953. He only accepted the England job on the insistence that he, and not a collection of blazered administrators, would select the team. The team would be his creation and not the patchwork side of a dusty selection committee. He was not even the first choice for the post but was approached by the FA after Burnley's Jimmy Adamson had turned it down. Ramsey had proved his remarkable managerial skills at Ipswich, who he led from obscurity in Division Three South to the first division title in just five years through shrewd organisation of limited resources. (Ramsey would show the same resourcefulness in 1966 when, realising that England lacked truly world-class wingers, he dispensed with those he had and created the then radical 4–3–3 "wingless wonders" system.)

His dedication was legendary. After Ipswich had been crowned Division Two champions he went straight off to watch the club's juniors play, leaving the team and the rest of the club to do the celebrating.

With England he realised the importance of trying to build up camaraderie and succeeded

*Sir Alf explains what went wrong in Mexico*

persuaded that he was on the wrong track. The 1965/66 season began in a way which gave no one good reason to expect that Ramsey would deliver his "millstone" promise. A 0–0 draw in Wales was followed by a 3–2 defeat to Austria at Wembley and a narrow 2–1 win over Northern Ireland.

The Wembley defeat was the lowest point in those early years, but it was to be England's last defeat for 20 matches. For Ramsey had hit upon a formula which would win him the World Cup: the 4–3–3 formation.

in fostering a club spirit in the national squad. He may have lacked Winterbottom's charm and public relations skills, and could often be abrasive to outsiders, but he developed a strong bond with his players who he protected with unwavering loyalty. To many, Ramsey seemed dispassionate and cold – an impression which was reinforced during England's World Cup triumph in 1966, when he sat motionless and poker-faced on the bench at the final whistle as all around him jumped for joy. But those who knew him would say he was a far more sensitive character than his surliness would suggest, claiming that his reserve was just a protective shield against criticism.

Ramsey was born in Dagenham, Essex, and apparently never lost his taste for jellied eels, but it was one of the contradictions of the man that he took elocution lessons to replace his strong estuarian accent with a more gentrified mode of speech – even though he was never more comfortable than with people of his own background. He was always immaculately turned out with barely a hair out of place, even on the training ground, and was a stern disciplinarian, though rarely unreasonable.

In 1967 he was knighted after guiding England to its finest hour in the 4–2 triumph in the World Cup final at Wembley on 30th July 1966. The team he took to Mexico four years later was even stronger, but lost to the Germans after extra time in the quarter-finals, despite being two goals up with half an hour to go. England failed to qualify for the 1974 finals after the notorious 1–1 draw with Poland at Wembley, when England bombarded the Polish goal in a vain search for the decisive winning goal. Ramsey paid the price for the freakish failure and was sacked. He returned to management briefly with Birmingham City, and later had a short spell as a consultant to Greek outfit Panathinaikos before retiring to the modest house in Ipswich he had owned since the mid-1950s.

**England record P113 W69 D27 L17 F224 A99**

The radical new system dispensed with orthodox wingers and placed the emphasis on teamwork rather than individual flair. He first tried the formation, which saw Bobby Charlton switching to a more influential role in the centre, in England's 1–0 win over West Germany in Nuremberg during the summer. Ramsey, though, did not discard his wingers there and then and his final squad would include three wide players: Ian Callaghan, John Connelly and Terry Paine. He kept all his options open, but in 4–3–3 he had discovered a way of making England extremely difficult to beat.

Ramsey was looking not just for his ideal 11 players but his ideal 22. "In the past, England have been too reliant on players who later became injured or lost form. I have said it many times since taking over as a manager: I want a squad, not a team, with players ready for first team action when I call them," said Ramsey, who actually made an average of just one change per match in his early years. For Ramsey there was little room for sentimentality. Winning the World Cup was all that was important and individual concerns had to be subordinated to the collective cause. The England Under-23s proved to be invaluable to him as he was able to draw upon a pool of players with international experience. Geoff Hurst and Martin Peters, key figures in England's eventual triumph, were both hastily summoned from the Under-23s in the few months before the finals. (Hurst made his debut for the senior side in February and Peters as late as May). Alan Ball and Nobby Stiles, whose tireless running and constant harrying of opponents became pivotal to Ramsey's game plan, had been called up a year earlier.

When England went on their final warm-up tour they were a settled side with only a few positions in doubt. Greaves, the greatest goalscorer of his generation, was back after a bout of hepatitis which had ruled him out for ten weeks. His remarkable scoring rate at both international and club level should have made him an automatic choice ahead of Hurst and Roger Hunt. There was also speculation that Bobby Moore's place was under threat from the less

## BOBBY CHARLTON

| | |
|---|---|
| Position | Forward |
| Caps/goals | 106/49 |
| Debut | v Scotland (4–0) |
| | in Glasgow |
| | 19th April 1958 |
| Last match | v West Germany |
| | (2–3 aet) in Leon, Mexico |
| | 14th June1970 |
| Clubs | Manchester United, |
| | Preston |

In 1995 a British Embassy spokesman in Morocco said: "A visit by the Prince of Wales is big news, but not as big as Mr Charlton's." Bobby Charlton played his last match for England in 1970 but he remains a sporting icon revered throughout the world not just for his outstanding athletic ability but also for his unimpeachable sportsmanship. Comparisons between players are

*Bobby Charlton:*
*revered throughout the world*

talented but more combative Norman Hunter of Leeds. England returned from their European tour full of confidence after beating Finland 3–0, Norway 6–1, Denmark 2–0 and a tough Poland side 1–0. Greaves scored four in Oslo prompting himself and many observers to believe he was back to his best.

When England returned from the tour on Wednesday July 6th Ramsey allowed his players to return to their families for two days before reassembling on the Friday to prepare for the opening game against Uruguay on the Monday.

Ramsey would say later that the decision to let the players go home to relax was one of the most important decisions he made during England's preparations. He felt also that the organisers' decision to stage the event in July rather than any earlier was to England's advantage as it would give his players time to recuperate after a typically gruelling English season. The FA managed to extract guarantees from the clubs that their England players would be given two weeks' complete rest before meeting up for intensive training at Lilleshall.

A strict routine was established at the England camp. Two afternoons per week were set aside for the press, but there were to be no other intrusions. And there was to be no creeping down the road for

often odious as different positions demand different skills, but it can be easily argued that Charlton's all-round talent makes him the best player ever to represent England. Such were his gifts that by the time of his retirement, nobody could say for sure whether his best position was midfield general, winger or centre-forward.

A strong runner blessed with a powerful long range shot with both feet, Charlton was also a good distributor of the ball. But he was at his most dangerous when he would take out a defender and prise open the opposition with his mesmerising body swerve.

Born into a football-obsessed mining family in Northumberland, Charlton and his elder brother Jackie were taught the game by their mother, the sister of the great Newcastle and England centre-forward Jackie Milburn. He joined Manchester United as a 15-year-old and scored twice on his league debut in 1956 against Charlton (causing great mirth among the newspaper headline writers of the day). He survived the Munich air disaster of 1958, when the plane carrying the United team back from a European Cup match in Belgrade hit a building at the end of a snow-bound runway, leaving 23 dead. The horrifying experience made a profound impact on the shy 20-year-old Charlton who became even more introverted.

Nonetheless, his career continued to flourish, although he was controversially dropped after England's 5–0 defeat to Yugoslavia in Belgrade later that year. He was named in the squad for the 1958 World Cup in Sweden but did not play a single game. Charlton played in the three subsequent World Cups but was at his best in England's 1966 triumph when he was at the peak of his considerable powers, scoring both goals in the 2–1 semi-final win over the highly-fancied Portuguese. The mid-1960s were golden years for Charlton: he not only won a World Cup winners' medal with England and a European Cup winners' medal with United in 1968 but was also named European Footballer of the Year in 1966.

His last match for England came when he (along with Martin Peters) was subbed in the ill-fated defeat to West Germany in the quarter-final of 1970, when England threw away a two-goal advantage to lose 3–2 in extra-time. In the twilight of his playing days he appeared briefly for Preston and even managed them for a short time before a dispute led to his resignation. He took a path rarely trodden by footballers when he became a director of Manchester United and also established a sports school. He was knighted in 1994 in belated recognition of his contribution, not just to sport but to sportsmanship.

## BOBBY MOORE

| | |
|---|---|
| Position | Left-half |
| Caps/goals | 108/2 |
| Debut | v Peru (1–4) in Lima |
| | 20th May 1962 |
| Last match | v Italy (0–1) at Wembley |
| | 14th November 1973 |
| Clubs | West Ham, Fulham |

"The best defender in the world" was Pele's tribute to Bobby Moore, England's World Cup winning captain of 1966. But when he died in 1993 at the age of 51, it was not just football fans who mourned his passing. Everyone in England knew Bobby Moore not only as a great athlete, but as an embodiment of all that is best in sport. Moore captained England in all but 17 of his 108 internationals with a calm authority that inspired rather than demanded respect. His dignity was never better illustrated than when he was arrested in Bogota on a bogus charge of stealing a bracelet from a jewellery store during England's preparations for the 1970 World Cup in Mexico. The news that the captain of the reigning World Champions was

a suspected thief naturally raced around the world, but Moore handled the whole ugly affair with composure, never betraying any sign of pressure on or off the pitch.

This coolness was his hallmark as a player, calmly going about his business even when others were losing their heads. His languid, unflappable style often led to accusations, mainly towards the end of his club career, that he wasn't trying. But the keys to this unhurried approach were his intuitive reading of the game, his measured distribution and his exquisite timing in the tackle. He was the personification of the big match temperament but if there were weaknesses, they were his lack of pace and his suspect ability in the air.

Born in East London, Bobby Moore joined local giants West Ham, making his debut at the age of 17, and quickly caught the attention of the England set-up. By the time he made his debut for the senior side in the immediate build-up to the 1962 World Cup, Moore had accumulated a considerable amount of experience of international competition having played 18 times for England Youth and eight times for the Under-23 side. He was one of the few players to emerge from the Chilean experience with any credit and established himself as a regular in the side.

He took over the captaincy from Jimmy Armfield but often found himself in conflict with Alf Ramsey. There was even speculation that Norman Hunter of Leeds might replace him for the 1966 World Cup, but they settled their differences and a mutual respect grew. Moore was named Player of the Tournament in 1966 and it is the picture of him, carried aloft on the shoulders of his jubilant teammates and clutching the Jules Rimet trophy, that became the enduring image of England's finest hour.

a pint – to the great frustration of Jackie Charlton. There were daily medical checks and weight sessions and even foot inspections with instructions to players on how to cut their toe-nails (the fear being that a careless snip of the scissors may lead to infection in the foot, the prize asset of the soccer player). Nothing which could possibly jeopardise England's chances was overlooked.

With a stable, experienced and harmonious squad, immaculate preparation, as well as the boon of home advantage, England's chances of winning the World Cup were as good as they ever would be. Ramsey had developed a solid, efficient side which had lost only once in just over two years. They were essentially a defensive team with a spine of truly world class players in Gordon Banks, Bobby Charlton and Bobby Moore. But the squad's greatest strength lay in its comradeship, the sense of all-for-one and one-for-all so shrewdly developed by Ramsey. The taciturn England boss, often prickly with the press and offhand to outsiders, had put his faith in a select group of players who returned his loyalty with interest.

England were to play all their matches at Wembley

## NORBERT 'NOBBY' STILES

| | |
|---|---|
| Position | Right-half |
| Caps/goals | 28/1 |
| Debut | v Scotland (2–2) at Wembley 10th April 1965 |
| Last match | v Scotland (0–0) in Glasgow 25th April 1970 |
| Clubs | Manchester United, Preston |

An instantly recognisable figure on the pitch with his toothless grin and rolled-down socks, Stiles was one of the least technically gifted and most criticised players ever to pull on an England shirt. But his constant harassing, ferocious tackling and ball-winning skills made him an invaluable asset in England's 1966 World Cup campaign.

His selection provoked widespread criticism but he justified his place when it was realised that without Stiles (or Alan Ball), the likes of Bobby Charlton would never see the ball. His performance in the semi-final against Portugal when he marked the outstanding Eusebio out of the game was a crucial factor in England's ultimate triumph.

He had to wear contact lenses after his vision was affected when he was knocked down by a bus as a youngster and his notoriously poor eyesight was often used as an excuse for some of his more injudicious challenges. In the group matches he incurred the wrath of the FA's international committee who demanded he was dropped for a crippling tackle on Simon of France. Ramsey refused to comply and said that if Stiles went, he went. The ultimate defensive midfielder.

*Nobby Stiles:*
*more grit than grace*

and like most host nations were accused at various points of the tournament of being given special treatment by the organisers and referees. (The French sports paper *L'Equipe* ran a cartoon after the group matches picturing Bobby Charlton driving in a Rolls-Royce as the referee cleared opposition players out of his way).

With the Jules Rimet trophy safely under lock and key, the 1966 World Cup finals were ready to start. To the immense embarrassment of the FA, the famous gold statuette had been stolen from an exhibition at Westminster Central Hall four months earlier. But they were spared the world's eternal scorn by a black and white mongrel called Pickles who found the trophy wrapped in newspaper under a hedge in a south London garden.

## v Uruguay (0–0)

Not for the first or last time, the opening match of the World Cup finals was a dreadful spectacle. The match was doomed from the outset as the South Americans strung nine men across the back and invited England to beat their heads against a defensive wall. The fears of those expecting a tournament to be marred by negative tactics seemed to have been borne out, although ten goals in three games the next day partially allayed those worries. England had 15 shots on goal, but Greaves and Charlton, their most likely sources of a breakthrough, were marked out of the game. The frustration of playing against a team determined only to avoid defeat did at least remind the players that industry and patience were going to be essential qualities over the coming weeks. Some commentators felt the match highlighted England's lack of imagination coming forward with the *Daily Mail* warning: "England played with endless heart as we knew they would.... But this never will be quite enough." The next day Ramsey took the players to Pinewood studios where Sean Connery was filming the latest Bond movie. "Instead of getting us uptight and tense, Ramsey put us in a relaxed state of mind for the game against Mexico," said Nobby Stiles.

*Greaves and Moore share a joke with Sean Connery and Yul Brynner as England relaxed with a visit to the set of the latest Bond movie*

**ENGLAND:** The Official F.A. History

## v Mexico (2–0)

England started off against Mexico much as they had left off against the Uruguayans: running in vain at a packed defence. But when the breakthrough came, it did so in spectacular fashion as Bobby Charlton picked up the ball in his own half and surged towards goal. With the Mexican defenders backing off, Charlton unleashed a thunderous shot from 25 yards that flew into the top left corner. And it was Charlton who set up England's second with a through ball to Greaves, whose shot rebounded for Hunt to score from close range. Not everyone, though, was impressed. Hugh McIlvanney in *The Observer* insisted: "Unless there is a dramatic injection of imagination in midfield and of vigorous initiative in attack, the dreams that have been cherished over three years of preparation are likely to dissolve miserably." But if McIlvanney was worried about England's poverty of ideas, he was positively coruscating about Mexico's abject display. "On the evidence of this performance Mexico have about as much right to be in the World Cup as the Isle of Man has to be on the Security Council," he suggested.

## v France (2–0)

France needed a handsome win to reach the quarter-finals after defeat to Uruguay and a draw with Mexico,

*Bobby Charlton fires England into the lead with a 25-yard thunderbolt*

*Bobby Charlton (centre), Roger Hunt (right), scorer of England's second goal, and Jimmy Greaves at Wembley*

*England's Ian Callaghan wrongfoots Jacques Simon during the 2–0 win over France*

but they never threatened a steadily improving England after an early injury to the influential Robert Herbin. Hunt scored after 37 minutes from a suspiciously offside position, turning in a header from Jackie Charlton that had cannoned back off the crossbar. As England celebrated, France's Jacques Simon lay prostrate after an ugly challenge from Stiles, who later admitted it was a bad tackle but claimed he had simply timed it wrong. The FA and some quarters of the press called for the Manchester United midfielder to be dropped for the potentially explosive encounter with Argentina. But the ever-loyal Ramsey issued an ultimatum: "If Stiles goes, I go," and the FA backed down. England were through to the quarter-finals but Ken Jones of the *Daily Mirror* was one of many who held out little hope of an ultimate triumph.

"This time there can be no excuse," he said. "There were no barricades in front of them smothering every attempt at build-up and breakthrough."

## Quarter-final v Argentina (1–0)

Ramsey called the changes for the match with Argentina who were regarded as one of the strongest teams in the finals. Winger Ian Callaghan was dumped in favour of Alan Ball, who was brought in to deal with the threat of Marzolini down England's left flank. Stiles was assigned to man-mark the dangerous Ermindo Onega while Greaves, who had failed to score in the group matches and had injured himself against France, made way for the more powerful Hurst.

The match was quickly embroiled in controversy when the early efforts of the German referee Rudolf

Kreitlein to impose some moral authority on the game backfired with famous consequences. Kreitlein took the name of an Argentinian in the opening minutes, incensing Argentine captain Antonio Rattin, who argued with the official for the next half hour. Fed up with his constant haranguing, Kreitlein ordered Rattin off after 36 minutes. Brian Glanville in *The Sunday Times* said that Kreitlein booked so many Argentinians that "one was reminded of a schoolboy collecting railway engine numbers. At last, possibly because he had no pages left, he abruptly ordered off Rattin". Rattin, however, refused to go and ten minutes passed while officials and policemen came onto the pitch to mediate. Finally with boos and a chorus of "Why are we waiting?" ringing in his ears and pieces of fruit showering down on him, Rattin walked.

At the end of the match Kreitlein had to be protected by police from the Argentine players, and

*Argentina captain Rattin refuses to leave the field*

*Bobby Moore assesses the options against Argentina*

*Below: referee Rudolf Kreitlein is given police escort off the pitch at the end of the game*

Ramsey was so disgusted by their behaviour that he tried to forcibly stop his players swapping shirts. As the England players celebrated their victory with champagne, a chair was thrown through the glass door of their changing room and several of the Argentinian players tried to force their way in for a fight. Ramsey described England's opponents as "animals" but later retracted his comments under pressure from the FA. The episode sparked a furious row with the South American countries threatening to pull out of FIFA at what they saw as a thinly-veiled European conspiracy. (On the same day at Sheffield, Uruguay had been beaten 4–0 by West Germany after having two players sent off by an English referee.) Amid all the controversy, England had slipped into the last four, but

only after a long struggle to break down their tough, talented opponents. The only goal of the game was straight out of the West Ham coaching manual, with Peters whipping over a cross from the left for Hurst to head in at the near post 12 minutes from time.

## Semi-final v Portugal (2–1)

In contrast to the horrors of the Argentina match, England's semi-final encounter with a brilliant Portugal team was a celebration of open, attacking football and good sportsmanship. "It is indeed remarkable that any football match, far less one played in the tense atmosphere of this competition, could proceed in such a gentlemanly fashion," said John Rafferty of *The Scotsman*. In what was arguably the best game of the series, no foul was committed until the 23rd minute and none by Portugal for nearly an hour.

The Portuguese were the new favourites after Brazil had bowed out, the victims of some ruthless

*Ramsey tries to stop the players swapping shirts*

*England right-half Nobby Stiles (right) and goalkeeper Gordon Banks embrace after beating Portugal 2-1*

treatment in the group stages. Central to England's success on the day was the performance of the much-maligned Nobby Stiles, who shadowed the ever dangerous Eusebio like a private detective. But it was Bobby Charlton who took the glory with one of his finest displays for England. He scored both England's goals, the second a thunderbolt hit on the run from the edge of the area which was so sweetly struck that several Portuguese players felt moved to shake his hand. Eusebio ensured an uneasy closing period for England when he scored from the spot after Jackie Charlton had handled on the line. Several England players wept with joy at the sound of the final whistle, while some commentators used the occasion to take a potshot at England's critics. "This performance rammed

**ENGLAND:** The Official F.A. History

the words of censure down the ranting throats of the defeated and envious teams from South America and Europe," wrote Desmond Hackett in the *Daily Express*.

## Final v West Germany (4–2 aet)

"No more gripping finale could have been offered as a product of the script-writer's art," said the FA's official report into the 1966 tournament. "If it had been fiction instead of fact it would have been regarded incredulously." It is unlikely that any of the 600 million people worldwide who watched or listened to the match would contest the report's conclusion. With an equaliser in the last minute of normal time, a goal which was still being disputed over 30 years later and victory only sealed with the last kick of the three-week tournament, the 1966 World Cup could not have ended more dramatically.

Both sides were unchanged from the semi-finals, meaning that Greaves, the deadliest marksman of his day, was left out. (He was so upset by his omission that he could not bring himself to attend the post-match banquet). Germany's manager, Helmut Schoen, decided to give Franz Beckenbauer the task of policing Bobby Charlton, a policy which many felt may have cost Germany the Cup as they missed the sweeper's creative talents coming forward.

The Germans scored first after 12 minutes when Helmut Haller swept home an uncharacteristically weak clearing header by Ray Wilson. The quick thinking of Moore led to England's equaliser five minutes later when he whipped over a free-kick for Geoff Hurst to head in with the Germans still taking up their positions. England were the stronger side in the second half and, roared on by a naturally partisan Wembley, they took the lead. The flame-haired Ball, whose endless running and stamina proved crucial before the game was out, won and took a corner 12 minutes from full-time. The ball ran to Hurst, whose

*The teams line up before the start of the final, one of the most dramatic matches of all time*

## MARTIN PETERS

| | |
|---|---|
| Position | Midfield |
| Caps/goals | 67/20 |
| Debut | v Yugoslavia (2–0) at Wembley 4th May 1966 |
| Last match | v Scotland (0–2) in Glasgow 18th May 1974 |
| Clubs | West Ham, Tottenham, Norwich |

*Peters jumps for joy after scoring England's second goal in the 1966 World Cup final*

Martin Peters was one of the West Ham triumvirate who played such a crucial part in England's 1966 World Cup campaign: Moore the leader and defensive rock, Hurst the hat-trick hero and Peters the all-round midfielder with uncanny positional sense who scored the "other" goal in the final. Alf Ramsey, who gave him his debut just two months before the finals, described him as ten years ahead of his time in terms of tactics and vision (prompting the terrace joke that Ramsey ought to wait another ten years before playing him). Regarded as a "modern" footballer with not just a bit but a lot of everything, Peters became Britain's first £200,000-player when he signed for Spurs in 1970. Peters had many qualities. He was fast, had a powerful right foot, a good head, an accurate pass, read the game well and, like David Platt 20 years later, had an ability to appear in goalscoring positions almost unnoticed. Although he was happiest on the left side of midfield, he was a player of great versatility whose all-round gifts made him one of the original "utility" players. He had a superb understanding with Hurst for club and country, and when he retired it was fitting that their partnership continued in the motor insurance business.

blocked shot fell to Peters to sweep England into the lead and to what seemed certain victory. But disaster struck in injury time when Jackie Charlton was adjudged to have fouled Held outside the area. Lothar Emmerich's free-kick fell to Weber, who pounced from six yards to stun Wembley into silence and send the game into extra time.

"You have beaten them once. Now go and do it again," was Ramsey's simple exhortation to his exhausted players.

Over 30 years on, there is barely a person in all of England who does not have at least some idea of what happened next. In the first half of extra time, Hurst struck a ferocious shot which cannoned downwards from the underside of the crossbar onto the goal-line (or thereabouts) and back into the six-yard box. Hurst

and the other England players cried "goal", but referee Gottfried Dienst of Switzerland was not so sure. He trotted over to his linesman on the right, a Russian by the name of Tofik Bakhramov, who was about to earn himself a place in the hearts of every Englishman. It was a goal, he told Dienst, who promptly pointed to the centre spot to the delight of a nerve-wracked Wembley.

Even now, after years of exhaustive slow-motion replays, no one is any the wiser, even though a team of Oxford scientists in 1996 claimed to have proved that the ball did not cross the line. The FA report published in 1967 was admirably patriotic in its judgement of events. "There is nothing controversial now about England's third goal, the one which would have been debated as long as football is played, if the

*Was it over the line? England's third goal is still disputed today*

human eye alone had been left to confirm or disprove the decision of the Swiss referee, Mr Gottfried Dienst, or the Russian linesman, Mr Tofik Bakhramov," it said. The report claimed that the official film of the tournament "Goal! World Cup 1966" demonstrated the indisputable authenticity of the goal: "The probing motion picture cameras established unquestionably the validity of the goal."

Three things, though, can be asserted with confidence. First, there is no way Mr Bakhramov, standing 50 yards away, can have been expected to make a considered judgement on a matter of fractions of an inch with the ball travelling at about 80mph. He may even have blinked at the decisive moment. Secondly, England scored a fourth goal anyway and on balance were the stronger team over the 120 minutes. Thirdly, there need never have been any argument if Roger Hunt had simply slotted the rebounding ball into the net instead of celebrating. Hurst sealed the famous win in the last minute when he burst past the exhausted German defence to blast a left-foot shot into the back of the net.

The phlegmatic Ramsey sat motionless and poker-faced on the bench as all around him jumped with joy at the sound of the final whistle. Moore, who was later voted Player of the Tournament, climbed the famous 39 steps to collect the golden trophy from Queen Elizabeth II. Both teams jogged a lap of honour, with the Wembley crowd cheering the Germans almost as loudly as the England players. Moore, clutching the most coveted prize in world football, was hoisted onto the shoulders of his teammates as Wembley celebrated England's finest hour. "Maybe those fellows were right when they said God was an Englishman," said Scotsman Hugh McIlvanney in *The Observer*. The England team was mobbed by jubilant crowds on the ten-mile journey to the post-match banquet at the Royal Garden Hotel in Kensington. Amid scenes of celebration not seen since VE Day 21 years earlier, the crowd demanded multiple appearances of the team on the hotel balcony. The following day the hotel management

had to call in builders to repair the masonry which had been chipped away in large quantities by souvenir-seekers.

Ramsey was widely credited with England's success.

"England's glory…was the result of the most patient, logical, painstaking, almost scientific, assault on the trophy there has perhaps ever been – and primarily the work and imagination of one man," wrote David Miller in *The Sunday Telegraph*. Brian

**ENGLAND:** The Official F.A. History

Glanville in *The Sunday Times* was of like mind,
writing: "A manager who can instill this kind of spirit
in a team, can bring them to this level of fitness, can
endow them with so concrete a defence, so persistent
an attack, deserves the highest possible credit...
The England team's triumph is inseparable from
his own."

*The victorious England team show off the Jules Rimet trophy*

## GEOFF HURST

| | |
|---|---|
| Position | Forward |
| Caps/goals | 49/24 |
| Debut | v West Germany (1–0) at Wembley |
| | 23rd February 1966 |
| Last match | v West Germany (1–3) at Wembley |
| | 29th April 1972 |
| Clubs | West Ham, Stoke, |
| | West Bromwich Albion |

Given his chance of immortality by England manager Alf Ramsey who bravely chose him ahead of the great Jimmy Greaves, Geoff Hurst seized his opportunity by plundering a spectacular hat-trick against West Germany in the 1966 World Cup final. One with his head, one with his left foot and one with his right, Hurst's is the only hat-trick to be scored in a World Cup final. His second goal, England's third in the 4–2 win, is perhaps the most controversial goal in the history of international football. His thumping shot cannoned down off the crossbar and, according to the Russian linesman, over the line.

Hurst, whose father played for Oldham Athletic, started his football life as a run-of-the-mill wing-half before West Ham manager Ron Greenwood converted him, at a stroke, into a potentially great player by playing him as a striker. Hurst quickly stood out as a powerful and energetic runner with an astute positional sense, constantly creating space for his colleagues to pick him out. West Germany can't say they weren't warned about Hurst as he made his debut against them a few months before the World Cup finals, but he lost his place on England's final warm-up tour and then regained it in the quarter-final against Argentina, when he scored with a towering header.

After retiring, he managed Chelsea briefly but ironically was shown the door after the club went a long stretch without scoring. He also played cricket for Essex.

*Hurst:*

*the only player to score*

*a hat-trick in a World Cup final*

## ALAN BALL

| | |
|---|---|
| Position | Midfield |
| Caps/goals | 72/8 |
| Debut | v Yugoslavia (1–1) in Belgrade 9th May 1965 |
| Last game | v Scotland (5–1) at Wembley 24th May 1975 |
| Clubs | Blackpool (twice), Everton, Arsenal, Southampton |

*Ball, third from left, a key figure in England's triumph*

If Alan Ball was the type of man who let criticism undermine his self-belief, then England may never have won the World Cup in 1966. When he was a youngster on the books at Bolton Wanderers he was told that he was not big enough to be a professional footballer but he might make "a good little jockey". But he was said to be so devoted to football that as a teenager he made no effort to get rid of his spots in the hope that girls would keep their distance and thus not distract him from "the beautiful game".

Lacking the speed and strength to make a striker and the technical skills to be a playmaking midfielder, he was rejected by Bolton and then Wolves before Blackpool recognised his qualities as a tenacious ball-winner. Ball, whose father played for Birmingham City, was instantly recognisable on the pitch with his fiery red hair, socks rolled down and elbows pumping as he careered around every inch of the turf during the 90 minutes. His tireless running and fanatical commitment to the team cause won him a call-up to the England Under-23 side before making his bow in the senior side at the age of 19. A year later he was collecting a World Cup winners' medal after producing arguably the key performance during England's 4–2 win over West Germany in the final. Ball forced and then took the corner which led to England's second goal before setting up the third. His stamina was a vital factor in the energy-sapping half hour of extra time as Ball more than repaid the faith shown in him by England manager Alf Ramsey.

He went on to twice break the British transfer record but his natural aggression often found him in trouble with referees and FA disciplinary commissions. Ever combative, he is the only player to be sent off twice in England colours, first for the Under-23s against Austria in 1965 and then for the senior side against Poland in 1973. He went into management with Exeter, Southampton and Manchester City but with only moderate success.

# 1967–1974

## DON'T MENTION THE GERMANS…OR THE POLES

*The toast of the country after steering England to glory in 1966,*
*Ramsey now faced the task of keeping his team at the top.*
*But against West Germany in 1970 and Poland in 1973*
*Sir Alf discovered that what goes up,*
*must eventually come down.*

Ramsey was made a knight of the realm in the New Year's Honours list as England luxuriated in the knowledge that for the next four years the rest of the world would have to acknowledge them as "England, the World Champions of football". It has been said that victory in 1966 was the worst thing to happen to English football because it set an impossibly high benchmark by which all future campaigns would be judged. Anything short of winning the event could only be regarded as a failure, the argument ran. It was not a theory, however, which was preoccupying England's jubilant players and fans in the period between the Wembley triumph and Mexico 1970. But it was a truth which eventually caught up with Ramsey that from the peak of winning football's ultimate event, the only way was down. England might have stayed there for another four or even eight years – but if they didn't, their efforts would be construed as failure.

The national team was certainly not in decline when they arrived in Central America to defend their crown. If anything, they were stronger and certainly more experienced and confident than when they won. They were joint favourites with Brazil who would be remembered as one of the greatest sides of all time. When the two giants of world football clashed in the group matches there was little to separate the teams except a vivid contrast in styles and a single Brazilian goal. The two teams were destined to meet again in the final until England's extraordinary, unlikely exit at the hands of West Germany in the quarter-finals.

The morale-crushing defeat to Franz Beckenbauer's side marked the end of a mini Golden Age in English football. It was followed by the 1970s – an altogether darker age in which the national team would fail to reach the World Cup finals of 1974 and 1978. Even the glittering success of English club sides in Europe during that period was marred as the country's burgeoning band of hooligans found new enemies and new battlefields across the Channel.

Ramsey's tactics were considered to be increasingly cautious after 1970 and his preference for grafters rather than artists attracted mounting criticism. Finally, the man who had led England to their finest hour, paid the price for the country's traumatic failure to qualify for the 1974 World Cup finals. Sir Alf Ramsey, the toast of all England eight years earlier, was sacked. Ramsey's cause was not helped at a time when he needed all the friends he could get when he fell foul of the powerful Professor Sir Harold Thompson, then an FA vice-President and later its Chairman. The Old Etonian's patrician manner rankled with Ramsey who did his career prospects no favours by once telling him to stub his cigar out when he had wandered into the England players' breakfast room in a thick cloud of silver smoke. Ramsey was a great football manager and a man of immense loyalty to his players, but he was no diplomat.

England lost their first match after the World Cup as well as their 19-match unbeaten run in a 3–2 defeat to Scotland at Wembley in April 1967. The Scots claimed the victory made them the unofficial world champions and their fans celebrated by cutting up sods of Wembley turf to keep as souvenirs.

But it was a hollow victory for the Scots as England were forced to carry three injured players for much of the match and even had to play Jackie Charlton at centre-forward. The following year the two sides drew 1–1 at Hampden as England secured a meeting with Spain in the quarter-finals of the European Championship. England won the two-legged encounter 3–1 on aggregate to reach the semi-finals – their best peformance in the competition, Terry Venables' side matched the achievement in 1996.

En route to Florence where they would face Yugoslavia, England stopped over in Hanover for a friendly against West Germany. The England players took to the pitch wearing stiff, new boots after being paid by German boot manufacturers to sport their

*The squad Ramsey took to Mexico was said to be stronger even than their predecessors in 1966*

Used to a thicker-skinned breed of pressman back home, Ramsey had inadvertently stored up trouble for his team for their return the following year.

Engine England's final preparations for the defence of their crown were unsettled shortly before the start of the tournament when Bobby Moore, the golden boy of world football, was arrested in Bogota on what later transpired to be a bogus charge of stealing a cheap bracelet from a jewellers' shop. The episode was disturbing for everyone, it seemed, apart from Moore himself who, despite spending four

*4th May 1970: Alan Ball leads Bobby Moore,*
*Emlyn Hughes, Keith Newton, Tom Wright,*
*Jack Charlton, Peter Osgood, Brian Kidd*
*and Alex Stepney from Whites Hotel, London,*
*for the airport*

products. They lost 1–0 as the Germans triumphed over their World Cup adversaries for the first time in 38 years of trying.

Four days later, they lost an ill-tempered clash with Yugoslavia by the same score as Alan Mullery became the first ever England player to be sent off after kicking an opponent.

England, who as holders qualified automatically for Mexico, went on a tour of Central and South America in the summer of 1969 with a view to getting a feel of the conditions they could expect a year later. England drew 0–0 with Mexico in Mexico City, beat Uruguay 2–1 in Montevideo and lost 2–1 to Brazil in Rio. But perhaps the most significant episode of the trip took place in Mexico where Ramsey's abrasiveness towards the local press succeeded in stirring up animosity towards the England team.

**ENGLAND:** The Official F.A. History

days in a Colombian jail, handled the whole affair with remarkable dignity and equanimity. Nowhere were the charges more forcibly denounced than in the Colombian press which claimed the arrest of the England captain was just another example of recent efforts to extort money from the rich or famous.

Following strong diplomatic pressure Moore was finally released and the charges later dropped as the so-called witnesses to Moore's light-fingering failed to provide the necessary evidence. In spite of the scandal, England arrived in Mexico highly confident of retaining their title. Ramsey's first choice eleven were an experienced side with only Francis Lee and Terry Cooper having collected less than 20 caps. The team was as strong defensively as it was four years earlier, still as methodical but with a bit more tactical variety. Banks, Moore, Hurst and Ball were probably better players than when they had played so crucial

**Jimmy Greaves went to
Mexico in 1970 – for the
World Cup Rally**

a role in England's 1966 triumph, and Bobby Charlton and Peters were still a feature although several critics voiced their opinion that both players were living off their reputations.

"We all felt, including Alf, that we were probably the strongest squad England had ever had in their whole history – stronger even than in 1966. We were convinced we could win it," recalled Alan Mullery, who had earned himself a regular place ahead of Nobby Stiles.

Ramsey's men may have been top of the pops in England with the single "Back Home", but they were soon hitting all the wrong notes in Mexico. As world champions, England were the team to beat and they fully expected to be subjected to great scrutiny from world media waiting to report their every failure or slip-up. But there was added animosity with the South America v Europe row, sparked by England's controversial quarter-final with Argentina in 1966, still fresh in the mind.

Ramsey's awkwardness with his Mexican hosts and his prickliness with the press further

*The Charlton brothers rest during training in Mexico City*

undermined England's chances of having garlands placed around their necks on arrival. The squad's image was not helped as the team disembarked from the aircraft – Jeff Astle of West Bromwich Albion had to be helped from the plane after drinking heavily to overcome his fear of flying. With Moore recently accused of theft and now pictures of an England player arriving apparently drunk, the press had a field day.

Ramsey had clearly not been on a crash diplomacy course with the Foreign Office since his last trip to Central America and once again he managed to offend Mexican sensibilities when the team arrived at their base in Guadalajara. The players were banned from talking to the press, and while most nations, especially the savvy Brazilians, saw the common sense in trying to charm their hosts, the England camp provided an object lesson in how not to make friends and not influence people. As the squad withdrew into its self-made bunker, an English frozen food company flew in a month's supply of beefburgers, sausages and tomato ketchup. England even had their own bus and driver flown over.

Like everyone else, England would also have to contend with the heat and altitude, but to make matters worse, Ramsey's men were drawn in the toughest group with Brazil, whom England had not beaten for 14 years, Czechoslovakia and Romania.

*The greatest save of all time?*
*Banks keeps out Pele's bullet header*

**ENGLAND:** The Official F.A. History

England came through their opening match with a 1–0 win over a physical Romanian side courtesy of a goal from Hurst. The clash with Brazil five days later was one of the most eagerly awaited encounters in the history of the World Cup. It was billed as the "moral final" and the joint favourites to win the competition did not disappoint the biggest ever TV audience for a football match. Pele, Rivelino, Tostao, Gerson, Jairzinho and Carlos Alberto made the Brazil team of 1970 one of the greatest football teams of all time and certainly the best attacking side in the tournament. England, the holders, could boast the most accomplished defence in the world and were no slouches in other departments. The England players were a little bleary-eyed on the morning of the match after being kept awake all night by a crowd which had

## GORDON BANKS

| | |
|---|---|
| Position | Goalkeeper |
| Caps | 73 |
| Debut | v Scotland (1–2) at Wembley 6th April 1963 |
| Last match | v Scotland (1–0) in Glasgow 27th May 1972 |
| Clubs | Chesterfield, Leicester, Stoke |

The man they knew as "Banks of England" was one of the greatest goalkeepers the world has ever seen. Never a flashy player but always brave and unflappable, Banks kept a remarkable 35 clean sheets in his 73 internationals, including a record

seven in a row up to the 1966 World Cup semi-final v Portugal when he was beaten by a Eusebio penalty. He produced what is widely considered to be the greatest save of all time in the group match with Brazil in the 1970 World Cup in Mexico. A close-range header from Pele seemed destined for the back of the net and the great Brazilian was said to be shouting "goal" as the ball rocketed towards the bottom left of Banks's goal. But the England keeper hurled himself to the foot of the post and somehow scooped the ball to safety. (An enduring trivia question arising from the episode is: did Banks deflect the ball around the post or over the crossbar?)

Illness forced him out of the famous quarter-final against West Germany that year with dire consequences for the reigning champions. His replacement, Chelsea's Peter Bonetti, took much of the blame as England threw away a two-goal lead to crash out 3–2 after extra time. Banks was never seduced into joining one of the more "fashionable" clubs and was content to spend his career first with Chesterfield and then Leicester and Stoke. In 1972 he was awarded the OBE and named Footballer of the Year, but his international career was ended that year by a car accident in which he lost the sight in one eye. He ended his playing career with Fort Lauderdale in USA and was still good enough to be voted the country's best goalkeeper despite his eye problem. He later had a brief spell as manager of Telford and became a partner in a Stoke-on-Trent plant hire firm. The only weakness in his game was said to be his kicking.

throughout. Moore had probably his best game for England, tackling everything that moved with exquisite timing. But the match will always be remembered for THAT save by Banks from Pele. The Brazilians, though, eventually found a way of beating "Banks of England" when Jairzinho scored on the hour, but it was only after Astle snatched his shot to miss an open goal and Ball had crashed the ball against the crossbar that England were beaten. Pele and Moore swapped shirts and those who had watched a match of outstanding quality were convinced they would see the two teams meet again in the final.

England beat Czechoslovakia 1–0 to go through to the quarter-finals where they would face West Germany in Leon for a replay of the 1966 final. The most significant moment of the encounter probably happened a few days earlier when Banks took a long refreshing gulp from his bottle of beer. England's goalkeeper was struck down by a stomach bug and

gathered outside their hotel chanting for Brazil and honking car horns. At the demand of the television executives, the match kicked off at noon under the high Mexican sun when not even local dogs would venture out of the shade.

A classic encounter was won by a single Brazilian goal, but England matched their dazzling opponents the inexperienced Peter Bonetti was called in at an hour's notice to play his first competitive game for four weeks. Bonetti, so outstanding for Chelsea in the previous season, had a game that he and all England would want to forget. England knew that their famously tight defence would have to be at its best to keep out a German side who had scored ten goals in the group matches. Both sides featured five players from the 1966 final and England had the confidence of knowing that they had only lost to Germany once in nine encounters since 1930.

Ramsey's men looked set to maintain their dominance as they went into a 2–0 lead inside 50 minutes, with goals from Peters and Mullery, after producing their best football of the tournament. Beckenbauer reduced the deficit on 68 minutes, when his harmless-looking shot from an unpromising angle squirted under the nervous Bonetti. There followed the end of one of the great international careers when Bobby Charlton trotted off to be replaced by Colin Bell, and then Peters, largely anonymous during the tournament, was replaced by the up-and-at-them Norman Hunter.

An England side under Ramsey had never thrown away a two-goal lead and there was still no reason to panic. Whether or not Ramsey was right to disrupt the rhythm of his side remains a moot point, but with ten minutes to go, Seeler equalised with a freak header as Bonetti stood helpless in no-man's land. Ramsey told his players before extra-time in the 1966 final: "You have beaten them once. Now go and do it again." But on this occasion, whatever he said failed to work.

After Hurst had a goal mysteriously disallowed, Müller struck a close-range volley after 108 minutes which flashed past Bonetti, who had frozen on his goal-line. The world champions were dethroned and England had kicked their last balls in a World Cup for 12 years. It was no use telling Ramsey and his players that they were the victims of a freak match and some dubious goalkeeping. England were the second best team in the tournament, but they were going home early.

England's decline as a major force in world football during the 1970s did not begin immediately. Comforted by the widely held view that they had been unfortunate in Leon, they won six out of seven of their internationals the following season and would lose just twice in the two years after Mexico. But a 3–1 defeat at Wembley in April 1972 in a European Championship clash against West Germany, their new bogey team, suggested that England were no longer the power they were. The end of an era seemed to have arrived when Hurst, the hat-trick hero of 1966, trudged off his most

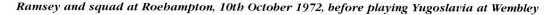

***Ramsey and squad at Roehampton, 10th October 1972, before playing Yugoslavia at Wembley***

*18th October 1973: England goalie Peter Shilton cannot bear to watch as Alan Clarke prepares to take the penalty against Poland*

famous stage, head down, after being substituted.

A few weeks later fortress Wembley was breached again as Northern Ireland triumphed 1–0. In January 1973 England's World Cup qualifying campaign got off to a shaky start when they were held to a 1–1 draw at home to Wales two months after they had scraped a 1–0 win in Cardiff.

England succeeded in upsetting Scotland's centenary celebrations with a 5–0 triumph at Hampden Park, with Moore winning his 100th cap. But their qualifying campaign hit the rocks that summer when they lost 2–0 to Poland in Katowice on 6th June. Alan Ball was sent off for getting involved in a scrap and appearing to knee a Pole in the groin, as England slid to their first defeat in a World Cup qualifier.

England were still favourites to qualify when they welcomed Poland to Wembley on 17th October. England needed to win but with a team composed of Shilton, Madeley, Hunter, McFarland, Hughes, Bell, Currie, Clarke, Chivers, Channon and Peters, there seemed little reason to fret. Brian Clough and his managerial side-kick Peter Taylor were certainly not worried. With words that would haunt England for years to come, Clough described Polish goalkeeper Jan

Tomaszewski as a "clown", while Taylor called their opponents "donkeys".

England bombarded the Polish goal from the outset only to find that the "clown" between the posts had also found time to become an outstanding goalkeeper. While England were guilty of some spectacular misses, Tomaszewski produced a string of spectacular saves to frustrate wave after wave of England attacks. Twelve minutes after the break, Poland scored with virtually

**ENGLAND: The Official F.A. History**

their first venture into enemy territory, meaning England would have to score twice to qualify. They levelled six minutes later through a Clarke penalty, and a second goal seemed just a matter of time as they continued to lay siege to the Polish goalmouth. In a desperate last gamble Ramsey threw on Derby's Kevin Hector with two minutes to go, and it almost paid off as the substitute headed just inches wide with seconds left on the clock. At the sound of the final whistle, some England players fell to their knees while others wept. A combination of Tomaszewski's brilliance, some poor finishing, grim Polish defending and downright bad luck had denied England a place in the finals.

The critics said it should never have come to that. "END OF THE WORLD" was the next day's headline in one paper. "I have never played in a more one-sided game in my life," said Hunter, playing in place of Moore for the first time and whose mistake led to Poland's goal. England, the champions of 1966 and the joint favourites of 1970, would not be going to West Germany in 1974, although Haiti, Zaire and Australia would.

Inevitably, a period of frenzied soul-searching began. Some argued that Ramsey had been too negative in his tactics over the previous few years while some said he had no idea how to use substitutes and that he was unable to cope with the demands of football in the modern age. Others complained about the poor preparations for international games, the standard of coaching, the problems at grass-root levels and so on… Amid all the recriminations, it was almost overlooked that England had overwhelmed the Poles for 90 minutes and had come within inches on a host of occasions to scoring the crucial second goal.

Nobody was calling too loudly for the head of Ramsey, the man who had steered England to its greatest moment eight years earlier and who was unquestionably one of football's great managers. But accepting the need for fresh impetus, the FA sacked Ramsey on 1st May 1974. The news was said to have shocked football's first knight, and many felt he should have been given the chance to step down of his own apparent accord.

**_Poland celebrate as England are eliminated from the World Cup_**

# 1974–1977

# THE DARK AGES

*England turned to Don Revie, the outstanding club manager of his generation, in a bid to revive the fortunes of the national team. But his three years in charge saw England slump to a new low before he abandoned his post amid cries of "traitor" in the middle of England's World Cup campaign.*

Joe Mercer took over the England job on a caretaker basis until the end of the season and managed to replace the scowl on the face of English football with a smile by his relaxed, cheerful manner. (Mercer's insistence on players being happy was said to have been so great that he dropped the gloomy-looking Stoke left-back Mike Pejic in fear that his face might depress the rest of the team.) There was, however, only one serious contender for the permanent job: Don Revie.

Revie was confirmed as Ramsey's successor on 4th July 1974 when he put pen to a five-year contract. Revie was in no doubt that he could reproduce his club success at international level. "I made the first move. They did not contact me. I fancied being England manager," he said after his appointment. England would not lose under Revie until their tenth game, and the 2–1 defeat to Czechoslovakia in October 1975 was followed by a 1–1 draw with Portugal in Lisbon which ended English hopes of qualifying for the finals of the European Championship. (The Czechs went on to win the event after a penalty shoot-out against West Germany.)

**17th November 1976, England v Italy at the Olympic Stadium. Bettega scores the second goal**

During that time signs of unrest in the England camp began to emerge. Kevin Keegan stormed out of a training session after Revie had dropped him from the side that drew 0–0 with Northern Ireland. He returned the next day, but he was not the only player to show his disapproval of the new regime. A year earlier, Stan Bowles, the prodigiously talented but wayward star of Queens Park Rangers, had also walked out while Ipswich's Kevin Beattie decided to go and stay with his mother rather than meet with the Under-23 squad. These incidents were blips rather than crises, but the failure to qualify for the European finals was certainly a heavy blow to morale.

Part of the problem seemed to be Revie's inability to establish a settled side. Players came and went with such regularity that by the 1976/77 season one newspaper was suggesting that Revie ought to hand over the responsibility of team selection to the Wurzels, who were topping the charts with "Combine Harvester" at the time. The decisive date in the Revie

## JOE MERCER (1974)

Joe Mercer's interregnum after the departure of Ramsey and the arrival of Revie was a happy but all too brief period for the national team in a decade that most England fans will want to forget. Depression had set in following England's unthinkable failure to qualify for the 1974 World Cup finals which led to the sacking of the man who had led England to glory in 1966. But with his banana smile, bandy legs and irrepressibly cheerful nature, Mercer provided some much needed comic relief. England lost just one of seven matches during the Mercer months – to Scotland – and after the disaster of the Revie years it can only be wondered what "might have been" had Mercer been appointed in his place.

A distinguished playing career with Everton, Arsenal and England was interrupted by World War Two. As manager of Manchester City he struck up a highly successful partnership with the flamboyant Malcolm Allison and together they led the Maine Road club to promotion to the first division before landing the league title, the FA Cup, the European Cup Winners' Cup and the League Cup.

**England record P7 W3 D3 L1 F9 A7**

*Mercer provided
a brief period of comic relief*

## DON REVIE (1974–77)

Somehow Don Revie's moody demeanour and hunched shoulders have come to capture the dark mood of English football in the 1970s, when the national side failed and hooligans went on the rampage. Revie's is a strange story. The man who never walked away from a challenge as a player or as a highly successful manager with Leeds, walked out of the national side in the middle of the qualifying campaign for the 1978 World Cup. To the disgust of the FA and the country at large, Revie dumped England to take an infinitely more lucrative job as manager of the United Arab Emirates. Revie did not help his cause by breaking

the news of his departure to a national newspaper before informing the FA. Nor was his image helped by the cloak-and-dagger manner in which he negotiated the deal with his Arab employers. The words "greed" and "treachery" were to come easily to the headline writers on Fleet Street.

Middlesbrough-born Revie started his playing career with Leicester before he moved to Hull City, Manchester City, Sunderland and finally to Leeds, where he was to establish himself as a hero. He enjoyed his greatest success as a player at Maine Road, where he developed into one of the most creative forwards of his generation, winning six caps, and was named Footballer of the Year in 1955.

*Italian joy as England watch their World Cup hopes go up in smoke*

years was 17th November 1976, when England lost 2–0 to Italy in Rome in a World Cup qualifier. Italy were no longer frightened of England, having beaten them for the first time in 40 years of trying in 1973. England, though, held the psychological advantage after coming back from two goals down to beat the Azzurri in a bicentennial game in America five months earlier. Italy's coach Enzo Bearzot chose seven Juventus players for the qualifier in Rome, but for the first half an hour his young side struggled to break down a steadfast English defence composed of Hughes, Mills, McFarland and, strangely, Clemence.

Italy went in front ten minutes before half-time, when Antognoni's free-kick took a wicked deflection

Revie's distinguished playing career was followed by a period of outstanding achievement as manager of Leeds where it is still not possible to hear a bad word said about him. Revie took over as player-manager with the Yorkshire club struggling in the lower half of the second division. Within a few years Leeds would be the most feared team in the land, with a reputation for tough, no-nonsense football. After winning promotion in 1964 Leeds did not finish out of the top four over the next ten years. During that time they won the league title in 1969 and 1974 and were runners-up in 1965, 1966, 1970, 1971 and 1973. They won the League Cup in 1968, the FA Cup in 1972 and were FA Cup runners-up in 1965, 1970 and 1973. They won the European Fairs Cup in 1968, having been losing finalists the year before as they were in the Cup Winners' Cup in 1973.

Revie's intensity and scientific approach to the England job made him similar to Ramsey. But whereas his predecessor succeeded in generating a club spirit at national level, Revie failed. His meticulously compiled dossiers on the opposition served only to confuse and often demoralise his players. He watched Italy no fewer than seven times in the run-up to England's 2–0 World Cup qualifying defeat in Rome in 1976 and baffled the team with his over-egged analysis of the Italians' strengths and weaknesses. And unlike Ramsey, who was loathe to upset the rhythm of his team by making sweeping changes to the line-up, Revie was erratic in his selection. Revie had all the right credentials for people to believe he would be a resounding success in English football's highest office. He arrived on the back of a 29-match unbeaten run at Leeds with England expecting, rather than simply hoping, that the glory days would quickly be back. Three years later his name was a dirty word in English football, a synonym for treachery, greed and failure.

*Praying for success:*
*Revie's coaching methods often*
*baffled England's players*

**England record P 30 W15 D 8 L7 F52 A16**

*Ray Clemence, Mick Channon*
*and Kevin Keegan leaving*
*Heathrow... on England duty*

on its way into the back of Clemence's net. England
seemed happy to suffer defeat by a single goal in the
belief (a correct one as it turned out) that they could
beat the Italians by a greater margin in the return
match at Wembley. But the apparent unwillingness
to look for an equaliser cost them dear in the end as
Bettega scored a second for Italy with a flying header
12 minutes from time. The mathematics now meant
that England would have to score a hatful when the
two teams met 364 days later. Revie knew England
had almost certainly blown their chances of going
to Argentina, and he knew who would have to pay
the price.

Confidence in the England camp was further
deflated when Holland came to Wembley early
in the new year. England were played off the park as
the men in orange gave their hosts a lesson in the arts
of "Total Football". Wembley was fast losing its
reputation as the impregnable citadel of world football
and at the end of May the Welsh came and plundered

**ENGLAND:** The Official F.A. History

a 1–0 win in the Home Championship. But it was a 2–1 defeat to the Scots a few days later, as well as the events that immediately followed the match, that prompted a sense that England had lost control. Wembley looked like a drunk Bay City Rollers concert as Scotland's tartan-clad fans poured onto the pitch to celebrate their first win at the home of English football for ten years. The goal frames were pulled down, nets ripped out and the turf cut up. In central London, Scottish fans danced in the fountains at Trafalgar Square. England, faced with failure to qualify for the World Cup finals, were now beaten in their own back yard by the Auld Enemy and the behaviour of the visiting supporters served only to indulge England's sense of humiliation.

Revie's popularity had been in sharp decline for some time when he outraged English football by announcing his resignation in the *Daily Mail* on 12th July 1977. The first the FA knew of Revie's decision was when they sat down to breakfast that morning. England were in the middle of a World Cup qualifying campaign – albeit one which had run out of hope in Rome eight months earlier. But what made Revie an instant hate figure was the fact that he had negotiated

*Scottish football supporters invade the pitch at Wembley Stadium and pull down the goalposts after a 2–1 victory over England in the 1977 home international*

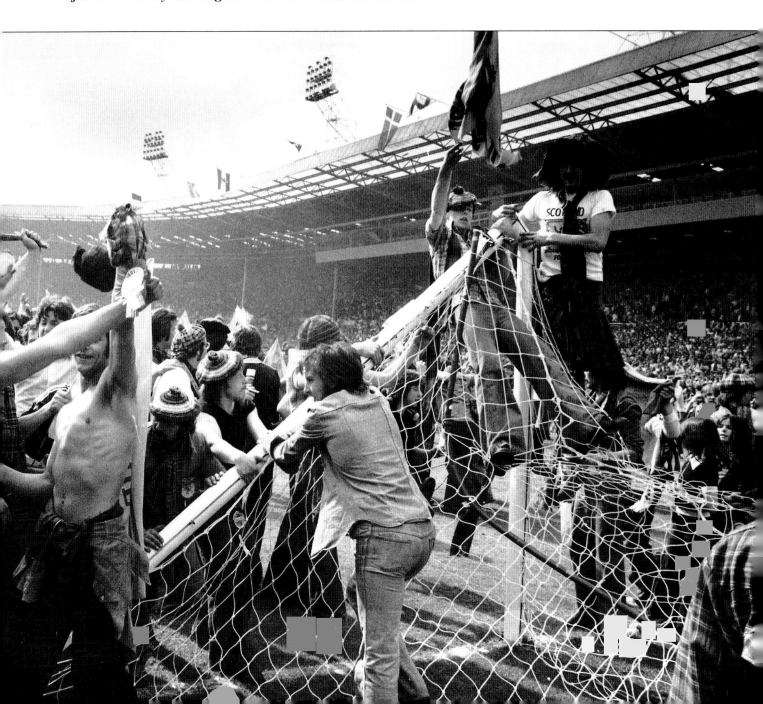

a lucrative deal to manage the United Arab Emirates while he was still in the England job. The press and England's despairing football public pointed the finger at Revie and cried "traitor!". The sense of treachery was compounded by the cloak-and-dagger manner of Revie's behaviour. As England set off on a summer tour of South America, Revie told the FA he was going on a "spying" mission in Europe and would join up with the team later. In fact, Revie got on a flight to Dubai (wearing dark glasses and with his collars turned up) to sort out the details of a contract with the UAE.

When the news broke, there was not a forgiving voice in the land – except in Leeds. "Don Revie's decision does not surprise me in the slightest. Now I can only hope he can quickly learn how to call out bingo numbers in Arabic," said Alan Hardaker, the secretary of the Football League. The papers, frustrated by years of failure on the pitch, went for all-out attack. It was open house in the personal abuse departments on Fleet Street. "TRAITOR!", "CHEAT!", "DESERTER!" screamed the back and front pages. The reputation Revie had built up so carefully in his years with Leeds was shredded by a press who had come to know him as "Don Readies" after his requests for cash in return for interviews.

Sir Harold Thompson, the man who brought down Ramsey and now Chairman of the FA, was distinctly unimpressed by the behaviour of his most important employee. Revie was suspended from English football indefinitely and the FA launched legal action. When the matter came to court, Revie won a joyless victory over the FA when the judge, Mr Justice Cantley, "with regret" ordered the FA to lift their ten-year ban on him. The court found Revie guilty of bringing the game into disrepute, with Mr Justice Cantley declaring the behaviour of the England boss was "a sensational, outrageous example of disloyalty, breach of duty, discourtesy and selfishness."

The Revie era, the saddest and darkest period

## EMLYN HUGHES

| | |
|---|---|
| Position | Defender |
| Caps/goals | 62/1 |
| Debut | v Holland (1–0) in Amsterdam 5th November 1969 |
| Last match | v Scotland (2–0) in Glasgow 24th May 1980 |
| Clubs | Blackpool, Liverpool, Wolves, Rotherham |

in the history of the national team, had ended in spectacular disaster. His attempts to restore the England team to its former glory by fostering the "Leeds spirit" in the squad had flopped. At Leeds, the team had picked itself. Revie had not needed to go out of his way to create a tight-knit family atmosphere among a group of players who week in, week out trained, played, ate, drank and socialised with each other. That was impossible with the national side and his notorious efforts to generate a club spirit by playing carpet bowls and bingo were merely greeted with amusement by the players.

Revie was lucky if he had his players together for a couple of days before a game, and there were some who had sympathy for him. If England had a World

*Don Revie and his wife Elsie arrive at the High Court to continue the fight against his ten-year ban*

Emlyn Hughes, who captained England 22 times during an international career spread over three decades, three managers and 11 years, had the right pedigree for a top sportsman. His father was a Great Britain rugby league international, his aunt played hockey for England while his brother and uncle were also professional footballers. Hughes, nicknamed "Crazy Horse", was a fully-committed player capable of lifting a team with his enthusiasm. One of the great defenders of his generation and a key figure in the brilliant Liverpool team of the 1970s, he was a player who loved driving upfield into enemy territory. But Hughes only managed one England goal in 62 games. It came at Ninian Park in England's 3–0 win over Wales in 1972 – to the great annoyance of his Welsh father. He has the rare distinction of winning the trust of three successive England managers – Joe Mercer, Don Revie and Ron Greenwood, who all made him captain.

*Victory in Europe? You must be joking. Hughes and Keegan share a laugh with PM Thatcher before they left for the European Championships in Italy*

Cup game on the Wednesday, the players still had to play in a tough first division game on the Saturday. Players would turn up for England bruised, battered, exhausted and often injured. But if Revie was searching for the continuity and unity he had enjoyed at Leeds, it was difficult to understand his reasons for chopping and changing the England team as often as he did. Revie chose 52 different players during his 29 matches in charge, whereas Ramsey had used 95 in 113. Ironically, the only unchanged England side he fielded was in his last game against Uruguay in Montevideo.

Revie's obsessional fear of the opposition was another cause for complaint among the England players. Many felt that he undermined confidence going into a match by talking up the threat of England's opponents. The in-depth dossiers he prepared on the opposition became a joke, but they testified to an almost paranoid fear of the enemy. Revie would say later that his one regret was that he tried to assemble a team capable of playing attractive football instead of assembling "a real bastard of a team".

# 1978-1982

## SPAIN IS THE AIM

*Ron Greenwood was on the verge of a complete retirement
from football when he answered an SOS from the FA to take on
the sinking ship that was the England football team.
He originally took over on a caretaker basis and arrived with a reputation
as one of English football's deepest thinkers.*

The 55-year-old had established a name for himself as a champion of "the beautiful game" after nearly two decades at West Ham. His teams were always attractive to watch but, his critics would say, they never won much. Others said that "Reverend Ron" was too nice, too thoughtful, too cerebral and lacked the steel and motivation qualities of Brian Clough, his main rival and the people's choice for the permanent post. The controversial Nottingham Forest boss thought he was certain to get the job when he emerged from Lancaster Gate to declare he had had a "magnificent interview". Greenwood, though, was a popular choice with the players. "The family atmosphere had gone, but he brought it back," said Emlyn Hughes.

Greenwood decided, at first, that the old-fashioned use of wingers was the way forward and turned to the pacy Steve Coppell of Manchester United and the skillful Peter Barnes of Manchester City to execute his strategy. Greenwood, though, would be quick to realise that one of the many difficulties of managing the national side was that he had to fashion a single style of play with a group of players whose clubs played in a variety of ways. On the continent the task of the national manager was easier, he would observe, because the clubs generally played the same way – with a sweeper. Greenwood would not have the benefit of that formulaic style of

**ENGLAND: The Official F.A. History** ───────

play which different players could slip in and out of without disrupting the team's rhythm.

He was faced with an apparently impossible mission when Italy came to Wembley in November 1977 for a World Cup qualifier that England needed to win by as big a margin as possible to stand any chance of reaching the finals. Both teams had eight points but England had played five games

*"Reverend" Ron*
*explains a tactical point*
*to his England flock*

*Keegan scores England's first in*
*the impressive 2–0 win over Italy*

to Italy's four. Italy had a goal difference of plus four and had the luxury of playing Luxembourg in their final game. On the night, England were magnificent as they chalked up a 2–0 victory with a vibrant and imaginative attacking performance in which Keegan and Coppell were outstanding. In the end Bearzot's side only managed to beat Luxembourg 3–0 to squeeze through at England's expense by the narrowest margin.

Notwithstanding the failure to qualify, England got off to a good start under Greenwood who was handed the manager's job on a permanent basis – partly on the strength of England's excellent display against the Italians.

England reached the finals of the 1980 European Championship in Italy after seven wins and a draw from their eight qualifying games against Denmark, the two Irelands and Bulgaria. But Greenwood's side failed to progress after finishing third in a group of four. England drew 1–1 with Belgium, who went into the final (there were no semis), lost 1–0 to their Italian hosts before inconsequentially beating Spain 2–1 in their final match.

B ut if the European Championship had been a disappointment, the following season was a disaster. England's prospects of reaching their first World Cup finals since 1970 looked rosy enough when the draw grouped them with Hungary, Romania, Switzerland and Norway, especially as two of the five

teams would go through. A handsome 4–0 home victory over Norway was followed by the setback of a 2–1 defeat in Bucharest and an unconvincing 2–1 win over the Swiss at

*Manchester United's Steve Coppell gets a few words of advice from England manager Ron Greenwood*

*Tony Woodcock scores England's second goal in a 4–0 win over Norway at Wembley in 1982*

Wembley in November 1980.

Six months later the press was calling for Greenwood's head as England's form suffered a dramatic slump. The first five matches of the new year were all at Wembley and England failed to win one of them. They lost to Brazil, Scotland and Spain and drew 0–0 with both Wales and Romania. The baying for Greenwood's blood reached its peak when England crashed to a 2–1 defeat to Switzerland in Basle at the end of May. The result left England facing an uphill task to qualify and was made all the worse by the behaviour of the team's fans, who rioted inside the stadium. Greenwood made up his mind to resign, but would not tell his players until England had played Hungary in Budapest a week later.

As if stung into urgent action by the mounting hostility of their critics, England produced one of their best performances for years against the Hungarians. Trevor Brooking, who scored twice, together with Robson and Keegan were outstanding in the midfield as England revived their World Cup hopes with a sparkling 3–1 victory. Brooking's second goal, after 60 minutes, restored the visitors' lead and will be remembered as one of the sweetest strikes in England's history. The accomplished West Ham playmaker pirouetted on the left corner of the area and fired a fierce rising shot which came to an abrupt stop in the top left-hand corner of the Hungarian goalframe. In the post-match press conference Greenwood effused about beating the country whose teams in the 1950s inspired his whole philosophy about football, but on the plane home he dropped his bombshell about quitting. A hasty conference took place among England's senior players before Keegan and Brooking sat down with Greenwood and persuaded him to stay on before the plane touched down.

England could enjoy the rest of the summer in the knowledge that their qualification campaign was on the rails again, but it was not long into the new season before they were plunged back into despair. The unthinkable happened: England lost to Norway. It was the first defeat against the Scandinavians in their history and could not have come at a worse time, for it left England relying on a highly improbable set of results elsewhere in the group to qualify for Spain. Norway's historic 2–1 win was greeted with uncontained delight in Oslo's Ulleval stadium and prompted one of the most famous outbursts in the history of sports broadcasting. Norwegian commentator Borge Lillelien threw objectivity to the wind as he joined the celebrations of his fellow countrymen. Live on air he screamed: "We are the best in the world! We have beaten England! Lord Nelson... Lord Beaverbrook... Sir Winston Churchill... Sir Anthony Eden... Clement Attlee... Henry Cooper... Lady Diana. We have beaten them all. Maggie Thatcher can you hear me? Maggie Thatcher your boys took a hell of

*Brooking's brilliant goal in England's 3–1 win over Hungary in Budapest lodges in the frame of the net*

## KEVIN KEEGAN

| | |
|---|---|
| Position | Forward |
| Caps/goals | 63/21 |
| Debut | v Wales (1–0) in Cardiff 15th November 1972 |
| Last match | v Spain (0–0) in Madrid 5th July 1982 |
| Clubs | Scunthorpe, Liverpool, Hamburg, Southampton, Newcastle |

Rejected by Coventry City as a youngster, Kevin Keegan went on to become the best English player of his generation, and he provides one of the few reasons to look back on England in the 1970s with any sense of pride. He was not blessed with an abundance of natural gifts, but made himself into a great footballer through sheer determination. A stocky Yorkshireman with a fiercely competitive streak, he was nonetheless the most sporting of players.

He started his professional career with Scunthorpe before Bill Shankly spotted his potential and took him to Liverpool in 1971. Keegan quickly endeared himself to the Kop with his darting runs, bottomless appetite for the fray and his clinical finishing. By the time he left for Hamburg in 1977, he had helped Liverpool win the FA Cup, the UEFA Cup twice, the European Cup and three league titles. His determination to learn the language and absorb a new culture made him a great success at Hamburg, whom he inspired to the 1980 European Cup final against Nottingham Forest. Keegan might have been excused for thinking international football meant nothing more than playing against Wales since his first three caps and his first match as captain were all against the Principality.

He was twice named European Footballer of the Year, but had the misfortune to be playing during a poor era for the national team and was denied the

*Keegan beats Argentinian Jorge Olguin at Wembley in 1980*

chance of showing his talents at the World Cups of 1974 and 1978 while he was at the peak of his career. There were other low points. On an England tour in 1974, Yugoslav airport police beat him up after mistaking him for a hooligan. In the Charity Shield of 1974 he and Leeds' Billy Bremner were sent off for fighting. He once pulled his car over in a lay-by near Southampton where he was set upon by a group of yobs with baseball bats. He also produced a single, "Head over Heels", at the height of his big-perm-and-flares period in 1978, which reached the Top Ten.

Towards the end of his playing days he said he wanted to become Prime Minister but went to play golf on the Costa del Sol instead, before returning to manage Newcastle for five years. Always passionate, honest and thoughtful as a player, Keegan took the same qualities into management and was hailed as the "Messiah" after taking the club from the edge of extinction back to the top of English football.

a beating. Norway have beaten England at football."

The England camp was more muted as Romania and Hungary were now clear favourites to go through. Switzerland, however, came to England's unlikely rescue when they upset the odds and the Romanians in Bucharest. Other results went England's way and, to everyone's delight and disbelief, they went into their final match at Wembley needing only a draw against Hungary, who had already qualified. In the end, a goal from Paul Mariner early on proved more than enough as England reached their first World Cup since 1970, albeit in the most unconvincing way imaginable. In one of the weakest groups they had lost three and drawn one of their eight games. England were through, but no one was holding their breath for success in Spain.

To general amusement back home and annoyance everywhere else, England were seeded in the finals despite trailing Hungary in their qualifying group. (The rationale behind the seedings was based on pedigree rather than current form). Many people had not wanted England to be there at all because Britain was at war with Argentina over the Falklands. Calls were made for a British boycott which would also have meant the withdrawal of Scotland and Northern Ireland. An encounter with Argentina would obviously carry potent symbolism for the winners and losers, but there were also security fears for the players and the spectators. But when the Thatcher government showed no sign of demanding a withdrawal, the protests simply died away.

Politics could not keep its head out of the 1982 World Cup finals, as England headed for their base in the northern port of Bilbao amid fears that Basque terrorists would exploit the publicity potential of the tournament. The players were given round-the-clock armed protection and there was even a tank parked in their hotel car park.

Greenwood's men were as confident as they had been for a while when they arrived in Spain on the back of six wins and a draw in which they conceded just two goals. Just as Ramsey had done 16 years earlier, Greenwood saw no need for wingers and found no place in the squad for Laurie Cunningham or Peter Barnes.

But there were now grounds for cautious English optimism. Greenwood had assembled a solid defence with Kenny Sansom and Mick Mills at full-back, and in young Terry Butcher Greenwood had found a player worthy of comparison with Dave Watson, England's inspirational defender of the late 1970s. Alongside him in the centre of the defence was the accomplished Phil Thompson of Liverpool. In midfield, Manchester

*England jet off for Spain: Kenny Sansom, Steve Foster, Trevor Francis, Steve Coppell, Ray Clemence, Graham Rix, Joe Corrigan and Glenn Hoddle*

United's Bryan Robson was rapidly establishing himself as a world-class player, while in Trevor Francis and Steve Coppell England had two forwards of great pace and skill. Add to that the elegant and probing left foot of Graham Rix, the steadying influence of Ray Wilkins as well as the reassuring presence of Peter Shilton in goal, and England looked a far better side on paper than they had been for real in the qualifying games. Crucially, though, England's two most influential players of recent years would miss out on all but the dying moments of their fifth and final match. Brooking, England's stylish midfield general, and Keegan, a proven match-winner albeit one in decline, both arrived with injuries.

The tournament kicked off with the surprise defeat of Argentina by Belgium, and morale in the camp of the reigning world champions was not improved by the news that the Falklands had been recaptured by British troops.

England's first match was against France, who they had not played since 1969, but they made up for lost time when Robson scored one of the fastest ever goals in a World Cup, after just 27 seconds. The England players sweated off nearly a stone each in the sweltering heat but with two-goal Robson magnificent throughout, they swept to a convincing 3–1 victory.

A 2–0 win over Czechoslovakia and a 1–0 win over Kuwait booked England's passage into a second group stage, where they would face their Spanish hosts and West Germany, the winners of which would qualify for the semis. It was unfortunate for Kuwait that the World Cup Finals coincided with Ramadan – the more religiously observant of their players took the field on empty stomachs, refusing even to drink water during the interval. But if Kuwait had Allah on their side they also had Mr Aristizabal, the Colombian referee, who seemed determined to blow his whistle every time an England player so much as looked in the direction of the goal or the opposition.

England now faced West Germany, their conquerors in four of their last six encounters. The Germans were the reigning European champions and

were joint pre-tournament favourites with Brazil, having put together a 23-match unbeaten run between 1978 and 1981. But in one of football's great upsets, the Germans were beaten by Algeria – to the delight of all those who had little fondness for Jupp Derwall's negative and unimaginative team. But West Germany caused outrage when they reached the second group stage at the expense of the North Africans after a scandalous encounter with Austria, which was quickly dubbed the "Anschluss" match. Austria had already qualified, but the Germans needed to win to go through, which they did, 1–0, with their Austrian cousins blatantly making no effort to score. The build-up to the match with England turned out to be infinitely more entertaining than the game itself. Pele famously described Germany as "a team of ten robots plus Karl-Heinz Rummenigge". Neither side wanted to attack, knowing that defeat would almost certainly kill off their hopes of reaching the semi-finals. The match predictably ended in a goalless stalemate, although England survived a late scare when Rummenigge wobbled Shilton's crossbar with a thundering drive.

England needed to beat Spain by two goals to book a place in the semi-finals against France following the Germans' 2–1 win over their hosts a few days earlier. Amazingly, if England had matched the Germans' score, the two teams would have been forced to draw lots to determine who would go through. England dominated the match but were undone by their lack of a truly world class striker. Greenwood threw on Keegan and Brooking in a desperate last fling. Their presence had an inspirational effect as England stepped up their siege of the Spanish goal. As it was, the two substitutes both missed the best chances of the game in the dying moments. England were out, despite having won three, drawn two and conceded just one goal in their five games. It was certainly no consolation for the outgoing Greenwood that England had managed a remarkable 24 shots on goal against Spain's two.

*It's behind you.*
*England v West Germany*
*in the 1982 World Cup*

**ENGLAND:** The Official F.A. History

# RON GREENWOOD (1977–82)

Ron Greenwood was the thinking man's England manager. A football purist inspired by the great Hungary sides of the 1950s, Greenwood set out to play a continental-style passing game à la West Ham, who he managed between 1961 and 1975. The Hammers won the FA Cup and the European Cup Winners' Cup in the mid-1960s, but they never won the League under Greenwood and sceptics wondered whether his teams had the steel to challenge the very best. But there can be no doubting his qualities as a tactician and a coach. England were already indebted to Greenwood before he took over as manager as a 55-year-old in semi-retirement. At West Ham, he groomed Bobby Moore, Geoff Hurst and Martin Peters for international duty, converting Hurst from an ordinary midfielder to a world-class striker.

Ever willing to experiment, Greenwood was the first English coach to champion the revolutionary 4–2–4 formation as pioneered by the all-conquering Brazil side of the late 1950s and early 1960s. He was always looking around for new ideas and once fitted his players at West Ham with radio receivers during training so he could issue individual players with instructions.

After a playing career with Brentford and Chelsea that was interrupted by the war, he went on an FA coaching course where he was inspired by Walter Winterbottom, but like the first ever England manager, he would often unwittingly confuse players with his polysyllabic team-talks. He took England to the European Championship finals in Italy in 1980 and then to the World Cup finals in Spain two years later, where England did not lose any of their five matches and narrowly failed to reach the semi-finals. He suffered a torrent of criticism from the press during England's poor World Cup qualifying campaign but was talked out of resigning by the team's senior players.

**England record P55 W33 D12 L10 F93 A40**

*Ever the innovator, Greenwood issues instructions to West Ham players during training*

# 1982–1990

# THE ROBSON ROLLERCOASTER

*A common photographic image of Robson captures him head down, chin buried in his hands and forehead furrowed by intense, apparently painful thought. It was an image his critics liked to use to convey an impression of fatal indecision. But to his supporters the Robson pose caught the thoughtfulness of the man who would never come to an important decision lightly or dogmatically.*

For the second time in four years Brian Clough, the inspiration behind Nottingham Forest's European Cup triumphs in 1979 and 1980, was overlooked for the England job. Instead, the FA turned to Bobby Robson who, like Ramsey, had cut his managerial teeth not at one of the country's big clubs, but at Ipswich. On a shoestring budget, the former England wing-half had moulded the East Anglian club into a major force in English football. Under his enthusiastic guidance, Ipswich won the FA Cup and the UEFA Cup and finished outside the top six of the first division just once in his last ten years at the helm. The hope was that if Robson could build so much from so little at Ipswich, he would be able to work wonders now that he had the cream of the country's footballers at his disposal.

Robson's critics accused him of fatal indecision. But the charge looked weak when he made Kevin Keegan surplus to his requirements in naming his first squad. The dropping of the twice European Footballer of the Year sparked a storm of protest, but Robson insisted that he had to look ahead, not just to the 1984 European Championship but also to the World Cup in 1986. By then, he argued, Keegan would probably be playing golf.

His first challenge was to ensure England's qualification for the European finals in France from a group including Hungary (again), Greece, Luxembourg and Denmark. It looked an easy enough passage until England were held to a goalless draw by the Greeks at Wembley in March 1983. England had won 3–0 in Salonika, so the result was not a mathematical disaster, just a blow to morale. Six months later disaster did strike when the Danes plundered a 1–0 win under the Twin Towers and England, barring miracles, had blown their chance of reaching the finals. Predictably, the press took a dim view of England's efforts against a Scandinavian country – population five million – who had won very little on English fields since the

*Bobby Robson directs an England training session*

Dark Ages. It was their first ever victory over England, but they were an emerging force in world football and in Michael Laudrup, Preben Elkjaer and Jesper Olsen they had players that would grace any team. In France, as in Mexico two years later, any doubts about the quality of the Danes was emphatically dispatched. But no one, of course, was to know this on the morning of 22nd September when Robson and the rest of England woke up to headlines calling for his blood.

Nor was anyone to know that Robson's first defeat in a qualifying game would also be his last.

There followed an uncomfortable nine months for Robson during which England lost to Scotland, France and then to the USSR at Wembley. But the turning point came two days before the start of the 1984 European Championship finals in France when England entered the mighty Maracana stadium in Rio de Janeiro on 10th June. England had set off

## PETER SHILTON

| | |
|---|---|
| Position | Goalkeeper |
| Caps/goals | 125/0 |
| Debut | v East Germany (3–1) at Wembley 25th November 1970 |
| Last match | v Italy (1–2) at Bari 7th July 1990 |
| Clubs | Leicester, Stoke, Nottingham Forest, Southampton, Derby |

*Record-breaking Shilton flanked by Franz Beckenbauer and Bobby Moore*

Peter Shilton is England's most capped player and was probably the best goalkeeper in the world in his prime. Incredibly, he would have had even more than 125 caps were it not for Ron Greenwood's insistence on alternating him with Ray Clemence. His England career spanned two full decades and he would have played in a total of five World Cup finals but for England's failure to qualify in 1974 and 1978. Only Stanley Matthews had a longer career and played for England at an older age.

An obsessional trainer who learnt much of his art from his predecessor Gordon Banks, Shilton was said to be so determined to succeed when he was a youngster that he tried to stretch his arms by hanging off door ledges and climbing frames. He played a British record of 17 World Cup matches and his ten World Cup clean sheets are a competition record. Shilton, who was Footballer of the Year in 1978 and was later awarded the MBE, kept 66 clean sheets for England and was one game away from equalling Banks's seven consecutive games without conceding a goal. He found success harder to come by as a manager and was involved in running rows with Plymouth Argyle, who finally despaired of his financial problems and demands. Shilton left the West Country with an apparent determination to play for every team in England before retiring and was last seen between the sticks at Leyton Orient.

## BRYAN ROBSON

| | |
|---|---|
| Position | Midfield |
| Caps/goals | 90/26 |
| Debut | v Republic of Ireland (2–0) at Wembley 6th February 1980 |
| Last match | v Turin (1–0) at Wembley 16th October 1991 |
| Clubs | WBA, Manchester United, Middlesbrough |

If Bryan Robson did not walk into most people's all-time England team, he would almost certainly hobble there on crutches – and then claim he was as fit as a fiddle. One of the greatest midfielders England has ever produced, he was also one of the most injury prone – a testament to his almost frightening commitment to the cause. It seems amazing that for someone who spent much of his professional life in plaster, or in a sling or on an operating table, Robson still won 90 England caps, captaining the side on 65 occasions. In all, "Captain Marvel", as he was dubbed by the tabloids, suffered over 20 fractures or dislocations of some sort, including three broken legs in 1976. In spite of his medical record, Robson is England's fifth most capped player and seventh top-scorer with 26 goals.

Ferociously competitive and brave almost to the point of madness, Robson was a natural leader who

*Robson in action in the 1988 Rous Cup*

inspired his colleagues and put the fear of God into his opponents. Robson, who became Britain's most expensive player when he moved from West Bromwich Albion to Manchester United for £1.5 million in 1981, was a player without any obvious weakness. His ball-winning skills, thundering tackles, accurate passing and deadly shooting made him the first name down on Bobby Robson's England team sheet. (He was never once an England substitute.) Injury ruled Robson out of most of the World Cups of 1986 and 1990, leaving England fans to wonder whether his dynamism and drive may have given the team the extra impetus to reach the final. He was quickly brought into the England coaching set-up at the end of his playing days, and became manager of Middlesbrough.

on the summer tour of South America with no fewer than 19 players unavailable to Robson and with public confidence in the team at a low ebb. To everyone's astonishment, not least Robson's, England triumphed over a Brazil side who had been described by one paper as coming "from a different planet".

Staunch in defence and bold in attack, England had triumphed in world football's most daunting arena after Robson had gambled by playing two young wingers, John Barnes and Mark Chamberlain. Barnes scored a goal that even Brazilians recall with fondness.

*Robson led from the field after dislocating his shoulder against Morocco*

It was one of the great England goals and began somewhere near the halfway-line before Barnes, then with Watford, set off on a mazy run into the heart of the Brazilian defence. Quiet gasps of appreciation could already be heard as Barnes reached the edge of the area before he slotted in a goal worthy of its magnificent setting.

"It was an unbelievable performance," reflected Robson. "We were under immense pressure for the first 20 minutes but held firm before going on to win. It was one of the most important moments in my life."

A 2–0 defeat to Uruguay in Montevideo and a 0–0 draw with Chile followed, but England returned home with renewed confidence. There was a conviction that if they could beat Brazil in their own back yard then they could not be as bad as everyone had told them.

With the World Cup qualifiers set to start in the new season, Robson was comforted by the knowledge that he had some experienced players of world-class ability in Shilton, Robson, Sansom and Butcher, as well as some emerging talent in Gary Lineker, Peter

Beardsley, Chris Waddle and John Barnes. The expulsion of English clubs from European competition at the start of the 1985/86 season in the wake of the Heysel stadium tragedy would have significant consequences for the national team. England's players would no longer be able to experience football at the highest club level against teams of a style and quality they were likely to meet at international level. But it would be a few years before that inexperience would be obvious and England came through their relatively easy qualifying group – involving Northern Ireland, Turkey, Romania and Finland – without serious alarm. They finished top of the group after winning four and drawing four of their eight matches while scoring 21 and conceding two goals in the process.

Mexico was to host the World Cup for the second time in 16 years, but this time there would be 24 teams rather than 16, as well as a number of additional venues. The heat and altitude, of course, were still there, as the England players would discover on returning to the changing room at the end of matches up to a stone lighter and feeling dizzy and breathless. The squad was based in Monterrey, far in the north of the country near the American border, exactly where the organisers had hoped they and their more unruly fans would be. Avoiding the mistake of Ramsey in choosing to stay in a hotel in the centre of town, England decamped high into the Sierra Madre out of the way of midnight revellers.

England arrived for the World Cup finals on the back of an unbeaten run of 11 matches, including a win in Moscow that made them the first side to beat the Soviets behind the Iron Curtain for six years. Robson's 22-man squad was a mix of the tried and the untested, but there were doubts over two of England's potential match-winners. Tottenham's sublimely gifted Glenn Hoddle, the people's favourite, was still struggling to impose his outrageous talent at international level, and Bryan Robson, England's

heartbeat, arrived with a suspect shoulder that was only ever one bad fall away from dislocation.

England got off to a dreadful start. On a bumpy pitch in an eerie near-empty stadium, they lost 1–0 to Portugal, who scored 14 minutes from time with virtually their first serious attack. England's defence froze, or rather melted in the 100-degree heat, as Carlos Manuel pounced at the far post.

Three days later, it was Morocco's turn to embarrass the mother country of football in a goalless draw that left England's hopes of progress looking slim. Robson was quick to point out that a win over Poland was all England needed, but after struggling against the group's weakest two teams, no one was holding their breath – especially not at Monterrey's altitude – for an English victory.

The Morocco match was one England would want to forget, but it contained two episodes of significance. The dislocation-in-waiting finally happened when Bryan Robson crashed to the ground and, as his shoulder came out, all hopes of his continuing in the

*Hat-trick hero Gary Lineker scores his second in the 3–0 win over Poland*

World Cup campaign went with it. But if the injury to England's captain was entirely predictable, the same could not be said of the behaviour of fellow midfielder Ray Wilkins. The most even-tempered and civilised of footballers became the first Englishman to be sent off in the finals of a World Cup when, in a rare fit of petulance, he threw down the ball which unfortunately struck the legs of the man who carried the red cards. Wilkins ripped his shirt off in disgust at his own folly and left the field having skippered his country for just two minutes.

The fate of Robson and Wilkins turned out to be England's saving because the team was forced into a tactical rethink which would transform their fortunes. England's group had been dubbed the "group of Sleep" after producing just two goals in four games, but it ended with a flourish as England swept to a 3–0 win over Poland. The Poles' record in recent World Cups was impressive. They had reached the

*Lineker practises holding the cup*

last four in 1974 and 1982 and the last eight in 1978. Poland prompted disturbing memories for Englishmen still mindful of that autumn night in 1973 when England were denied a place in the 1974 finals by the acrobatics of Jan Tomaszewski, the Polish goalkeeper dubbed a "clown" by Brian Clough before the match.

Forced into a reshuffle, Peter Beardsley came in to partner Lineker in place of Mark Hateley upfront, while Trevor Steven took over from Waddle on the right and the workmanlike Steven Hodge and Reid joined the midfield in place of Robson and Wilkins. The results were spectacular. England were suddenly a team of brilliant footballers astounding their fans who were hoping at best that their heroes might sneak a 1–0 win. England went two better, with all three goals coming in the first 35 minutes and all from the boot of Lineker.

If ever Bobby Robson felt the need to express the view that "football was a funny old game", it was

**ENGLAND:** The Official F.A. History

as he walked from the field with a smile as wide as a Mexican sierra. Some say Robson hit upon his winning formula purely by chance, while others claimed it came about as the result of a changing-room revolt. But according to a later account by the sidelined Bryan Robson, the truth was a little more prosaic. The squad simply sat around with the manager on the eve of the match and everyone was invited to air their views on the best way forward. Between them it was agreed that England would play 4–4–2 rather than 4–3–3. His critics would say that the episode proved that the England manager had no clear strategy. His supporters would say it proved Robson was a reasonable, flexible man neither frightened nor too proud to let others have their say. Either way, England were suddenly a force to be reckoned with and Lineker had announced his arrival as one of the deadliest strikers in world football.

Though they scarcely deserved it on the strength of their overall group performance, England were rewarded with a match against Paraguay, the weakest side left in the tournament, in the next round. In the magnificent Aztec Stadium of smog-bound Mexico City, Lineker scored twice and Beardsley once as England won 3–0. The Paraguayans were rough in the second half and Beardsley actually scored his goal when Lineker was off the field receiving treatment for an injury to his face, which had collided with a Paraguayan elbow. The match was also a tricky one for the world's commentators, who were faced with two players called Gary Stevens, one called Trevor Steven and one called Steven Hodge.

Two convincing displays had liberated England's players from the fear of being put in the stocks of public opinion as they headed for a quarter-final clash with Argentina. The fixture carried plenty of history – most of it unhappy. Feelings were still running high after the Falklands War and sporting and diplomatic ties between the two countries remained cut. In football terms, memories were still fresh of England's controversial 1–0 win in the 1966 quarter-finals, when the Argentinian captain Rattin was sent off, prompting

*Lineker's six goals won him the Golden Boot award in the 1986 World Cup*

***Maradona's infamous "Hand of God"***
***pushes England to the brink of defeat***

South American allegations of a European conspiracy.

Argentina had Maradona, the best player in the world, who would make two unforgettable contributions to the game. The first half passed by without incident, but the second was only five minutes old when the match burst into controversial life. Hodge botched his overhead clearance from inside England's area and, as Shilton raced off his line to punch clear, Maradona launched himself at the ball and palmed it into the back of the net. The view from behind the stocky Argentinian made it difficult to see what part of his body had propelled the ball into the goal, but from the front or side angle, it was clear that the hand had prevailed over the head. Only England, though, were protesting and to no avail. Maradona protested later – but only his innocence, as he famously claimed that "the Hand of God" had done the dirty work. The referee had almost certainly been unsighted but the linesman looked well placed.

"I knew what had happened and the linesman looked at me and then just ran off up the touchline," recalled Shilton.

England were still in a state of annoyed bemusement, when five minutes later Maradona scored one of the greatest goals of all time. From just inside his own half, he set off on a bewildering run which left Reid, Beardsley, Fenwick and Butcher trailing in his light blue slipstream before he burst into the area, fooled Shilton and slid the ball into the back of England's net. Robson threw on his wingers Waddle and Barnes in desperation and the gamble almost paid off as England responded with verve to the double setback. Barnes was the inspiration behind England's fightback, delivering a perfect cross for Lineker to score from close range ten minutes from time. Moments later the Watford winger set up the chance of an identical second which Lineker came within millimetres of converting. But it was to be their last attack of the World Cup. England went home while Argentina went on to lift the trophy.

If the World Cup had been a qualified success for England, the European Championship finals in West Germany two years later were an unmitigated failure. England, who had recently destroyed Yugoslavia 4–1 in Belgrade, arrived as one of the favourites, but left as also-rans after limping to straight defeats to Jack Charlton's Republic of Ireland, appearing in their first major finals, eventual winners Holland, and then Russia. England had a number of good chances against the Irish but Lineker was unusually sluggish and wasteful and he was later diagnosed as suffering from

jaundice. Peter Shilton won his 100th cap against the Dutch, but he was powerless to stop the eventual champions, who swept to an ultimately comfortable 3–1 win as Marco Van Basten grabbed a hat-trick.

England were already eliminated by the time they faced the USSR, but far from salvaging any respect, they were completely outplayed, and slumped to another 3–1 defeat. It was an unhappy couple of weeks for English football with the riotous behaviour of a minority of fans adding to the gloom of events on the pitch. England fans were involved in running

***Stevens challenges for the ball during England's 2–1 defeat in the quarter-finals***

*Peter Beardsley and Kenny Sanson track*
*Holland's Frank Rijkaard during*
*England's disastrous European*
*Championships campaign*

clashes with German police as well as German and Dutch fans. Over 200 were detained and the images coming out of Germany were so bad that the FA was forced to withdraw its application to UEFA for the return to European competition of English clubs. Downing Street, meanwhile, called an emergency "hooligan summit" at which a drastic plan to combat trouble was drawn up.

Robson and the FA withstood the calls for the manager's head which followed England's wretched display – to the annoyance of the tabloid press who embarked on a campaign of vilification against Robson that reached an ugly climax at the start of Italia 90. England drew 0–0 with Sweden at the beginning of their World Cup qualifying campaign. The following morning the back page of one newspaper had a blunt message for the England boss: "IN THE NAME OF GOD GO". The paper accused Robson of not knowing who he was playing against after he had absent-mindedly said that a goalless draw against "Denmark" was not a bad result. Robson's forgetfulness was well known and he was once said to have called Bryan Robson "Bobby". "Bobby was

**ENGLAND:** The Official F.A. History

loyal to his players, professional and meticulous in his approach and had bags of enthusiasm," recalled Chris Waddle. "He also wanted us to have a good time and enjoy our football – but he could never remember players' names."

After England drew 1–1 with Saudi Arabia in Riyadh a month later, the Saudi manager said Robson was "not a good manager but he would make a good train driver". His comments were music to the ears of Fleet Street headline writers. "IN THE NAME OF ALLAH GO!" boomed one paper. If anything the

criticism that rained down on Robson served only to unite the England squad. He had always stuck up for them, individually and collectively, and now they would return the compliment.

In the end England reached the 1990 World Cup finals with ease during an unbeaten run of 17 games stretched over a period of 23 months. In their six qualifying games against Sweden, Poland and Albania,

*Mark Wright outjumps Niall Quinn during England's shock 1–0 defeat to Jack Charlton's Ireland*

## BOBBY ROBSON (1982–90)

Bobby Robson followed in the footsteps of another former Ipswich manager, Sir Alf Ramsey, when he took on the England job at the end of the 1982 World Cup after getting the nod ahead of the punters' favourite Brian Clough. The former England wing-half would ride his luck as well as some heavy criticism from the tabloids before he departed after taking England to within a penalty-kick of the 1990 World Cup final.

Eight turbulent years in charge began with England's failure to qualify for the 1984 European Championship in France. Relative success followed as England reached the quarter-finals of the 1986 World Cup before they fell victim to Diego Maradona's "Hand of God" goal. There was more European disaster two years later when England slumped to straight defeats to the Republic of Ireland, Holland and the USSR. But Robson had the last laugh on his critics when England reached the semi-finals of the 1990 World Cup in Italy, only going out to the Germans after a penalty shoot-out.

Robson grew up in a coal-mining community in County Durham, where he worked as an electrician in the local colliery before heading south to sign

England did not concede a goal, though they were second to the Swedes, who finished with one more point.

Despite England's streak of good form, the tabloid press continued to roast Robson. But it was the news pages and not the sports pages that were starting to hurt the England manager with a series of allegations about his private life. The pressure mounted in the countdown to the finals when it was revealed that Robson's England contract would not be renewed and that he would be joining Dutch side PSV Eindhoven. Some observers attacked Robson on the grounds that the haste with which he took his next career step was indecent and risked undermining the morale of the England players. Others felt that Robson had every right to sort out his future and that, if anything, the fact of his imminent departure created a focus and a determination among the players to give him a triumphant send-off.

*Tabloid target Robson gets away from it all*

for Fulham at the start of a successful playing career. He moved to West Bromwich Albion where his qualities as an attacking wing-half quickly brought international recognition. He played 20 times for England, but was dropped for nearly two seasons before being recalled in 1960, when he and old Fulham teammate Johnny Haynes provided the vital "2" in England's new 4–2–4 formation. But his international career ended after he picked up a minor injury and he lost his place to Bobby Moore.

His managerial career began with a brief, farcical spell at Vancouver Royals and a short six-month stint at Fulham, but it was only when he moved to Ipswich in early 1969 that he had his first real chance to prove himself. Like Ramsey before

him, he quickly reversed the fortunes of the modest Suffolk club who became a major force in European as well as English football over the next 13 years. Robson showed his resourcefulness in creating a successful team that played neat, incisive football, with Ipswich winning the FA Cup in 1978 and then coming close to winning a remarkable three trophies in 1981, but eventually settling for the UEFA Cup.

After his England years Robson headed for the continent where he continued to find success first in Holland with PSV Eindhoven, then in Portugal with Sporting Lisbon and FC Porto before Barcelona, the biggest club in the world, took him on as successor to Johann Cruyff. For both club and country Robson always tried to strike the right balance between direct and possession football while his enthusiasm, good humour and loyalty won him the affection and respect of the players.

**England record P95 W47 D30 L18 F154 A60**

The star of England's show would be the precocious Paul Gascoigne, described by Robson as both "daft as a brush" and "a rare talent". Everyone in the country already had a view of Gascoigne, the Mars Bar kid, who could do tricks only Brazilians and Dutchmen in the 1970s were meant to be able to do. He had just turned 23 before the start of Italia 90, but he was to become one of the players of the tournament after playing a crucial role in England's progress to the semi-finals.

The young Geordie found himself in experienced company on the flight out to Italy with Shilton, Butcher, Robson, Lineker, Waddle, Barnes and Beardsley at the peak, or thereabouts, of their careers. Add to that list the explosive Stuart Pearce at left-back and the speedy, unflappable Des Walker in central defence, and England had, on paper at least, a formidable side. Italia 90 would also see

## TERRY BUTCHER

| | |
|---|---|
| Position | Central defence |
| Caps/goals | 77/3 |
| Debut | v Australia (2–1) in Sydney 31st May 1980 |
| Last match | v West Germany (1–1) in Turin 4th July 1990 |
| Clubs | Ipswich, Glasgow Rangers |

Butcher belongs to the long line of towering, inspirational England central defenders that boasts the names of Jackie Charlton, Dave Watson and Tony Adams – one for each decade since Charlton in the 1960s. He was thrown in at the international deep end during the 1982 World Cup in Spain when he took over from Watson after just a handful of games. His career coincided neatly with the reign of England manager Bobby Robson, his boss at Ipswich, who saw Butcher, together with goalkeeper Peter Shilton and midfielder Bryan Robson, as automatic choices in his line-up. As committed as any player to have ever pulled on an England shirt, Butcher's physical and moral presence on the field were immense. The image of Butcher which most readily springs to mind is of a player with his head swathed in bandages, his shirt soaked in blood, screaming impassioned orders to his colleagues. Butcher was said to have developed as a left-footed player after burning his right foot as a youngster. The broken leg he sustained before the 1988 European Championship was a devastating blow

to England whose defensive frailty without his commanding presence was brutally exposed as England slumped to defeats to the Republic of Ireland, Holland and the USSR. He had a very good World Cup in Italia 90, helping England reach the semi-final against West Germany, after which he retired from the international scene. He won the UEFA Cup with Ipswich under Robson in 1981, before joining Glasgow Rangers, where his near maniacal devotion to the cause quickly endeared him to the Ibrox fans. He tried his hand at management with Coventry and Sunderland but with only moderate success. Now runs an 18th-century hotel outside Stirling and works as a part-time radio and TV pundit.

*Never surrender: Butcher after England's 0–0 World Cup qualifier against Sweden*

**ENGLAND: The Official F.A. History**

*Paul Gascoigne, the star of the show during England's 1990 World Cup campaign*

the emergence of David Platt as a world class performer.

The fear of trouble from England fans, which was fuelled by the shrill, alarmist rantings of sports minister Colin Moynihan, led to England being exiled to the island of Sardinia for their group matches. The Republic of Ireland, appearing in their first World Cup finals, provided the opposition in England's opening game just as they had in Germany two years earlier. Not helped by conditions more in keeping with Wigan in winter rather than Sardinia in summer, the two teams produced the worst match of the competition.

The Irish were in no mood to play beautiful football and, with a howling gale blowing in off the Mediterranean, the weather was in no mood to let England – if that had been their intention. A purists' nightmare ended 1–1 after Kevin Sheedy capitalised on a mistake by substitute Steve McMahon to equalise Lineker's scrappy opener.

After the match a number of other senior players approached the England manager about playing a sweeper against Holland in their next match. England could boast three world-class central defenders in Butcher, Walker and Wright. Robson, who said he had been contemplating the idea, agreed to play the system for the first time during his eight years in charge. The news provoked an uproar in the press, which insisted that trying out a wholly alien system in a crucial World Cup game bordered on madness. England, though, had been destroyed by Holland in the 1988 European Championship when not playing a sweeper exposed their squareness at the back. And determined that England would not be caught out again, Robson said he had faith in the experience and adaptability of his players and handed the sweeper's job to Wright. The gamble worked not just against Holland, but in the later stages of the tournament, although Robson would abandon the system whenever England found themselves a goal down. England were the better team against a Dutch side including Ruud Gullit, Frank Rijkaard, Ronald Koeman and Marco Van Basten. Lineker and Pearce both had goals disallowed but despite their domination England had to settle for a goalless draw.

To the disappointment of the players, Robson reverted to 4–2–4 (or 4–4–2 depending on which way you looked at it) for the 1–0 win against Egypt in their final group match. A dreary match in which England never reached the heights of their performance against Holland was settled by Wright's header from Gascoigne's free-kick.

England set off for Bologna to face Belgium in the next round as their fans arrived on the Italian mainland for the first time to the consternation of the forces of law and order.

Belgium had beaten England just once in 17 times of asking, but they were an experienced team with 530 caps between them and in the extravagantly gifted Enzo Scifo they had a midfielder as good as any in the finals. Amazingly an open, highly entertaining game which went into extra-time yielded just one goal, although Barnes had a sweetly-struck volley mysteriously disallowed, and the Belgians twice hit the post. But when the goal came after 120 minutes of gut-wrenching tension it was well worth the wait – not just for Englishmen, but for any neutral with a love of the beautiful things in football.

With penalties looking inevitable, the quick-thinking Gascoigne floated a free-kick into the Belgian area when others may have been tempted to play safe and keep possession. The ball dipped towards David Platt and, as it dropped over his shoulder, he pirouetted and volleyed across the face of goal and high into Preud'homme's net. Platt, a substitute for McMahon, had scored the goal of the tournament and

*England celebrates before the referee disallows Stuart Pearce's free kick*

England had matched their achievement of four years earlier by reaching the quarter-finals.

England now faced Cameroon, the darlings of the tournament who had beaten reigning champions Argentina in the curtain-raiser despite having two men sent off. Cameroon had lit up the group stages with their exciting brand of attacking and unpredictable football, but their occasional brutality in the challenge showed that they had not come to Italy simply to provide light entertainment. In the flamboyant 38-year-old Roger Milla they could also boast one of the deadliest strikers in the finals.

*England rattled as Belgium's*
*Enzo Scifo hits the post*

**ENGLAND: The Official F.A. History**

## GARY LINEKER

| | |
|---|---|
| Position | Striker |
| Caps/goals | 80/48 |
| Debut | v Scotland (1–1) in Glasgow 26th May 1984 |
| Last match | v Sweden (1–2) in Stockholm 17th June 1992 |
| Clubs | Leicester, Everton, Barcelona, Tottenham, Grampus Eight |

*Familiar pose: Lineker celebrates one of his 48 England goals*

Gary Lineker, football's outstanding exception to the rule that nice guys don't win, is second only to Bobby Charlton in the England goalscoring stakes. Many of his 48 goals were crucial to England's success, with 16 of them the only goal of the game and ten of them coming in Mexico 1986 and Italy 1990 – making him England's top-scorer in World Cup finals. Lineker was a player who knew his limitations and made the most of what natural gifts he had. Never a flamboyant player, he scored only a handful of goals from outside the area. But his great pace and superb positional sense made him the goal-poacher extraordinaire, the best England had seen since Jimmy Greaves in the early 1960s.

He began his career with his hometown club Leicester, before moving to Everton where he quickly caught the eye of England manager Bobby Robson. Lineker may have saved Robson his job two years later when his six goals in Mexico rescued England from a disastrous opening to their World Cup bid and won him the competition's Golden Boot award. 1986 was a great year for the young striker as he picked up the Football Writers' and Players' Player of the Year awards. He also kept England in with a chance of reaching the World Cup final when he equalised against West Germany in the 1990 semi-final with a typically predatory strike that sent the game into extra-time. And it was Lineker who ensured England's qualification for the 1992 European Championship finals with the goal that secured a draw in Poland.

He scored 23 goals in his first 25 internationals, but after recovering from a bout of jaundice, his remarkable strike rate slowed up a little. Lineker's international career ended on a controversial note in the finals in Sweden when manager Graham Taylor provoked a national uproar by substituting him with Arsenal's Alan Smith, a good club player but not in the class of the man he replaced.

The second half of his club career was spent with Barcelona, Tottenham and Grampus Eight in Japan. He made an impact wherever he played – even in Spain where he was often asked to play out wide or in Japan where a toe injury restricted him to just a handful of matches but where his sunny personality helped give a boost to the image of the game. Lineker, whose patriotic middle name is Winston, captained England 18 times towards the end of a career in which he was never booked for club or country. Feared around the world as a lethal finisher, Lineker was often on the receiving end of some rough treatment from defenders, but he retaliated in the only way he knew – by scoring goals. "He was the best finisher I've seen," said Bobby Robson. Now he works as a presenter for BBC Sport.

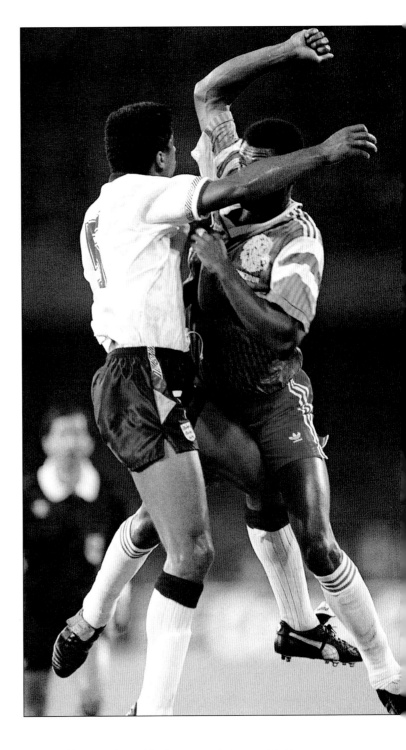

*Des Walker tussles with Cameroon's Oman Biyik*

England took the lead in Naples in their first ever match against sub-Saharan African opposition with a header by Platt on 25 minutes. But pre-match suggestions that England had a virtual walkover into the semi-finals looked badly off the mark as Cameroon responded by mounting a sustained assault on Shilton's goal.

England seemed to have ridden the worst when the Africans swept into the lead with two goals midway through the second half. Kunde converted from the spot for the equaliser after Gascoigne had brought down Milla, and then Ekeke mocked Shilton with a delightful chip. Robson immediately abandoned the sweeper system as England reverted to instinct in a frantic bid to avoid one of the greatest upsets in their history. In the end England had the vision of Gascoigne and the composure of Lineker to thank for saving them, two passes from the former leading to fouls in the area on the latter. Lineker kept his cool as his first penalty sent the game into extra time and his second ensured England reached their first World Cup

*Gascoigne beats Klaus Argentbaler during England's dramatic clash with West Germany*

semi-final since 1966. "Some bye that!" said Waddle as he headed down the tunnel.

England's recent record against West Germany was not good. They had won just twice in ten games since 1966 and not once in a competitive match. The Germans had looked the strongest team in the competition during the group matches when they crushed Yugoslavia (4–1) and the UAE (5–1) and drew 1–1 with Colombia. But they had started to show signs of fatigue through the knockout stages where they triumphed 2–1 over old rivals Holland and then scraped past the Czechs with the only goal of the game.

England, by contrast, had improved immeasurably since the dire showing against the Irish. The Belgians had been the equal of them and they stumbled against

**ENGLAND:** The Official F.A. History

*Chris Waddle with Lothar Matthäus as the semi-final heads for penalties*

Cameroon, but the manner of their comeback against the Africans suggested there was still plenty of fight in the team. The prize was now a place in the final against a relatively poor, negative Argentina side who looked ripe for a beating.

Far from retreating into their shells with the aim of keeping it tight and sneaking a goal on the break, both teams came out to play in what turned out to be the best match of the finals.

England hurled themselves into attack from the kick-off, Gascoigne testing Illgner with a sweet low volley early on. At the halfway mark England were certainly ahead on points with the Germans having rarely threatened Shilton's goal. Germany had the better of the exchanges early in the second half before they took the lead with a freak goal on 59 minutes. Thomas Hassler, who had been fouled by Pearce close to the right-hand corner of the England area, tapped the free-kick to Andreas Brehme. The German left-back blasted his shot straight at the on-rushing Paul Parker, only for the ball to arch high over England's

defensive wall and over a scrambling Shilton before coming to rest in the back of the net.

Robson again ditched the sweeper system as soon as England fell behind, bringing on Trevor Steven for Butcher, and they were back on terms nine minutes from time after a typically predatory strike from Lineker. Parker threw over a deep cross from the right, as much in hope as in expectation of finding a white shirt, but there was rare confusion among the German defence and Lineker pounced, sweeping the ball left-footed across Illgner and low into the corner.

Gascoigne was booked for an enthusiastic rather than malicious tackle on Berthold and began to cry as he realised that he would miss the final if England went through. The hyper-sensitive Geordie held his shirt to his reddening face as the tears, and the cameras, rolled.

Extra-time. Just as they had in 1966 and 1970 and just as they would in 1996, England and Germany needed another 30 minutes to settle their differences. The entertainment or tension did not relent during the additional period which began with Waddle thudding a wicked low drive against a post. At the other end, Buchwald did the same, while Klinsmann was guilty of a glaring miss.

Still nothing could separate the two sides and so the match would be decided by the lottery of a penalty shoot-out. England and Germany stood still. Parity continued for six penalties as Lineker, Platt and Beardsley saw their efforts matched by Brehme, Matthäus and Riedle.

But then disaster for England as Pearce crashed England's fourth against the legs of Illgner, Thon giving Germany the advantage moments later. With the eyes of the world upon him, Waddle was entrusted with the task of keeping England in the World Cup. Waddle, so close to being the toast of all England half-an-hour earlier, looked up, ran towards the ball before unleashing England's last hope of reaching the World

Cup final only to see his effort sail high over the bar towards the Union Jacks behind the goal.

Just as they had in 1986, England had lost to the eventual winners. "No team deserved to win because no team deserved to lose," said Franz Beckenbauer, Germany's coach.

England, though, were right to feel proud of their efforts. Robson's team, who lost the third place play-off to hosts Italy, had played some of the best football of the tournament, and the matches against Belgium, Cameroon and West Germany were three of the most entertaining games in the finals.

Robson retired in a blaze of glory as England flew home to be met with a tumultuous reception by fans in Luton, leaving them to wonder how they might have been received had they won it. Robson's courage in the face of hostile critics, undiluted loyalty to his players, willingness to adapt, and a good slice of luck had been rewarded.

*Lineker equalises to send the game into extra-time*

*Gascoigne wipes away the tears after his booking*

# 1990–1993

# BEST WE FORGET

*"You have to accept criticism as part of the job with England, but I think there is a difference between constructive criticism and personal criticism. I think all England managers, not just myself, have received too much personal criticism."*

– Graham Taylor –

**C**riticism was not something that Graham Taylor was accustomed to when he took charge of the national team after the 1990 World Cup. His achievements at Watford and Aston Villa had made him an outstanding candidate for the post. Under Taylor, Watford had risen from the depths of the old fourth division to the first in just five years. They were fourth division champions in 1977/78, third division runners-up the following year, second division runners-up in 1981/82 and, in their first season in the top flight, they finished runners-up to Liverpool. In 1984 they reached the FA Cup final but lost 2–0 to Everton.

Taylor then took over at Villa after they had been relegated to the second division in 1988, and brought them straight back up before steering them to second place – to Liverpool again – in 1989/90. Despite his record, the sceptics would complain that Taylor was taking over the highest managerial job in the land without ever having won a major trophy. It was also

*An excellent club record behind him, Taylor was all smiles when he took the England job*

pointed out that Taylor had never played football in the first or second division, let alone at international level, and that winning the respect of the players would be difficult. And although at Villa he abandoned the much-maligned long-ball game he had perfected at Watford, there were still worries about his tactical intentions at a time when English clubs were looking to ditch "route one" football in favour of a more picturesque route to goal.

## DAVID PLATT

| | |
|---|---|
| Position | Midfield |
| Debut | v Italy (0–0) at Wembley |
| | 15th November 1989 |
| Clubs | Crewe, Aston Villa, Bari, |
| | Juventus, Sampdoria, Arsenal |

David Platt may have failed to fulfil the high hopes of those who saw him as the next Bryan Robson, but he still proved to be the most influential member of the England team in the early 1990s. Platt never had the driving, combative qualities of "Captain Marvel", but, like his predecessor, he had a knack for making perfectly timed runs into scoring positions from deep. His scoring rate of 27 goals in 62 games is remarkable by anyone's international standards.

A tireless runner and tidy passer, Platt led England by a quieter example than Robson, but was an inspiration at a time in the history of the England team when inspiration was a rare commodity. At one point, it seemed as if he had been granted the copyright on England goals, scoring nine in nine games during the 1992/93 season.

His eagerness to improve his game saw him move to Italy after an impressive showing in Italia 90. It was there that, after a string of appearances as substitute, Platt caught the world's attention in one spectacular instance, when he produced a stunning overhead volley to settle England's match against Belgium.

*Platt: vital goals under Taylor*

Playing first for Bari, then Juventus and Sampdoria, Platt showed a professionalism rare among English footballers in Italy by enthusiastically immersing himself in the culture and language of the country.

His move to Arsenal at the start of the 1995/96 season took the total transfer money spent on him over the £20 million mark. But although he returned a technically more accomplished player, a recurring knee injury appeared to have reduced his effectiveness.

*Liverpool star John Barnes: unfulfilled genius?*

England lost just once in Taylor's first 23 matches, but they struggled to qualify for the 1992 European Championship finals in Sweden. The Republic of Ireland twice held them to a 1–1 draw, the Turks only succumbed by a single goal at Wembley and in Izmir, and it was only a last-ditch goal by Lineker in Poland that saw England through at the expense of the Irish.

England's ragged qualification for the finals turned out to be the high point of Taylor's tenure. From there it was a slow, painful descent into failure, controversy

*Carlton Palmer in action against Jonas Thern during England's 2–1 defeat to Sweden*

and abuse from the press and public. England would perform poorly in Sweden and then fail to qualify for the World Cup finals.

When he resigned in November 1993, Taylor bequeathed a team to Terry Venables that was low on confidence and short of direction to the point of disorientation. Taylor came to the job with a reputation as a likeable, open and honest character. He was convinced he could withstand the slings and arrows that would inevitably be thrown his way. But as England struggled on the pitch, post-match press conferences began to assume a gladiatorial feel, with Taylor often lashing out in self-defence.

With England heading for elimination from the World Cup, the latter months of Taylor's reign became sad ones for everyone with an interest in the fortunes of the national team. This was the case not least for the manager himself, who woke up to find himself caricatured as a root vegetable on the back page of the *Sun* newspaper following the defeat to Sweden that ended England's interest in the European Championship.

The decision to substitute Gary Lineker, England's golden boy and one of the deadliest strikers in world football, lost Taylor what few friends he may have had left on Fleet Street. Taylor's face was superimposed on a turnip under the headline "SWEDES 2 TURNIPS 1".

The accusation that the England manager was unable to cope with "stars" was first levelled after he dropped Gascoigne for the European Championship qualifier against the Republic of Ireland

*The end of the international road for Gary Lineker as he is substituted during England's defeat to Sweden*

***Alan Smith:***

***the man who replaced Lineker***

in Dublin. Taylor argued that Gascoigne, England's hero in Italia 90, might lose his head in an inevitably bruising encounter with the Irish. Taylor's reasoning looked even more suspect when the aging Gordon Cowans was named as the midfielder's replacement.

Gascoigne's omission raised eyebrows in some quarters of the press and all hell in others, but the criticism was mild compared to the outrage sparked by his decision to replace Lineker with Arsenal's Alan Smith. Taylor's apologists pointed out that Lineker, who was just one short of equalling Bobby Charlton's England record of 49 goals, had not scored in six games. But his critics countered that Smith had scored just twice during his brief and undistinguished international career. Lineker's subsequent reactions to the episode would suggest there was something more than mere tactics behind the most controversial decision of Taylor's reign.

But even the most hard-hearted of tabloid sub-editors winced at the sight of some of the criticism that rained down on Taylor in the wake of England's poor showing in Sweden.

Taylor won back some admiration when he emerged a few months later to admit he had made mistakes, and the FA further boosted his morale by giving him more than a token endorsement to carry on. The old Taylor enthusiasm seemed to be back, but in the first game of the 1992/93 season England were played off the park when they lost 1–0 to Spain in Santander. The *Sun* dug out its book on vegetables and depicted Taylor as a Spanish onion.

Taylor's overall record for England does not make bad reading, but it shows that the team rarely won matches when it mattered – not least in the quest to reach the 1994 World Cup finals. The qualifying group contained Holland, Norway, Turkey, Poland and San Marino, from which England were expected to go through with the Dutch.

England had won just two of their previous nine games when they began their World Cup campaign with a disappointing 1–1 draw at home to Norway. Six

*Platt is brought down on the edge of the area during England's defeat in Rotterdam*

months later Wembley saw England go 2–0 up against Holland inside 25 minutes, through Barnes and Platt. Dennis Bergkamp pulled one back, entirely against the run of play, with a goal of sublime skill, before England suffered a second blow when Gascoigne left

the field after his face came off worse in a collision
with Jan Wouters' elbow.

But England continued to control the match, and
looked to be heading for a crucial two points (which
would have all but buried Dutch hopes of qualification
following their defeat in Norway and a draw at home
to the Poles). But four minutes from time, Des Walker
was beaten for pace by Marc Overmars, prompting the
Sampdoria defender to grab hold of the Dutchman's
shirt just inside England's area. The referee pointed
to the spot, Van Vossen converted and England were
suddenly facing a serious struggle to make it to the
United States.

E ngland could restore their American dream if they
took three out of four points on the summer trip
to Poland and Norway. Poland, billed as the dark

*Gunnar Halle and Bjornebye in England shirts*
*after Norway's historic win in Oslo*

horses of the group had looked more like dark
donkeys in scraping 1–0 home wins over San Marino
and Turkey. But with reported win bonuses of £5,000
per man, they came out to play against England and
should have won at a canter. They took the lead in the
first half through Adamczuk and were heading for a
win before Ian Wright forced an error from goalkeeper
Bako, five minutes from time, to salvage a vital point.

England, who had looked tired and directionless
against the Poles, now faced a Norway side on a high.
The Scandinavians had arrived from nowhere as a
serious force in world football, and had taken Group

Two by storm with a series of early victories that left England, Holland and Poland scrapping for second place. In Thorstvedt, Halle, Bohinen, Bjornebye, Rekdal, Flo, Fjortoft and Leonhardsen, they could boast players of the highest quality. Taylor made last-minute, wholesale changes in personnel and tactics, opting for three centre-backs plus Carlton Palmer, with Lee Sharpe and Lee Dixon playing wide, Gascoigne and Platt in the middle and Ferdinand and Sheringham up front.

Taylor felt the need for a shake-up after the drab showing in Katowice but the new formation took everyone by surprise – including the players who spent the match chasing Norwegian shadows. England were dreadful and deserved to lose by more than 2–0. Taylor, to his credit, held up his hands. "We made a complete mess of it. I'm here to be shot at and take the rap. I have no defence for our performance," he said afterwards. But his candour and honesty did not spare him a roasting back home.

*Do I not like that: Taylor is restrained by a FIFA official as England lose 2–0 to Holland*

"NORSE MANURE!" screamed one tabloid, which threw in a picture of steaming dung just to rub the pun home. "OSLO RANS!" said another. Just when England fans thought it could get no worse, England lost 2–0 to the USA in Boston a week later, evoking terrible memories of England's stunning defeat to the Americans in 1950.

England beat Poland 3–0 at Wembley with a much-improved display at the start of the 1993/94 season raising the nation's hopes going into the now decisive clash with Holland in Rotterdam in October.

A draw would suit England, assuming they could put a hatful past San Marino. The tension in the build-up to the match was evident in the streets of the Dutch port, where the lunatic elements of each country's supporters were involved in skirmishes.

Inside the stadium the match was played at a furious pace. England found themselves under immense pressure early on, but they hit back with a string of counter-attacks as Dorigo struck the post and Adams and Platt both went close. But it was the Dutch who considered themselves unlucky not to be a goal up at the interval when Rijkaard had a goal disallowed for offside, despite television pictures showing he clearly was not.

Fifteen minutes after the turnaround, it was England's turn to feel a sense of injustice when the sluggish Ronald Koeman resorted to pulling down Platt just outside the area as the England player raced in on goal. If England proved wrong to claim it was a penalty, they were right to insist that the giant Dutchman should have been sent off for a blatant professional foul. But Koeman survived – with fatal consequences for England.

Two minutes later Ince had fouled Wouters on the edge of the England area and none other than R.Koeman came forward to take it. The Dutch free-kick specialist shot straight at Ince, who was booked for encroaching, but he was handed a second chance and made no mistake as he golf-chipped the wall and out of reach of the faraway Seaman. The man who should have been running the taps of the big bath,

was now running the length of the field in celebration.

Merson hit the woodwork moments afterwards, but Bergkamp quickly buried English hopes with Holland's second, though there was a suspicion of handball when he went to control the ball at speed. During all this, Taylor was in apoplectic mood on the touchline, berating officials as the obvious significance of the result began to sink in.

Holland still needed to win in Poland, which they

*Dennis Bergkamp scores Holland's second*

**ENGLAND: The Official F.A. History**

did on the same night England were hoping to run in a cricket score against San Marino (population 30,000). But the final humiliation came in Bologna, where England found themselves a goal down after just nine seconds. England went on to win 7–1, but Holland had beaten the Poles 3–1 to take second place. England would not be going to the States and the next day, the back page of the *Daily Mirror* featured a mock letter from the England boss to the FA in which he tendered his resignation with a blank space for Taylor to sign. Taylor took the hint.

If the vilification of Taylor had been excessive, not even his closest supporters could claim that England had been a great side under his supervision. When he took over, England were a strong team who had come within a penalty-kick of reaching the final of the World Cup, but the team he handed over to Terry Venables was weak, demoralised and directionless.

An outstanding club manager had found out that England was another country.

## GRAHAM TAYLOR (1990–93)

Graham Taylor came to the England post with a reputation for rescuing teams in trouble. So it might have been with some disappointment that he inherited a team that had missed out on a place in the 1990 World Cup final by the odd penalty-kick. His achievements at Watford and Aston Villa were outstanding by anyone's standards, although his critics would complain that ugly football was the price to be paid for his success. His three-and-a-half years in charge got off to a solid, if unspectacular, start and it was to be a year before England suffered defeat. But he sparked a storm of criticism when he took off Gary Lineker during England's 2–1 defeat to Sweden, which ended England's dismal campaign in the 1992 European Championship. Taylor could have been excused for thinking that he had thrown a pint of beer over the Queen Mother when he woke up to see the reaction of the press the following morning.

The decision to replace a national treasure with Arsenal's Alan Smith marked the turning point in his relationship with press and public. England slid from bad to worse over the next 18 months and finally missed out on qualification for the 1994 World Cup after failing to beat either Holland or Norway at home or away.

England rarely found their rhythm under Taylor, who used 59 players in his 38 games in a bid to build a new team without the old "spine" of Peter Shilton, Terry Butcher and Bryan Robson. But he was not helped by the absence for long periods of the injury-prone Paul Gascoigne, England's most talented player, or by his reluctance to use Peter Beardsley and Chris Waddle.

The son of a sports journalist, Taylor had an undistinguished playing career as a full-back with Grimsby and Lincoln before he was forced into early retirement by a hip injury. At the age of 28 he took over the manager's job at Lincoln, where his enthusiasm and meticulous planning helped the club win promotion to the third division. His qualities were spotted by Elton John, who took him to Watford, where Taylor overhauled the entire structure of the club. He transformed the club's

*England had just beaten San Marino 7–1, but could not stop Holland reaching the World Cup finals*

**ENGLAND:** The Official F.A. History

fortunes on the field by playing the "long-ball" game. It was not pretty, but Watford rose meteorically from the fourth division to the second, where they spent two seasons before winning promotion to the top flight and finished runners-up to Liverpool in their first season. In 1984 Taylor guided the club to the FA Cup final where they lost to Everton. All this was achieved on a shoestring budget. In 1987 he accepted the challenge of yet another rescue mission when he took over at Villa, who had just been relegated to the second division. Taylor ensured their return the following season, and in 1990 steered them to second place behind Liverpool.

**England record P38 W18 D13 L7 F62 A32**

# 1994–1996

# REVERSAL OF FORTUNE

*The appointment of Terry Venables*
*as the new England coach met with near universal approval.*
*But after restoring pride to English football, the ebullient Cockney*
*resigned to spend more time with his lawyers.*

Terry Venables may not have been good enough for Tottenham chairman Alan Sugar, but England were only too happy to find work for a man widely regarded as the best coach in the country. His appointment in January 1994 was unique in that its announcement was met with barely a murmur of disapproval from within the world of football. He seemed to have all the qualities needed to thrive in one of sport's most demanding jobs: the Cockney cunning and confidence of Ramsey, the tactical astuteness of Greenwood, the charm and PR skills of Winterbottom, the tough streak of Revie, the player-loyalty and boyish enthusiasm of

***England training at Bisham Abbey,***
***24th January 1996:***
***England coach Terry Venables***
***in the media spotlight***

## PAUL GASCOIGNE

| | |
|---|---|
| Position | Midfield |
| Debut | v Denmark (1–0) at Wembley |
| | 14th September 1988 |
| Clubs | Newcastle, Tottenham, Lazio, |
| | Glasgow Rangers |

A match-winner capable of turning the course of a game with the flick of a boot, Paul Gascoigne could yet be remembered as one of the great unfulfilled talents of world football. Without question one of the most gifted footballers ever to pull on an England shirt, Gascoigne has also proved to be one of the most frustrating.

During a career ravaged by serious injury and dogged by controversy, the hyperactive Geordie has been the subject of more negative than positive headlines in the nation's newspapers. His magical dribbling skills, together with his immense upper body strength, might have been better suited to an earlier era, but his enthusiasm, great vision and potency from deadball situations, would make him a great player in any age.

A glittering career seemed to lie ahead of him after an ebullient display in the 1990 World Cup. Some brave voices were even heard declaring that the highly-strung midfielder was ready to inherit the title of the world's best footballer from Diego Maradona. But since then he has shone only when injury and fitness have allowed. He was introduced slowly to international football by a shrewd Bobby Robson, who got the balance right between experience and over-exposure. But he showed his time had come in the build-up to Italia 90, when he set up three goals and scored a brilliant fourth in a 4–2 win over Czechoslovakia. At the World Cup, Gascoigne, the ultimate showman, thrived off the adrenalin and nervous energy that come from performing on football's biggest stage. The tears which he shed after being booked in the semi-final against Germany catapulted him to early stardom.

It was not long, however, before he became a victim of his own exuberance when, playing for Spurs in the 1991 FA Cup final against Nottingham Forest, he sustained a career-threatening knee injury after making a maniacal lunge at Gary Charles. He was out for over a year before he left for Lazio, where he promptly broke his right leg in training after just a handful of games for the Roman side. He returned to Britain to play for Glasgow Rangers, a yard or two slower, but remained central to the plans of England manager Terry Venables, who encouraged his maverick genius to use his vision rather than his dribbling to open up opposition defences.

"There's no nastiness in him. He might just say or do the wrong thing or burp at the wrong time. He'll always realise his mistake, but it's too late," said Venables. He was welcomed into Glenn Hoddle's team, but it remains to be seen whether Gascoigne's international career will be talked about more in terms of what was rather than what might have been.

Robson and the proven track record of Taylor. But despite his outstanding credentials, his appointment was still a brave act of faith by the FA, who knew they were employing someone whose legal and commercial tangles made him a likely source of negative publicity.

The FA's technical consultant, Jimmy Armfield, was charged with finding a successor, and he quickly discovered there was no serious challenger to Venables. The bookmakers soon stopped taking bets on the identity of the new coach and Armfield, who travelled up and down the country to canvas opinion, reported: "There was near unanimous backing for Terry."

Venables, though, was lucky in that he inherited a team that could not get much worse in terms of confidence and form. Failure to improve on the sad World Cup qualifying campaign would have constituted a crisis for one of the world's major football nations. The only way was up for Venables' England.

Venables rebuilt the team without ever making wholesale changes in personnel. His job was made easier by a long string of fixtures against mediocre opposition, which allowed the players to gradually feel their way back to the top. It also allowed Venables to experiment with a number of different formations, including the notorious "Christmas Tree" line-up, which gave the team a sense of tactical direction. His own ebullient confidence had a contagious effect on the England squad and restored a much-needed sense of self-belief.

## TERRY VENABLES (1994–96)

Terry Venables was never short of confidence. As a young boy growing up in Dagenham (also the birthplace of Sir Alf Ramsey), he wrote on the first page of his autograph book: "Terry Venables – manager of Tottenham". The son of a Tilbury docker and a Welsh mother, Venables was quick to make an impression on the world and before he was out of his teens he had signed for Chelsea, represented England schoolboys, turned himself into a plc and sung with the Joe Loss Orchestra at the Hammersmith Palais. Twenty-five years later he had become the first footballer to buy a major share in a top club when he formed a doomed partnership with Amstrad boss Alan Sugar to rescue Tottenham.

On the pitch Venables developed into a skillful midfielder but lacked the extra yard or two of pace to be a truly great player. After Chelsea, he went to Spurs and then QPR and Crystal Palace. During the early 1970s he went to a secretarial college to learn how to type before co-writing a novel with Gordon Williams *They Used to Play on Grass*, as well as the TV detective series *Hazell*. He also designed a board game. His earlier business interests included a tailor's in the West End, a grocery store and a company called Thingummywigs, which made wigs for women to wear over their curlers.

Venables succeeded Malcolm Allison as manager of Crystal Palace at the age of 33 and steered them from the third division to the first with a style that led many to believe the south London club would be the team of the 1980s. But he was soon on the move to west London, where he took over as manager of Queens Park Rangers, who he even tried to buy. He guided the Loftus Road club into the UEFA Cup as well as their first FA Cup final in 1982, before Barcelona recognised his potential. He arrived in Spain in 1984 amid doubts about his ability to reverse the fortunes of the world's biggest club, but showed he would not shrink from the challenge when he marched to the centre of the Nou Camp pitch, took the microphone and addressed the crowd in Catalan with a heavy Cockney lilt.

Venables learned Spanish as well as Catalan (he even released a version of Frank Sinatra's "My Way" in Catalan), as the papers back home dubbed him "El Tel". He was an instant success, as he guided Barcelona to their first league title in 11 years and

But if the players were happy, Venables was not and, in January 1996, he announced he would be retiring after the European Championship. There was no single reason behind the decision to quit, but a disagreement with Noel White, a member of the international committee, was certainly a factor.

FA chairman Sir Bert Millichip, chief executive Graham Kelly and the majority of the international committee all gave Venables their unqualified backing. But Liverpool director White and Oldham chairman Ian Stott went into print to express their worries about the negative headlines being brought by Venables' five court cases (these were a case for wrongful dismissal against Tottenham, libel actions against BBC *Panorama* and the *Daily Mirror*, a libel action by Alan Sugar against him, and an application by the Department of Trade and Industry to have him disqualified as a company director). White also angered the England coach by saying that he had to prove himself in the European Championship finals before a new contract could be considered – to which Venables replied that White wanted to back a horse after it had passed the post. The impending legal cases were also a worry for Venables, who feared England's World Cup qualifying campaign could be disrupted if he was constantly being called away from the training ground or from spying missions.

then to the 1986 European Cup final, which they lost to Steaua Bucharest on penalties. He returned to Tottenham as manager in 1987 and also bought a stake in the club. But his belief that he could achieve the same success in the boardroom as he had in the bootroom led to a power struggle with chairman Sugar, which would dog his career, not just with Spurs, but also with England. The clash with Sugar opened up a can of legal worms and eventually forced him to resign as England coach. But Venables could not stay out of football or resist a new business venture for long. A few months after he had quit the international scene, having guided England to the semi-finals of the European Championship, he bought first division Portsmouth for £1, and was appointed coach of the Australian national team.

**England record P23 W11 D11 L1 F35 A13**

*Venables: The people's and pundits' choice*

There was nothing spectacular about England's recovery under Venables, but by the time the team ran out at Wembley for the opening match of the 1996 European Championship finals against Switzerland they had proved that, at the very least, they were a tough side to beat. England had lost just once since Venables took charge – a 3–1 defeat to Brazil 12 months earlier – but there were still doubts about whether they were worthy of a place at the top table of world football. Without a competitive match since November 1993, England had rarely left the comfort of Wembley. On one of the rare occasions when they did venture overseas, it was with terrible consequences. The Dublin friendly against the Republic of Ireland in February 1995 was hijacked by a hardcore of neo-fascist hooligans who forced the abandonment of the game after 27 minutes. As hosts of Euro 96, England's reluctance to travel after the riot became more understandable.

There was a different type of controversy when the squad flew back from two final warm-up games in China and Hong Kong. Allegations that damage had

*Alan Shearer celebrates after scoring England's first goal against Scotland*

**ENGLAND:** The Official F.A. History

*Paul Gascoigne settles the "Battle of Britain" with England's second*

been caused to the Cathay Pacific Jumbo jet carrying the players home were followed by pictures of the team celebrating Gascoigne's 29th birthday in a Hong Kong bar. To the disappointment of the tabloid executioners Venables refused to pick out individuals for blame and the squad announced it was taking "collective responsibility" for the incidents. As a distraction from football matters the episode was the last thing Venables needed, but it did at least create a sense of solidarity as the players closed ranks on the world outside.

Euro 96 kicked off amid glorious sunshine and great expectations, but like so many curtain-raisers in major tournaments, England's match against

Switzerland was a huge disappointment. The home side had to settle for a 1–1 draw, but crucially Alan Shearer found the net with a thumping first-half strike that brought to an end one of international football's more inexplicable goal droughts, which had begun 20 months earlier.

It was not until England faced the Scots a few days later that the Championship came to life – from an English point of view – in a match billed as the "Battle of Britain". Fears of crowd trouble proved entirely unfounded (as they would for all but one night of the three-week event), as Wembley basked in sunshine and the reflected glory of victory over the Auld Enemy.

Scotland had the better of the first half before

Shearer got on the end of a superb cross from Gary Neville, to ram home an unstoppable close-range header, shortly after the interval. David Seaman kept England in front with a stunning save from Gordon Durie, but the turning point came moments later when England captain Tony Adams upended Durie. Gary McAllister's penalty was blocked by Seaman and, with the Scots momentarily dazed by the miss, England swept downfield. Substitute Jamie Redknapp released Gascoigne, but there seemed little or no danger as he advanced into the area, until he impudently lifted the ball over Colin Hendry and fired an unstoppable low volley beyond his Rangers' teammate, Andy Goram, in the Scottish goal.

Next up were the Dutch, the bane of England's 1994 World Cup qualifying campaign, but something of an unknown quantity at Euro 96, where their talent for "the beautiful game" was being overshadowed by their talent for destructive in-fighting. It turned out to be a match that confounded even the most optimistic of home fans, as Venables' men produced one of the great England

*Celebration time for Alan Shearer*
*and Steve McManaman*
*after one of Shearer's two goals*
*against Holland*

**ENGLAND: The Official F.A. History**

*David Seaman saves from Nadal in the penalty shoot-out against Spain*

performances. Holland were crushed 4–1, and for Venables, a great admirer of Dutch football, it was an especially sweet moment. Nobody could now accuse England of stumbling through the competition simply on the back of home advantage.

Football fever swept the country in the build-up to England's quarter-final against Spain. Some tabloid newspapers were criticised for taking England's cause to xenophobic extremes (as they would be even more forcibly in the build-up to the semi-final against Germany). The match proved to be a tightly-contested affair, which failed to yield many genuine chances, even in extra-time when the new "golden goal" rule produced a sense of caution rather than urgency. After 120 goalless, nerve-racking minutes, the match

was finally settled by the lottery of a penalty shoot-out. Seaman saved one, the other hit the bar, and Pearce buried the ghost of his miss against the Germans in Turin six years earlier as England triumphed 4–2.

Facing England in the semi-final were the mighty Germans, who they had not beaten in a competitive match since the 1966 World Cup triumph, and who had come through the earlier rounds with ominous and characteristic efficiency.

But if ever England had grounds for optimism

*Football's coming home:*
*England fans turn on the style*
*during the semi-final*
*against Germany*

**Shearer scores after just two minutes as the stunned Germans look on**

going into a match against their modern-day bogey team, it was now. The confidence which had grown steadily during Venables' two and a half years in charge had mushroomed dramatically after the destruction of Holland. Wembley, a good-natured riot of noise and colour in the earlier matches, would be an intimidating arena even for the most accomplished and experienced of opponents.

The Germans, moreover, had serious injury problems after a bone-shudderingly brutal clash with Croatia at Old Trafford in the quarter-finals. Jürgen Klinsmann, Germany's lethal centre-forward and former Tottenham favourite, had been carried out of the match with an ankle injury and was given no chance of being fit.

There were no such problems for England who, in the rejuvenated Alan Shearer, had a goalscorer as good

as any in the world. And it took just two minutes for England's deadliest striker since Gary Lineker to prove his menace. With the German defence still adjusting to the barrage of noise that filled Wembley, Shearer pounced with a close range header.

Surely now triumph over the Germans and a place in the final was just 88 minutes away? Not so. Fifteen minutes later Stefan Kuntz put Bertie Vogts' side back on terms after a mistake by Pearce. The most entertaining of all 31 matches in the finals went into extra-time where the "golden goal" rule finally came good, as Darren Anderton hit a German post at one end, Kuntz had a goal disallowed at the other, before Gascoigne just failed to get a foot to Anderton's cross.

Penalties. Again. Considering what was at stake it was incredible that parity continued for five penalties apiece before the unfortunate Gareth

Southgate stepped up to take the first of the sudden-death spot-kicks.

His only other penalty in a competitive match (for Crystal Palace) had hit a post, and he was to fare no better on this occasion as his shot was saved by Andreas Kopke. Andreas Moller delivered the killer blow to English dreams when he smashed the winning shot into the roof of Seaman's net.

Just as they had in the 1990 World Cup, England had lost out to Germany in the semi-final after 120 minutes of open play had failed to separate the two old adversaries.

*Gareth Southgate puts his head in his hands*
*after his sudden-death penalty miss*

# 1996–

# EARLY PROMISE

*The euphoria that followed England's impressive performance*
*in the semi-finals of Euro 96 had raised the stakes for Venables' successor.*
*No longer were England's followers hoping for success. They expected it.*

Glenn Hoddle, at 38, became England's youngest ever manager when he took over from Venables at the end of the 1996 European Championship. He had a difficult act to follow. The mood surrounding the national team was buoyant following the euphoria created by England's progress to the semi-finals of Euro 96. In restoring a sense of pride in the England team, Venables had also raised the stakes for his successor. But at least rebuilding confidence would not be one of Hoddle's tasks and the team he inherited had a shape, identity and, crucially, a taste of success. The former Chelsea and Swindon boss was almost alone in wanting the post after virtually every other candidate had ruled themselves out of the running for English football's most thankless job.

## ALAN SHEARER

| | |
|---|---|
| Position | Striker |
| Debut | v France (2–0) at Wembley |
| | 19th February 1992 |
| Clubs | Southampton, Blackburn, |
| | Newcastle |

Few would dispute Alan Shearer's right to a place in England's Hall of Fame, despite his relatively poor goal record for a centre-forward of just 15 goals in 34 games. Shearer went 13 games and 20 months without scoring a goal for his country between England's 2–0 win over USA in September 1994 and the opening game of the European Championship against Switzerland in June 1996. Any other player would have been dropped, but Shearer's outstanding ability and self-belief were so obvious in his performances for Blackburn that England coach Terry Venables never contemplated leaving him out.

Since rediscovering his scoring touch with a thumping shot into the roof of the Swiss net in England's 1–1 draw, Shearer has repaid the faith put in him with a string of commanding performances. He finished Euro 96 as top scorer, with five goals, and had scored ten goals in ten games up to England's 2–0 World Cup qualifying victory over Poland in Katowice on 31st May 1997. The 26-year-old Geordie has led from the front since being named England captain by new coach Glenn Hoddle at the start of the World Cup campaign in September.

"No money in the world can buy the feeling of putting on that white shirt, and I want to play every single game I can," said Shearer after his towering display in Poland prompted comparisons with Nat

Lofthouse's display in England's 1952 3–2 win over Austria in Vienna. Shearer scored after just five minutes and then withstood a physical battering from the Polish defence as he led the front-line with an authority that was an inspiration to his teammates.

"Alan has been the right choice on and off the pitch," says Hoddle. "He's always had a lot of pride in putting on an England shirt. He seems to really thrive on the responsibility."

Shearer is not bashful about his international ambitions. "I want to win 100 caps and to become England's top scorer," he says. "By the time I hang my boots up at 35 or 36, I want to be able to look back and say I gave everything, wanted to play every game and tried my best in every game."

His commitment to the England cause saw him

*Destined for greatness: Shearer on his way to becoming one of England's greats*

play through the pain barrier in England's 1–0 World Cup qualifying defeat to Italy at Wembley in February 1997, even though he needed a third groin operation in the space of 12 months.

Shearer began his career at Southampton and made his debut for England against France in 1992, before Kenny Dalglish took him to Blackburn Rovers, where he scored over 30 league goals in three consecutive seasons, helping the club win its first league title for 81 years in 1995. In July 1996 he became the world's most expensive player when he returned to his home town club of Newcastle for £15 million.

*Two-goal Shearer tussles*
*with Marek Jozwiak*
*during England's*
*2–0 win over Poland*

Ahead of Hoddle lay the task of ensuring England's qualification for the 1998 World Cup finals in France from a group which included the mighty Italians, the unknown quantities of Georgia and Moldova and the traditional stumbling block of Poland. Only one side would qualify automatically, although the best runner-up in the European groups would also go straight through. The other eight teams finishing second would go into the play-offs.

One of the reasons that Hoddle took the job was the talent he could see emerging. "There were clearly a lot of good youngsters around and an underbelly in the Under-21s that we could bring through."

But Hoddle took few risks at the start of England's qualifying campaign, which saw England clear potentially tricky hurdles against Eastern European opposition. England won 3–0 in Moldova, before Alan Shearer redeemed a poor performance against Poland at Wembley with two goals, after England had gone a goal down. England then won 2–0 in Georgia.

For England's crucial encounter against the Italians

*A downcast Gary Neville shakes hands*
*after England's 1–0 defeat to Italy at Wembley*

# GLENN HODDLE (1996–)

Perhaps Glenn Hoddle's relative lack of success as an England player gave him greater cause to succeed as the team's manager. Despite their love of open, attacking football, both Ron Greenwood and Bobby Robson failed to accommodate Hoddle's extravagant talents. He won a total of 53 caps over a nine-year period but rarely produced the performances that made him such an exceptional midfielder at club level.

After catching the eye as a youngster playing for Essex schools, Hoddle joined Tottenham as an apprentice in 1974, turned professional the following year and made his debut at the age of 18. He represented England Youth, the Under-21s and the "B" team before scoring on his debut for the senior team against Bulgaria in 1979.

Hoddle helped Spurs win consecutive FA Cups in 1981 and 1982 but left after the club's surprise defeat to Coventry in the 1987 final. He joined Monaco for £750,000 and played a major role in guiding them to the league title in his first year. It was while he was at the French club that he was inspired by manager Arsene Wenger to consider going into coaching.

He won his last England cap in England's 3–1 defeat to the USSR in the 1988 European Championship finals. He retired through injury but returned as a non-contract player at Chelsea in 1991. He took over as player-manager of Swindon that summer and steered them into the Premiership via the first division play-offs at the end of the 1992/93 season, when he scored in a 4–3 win over Leicester. A month later he joined Chelsea as player-manager and guided them to the 1994 FA Cup final against Manchester United in his first season.

*The guardian of English hopes:*
*Hoddle, the youngest ever*
*England manager*

at Wembley in February, he gambled by including the maverick talent of Southampton's Matt Le Tissier. England lost 1–0 and were barely given a sniff at goal after the Italians had seized an early lead with a lightning strike by Chelsea's Gianfranco Zola. Hoddle had his first experience of tabloid fury the following morning and was widely pilloried for playing Le Tissier. Defeat, England's first in a competitive match at Wembley for 14 years, increased the pressure for England to get at least a draw in Poland where they had not won since 1966.

Georgia had been beaten 2–0 at Wembley a month before England set off to face the Poles, in the intimidating stadium of Katowice, for a match Hoddle admitted "was the most important game we've had". Hoddle's plan was to attack and he named Gascoigne, David Beckham and Robert Lee in his midfield. But it was to be his captain, Alan Shearer, who would stand out from a magnificent team performance as England swept to 2–0 victory that virtually guaranteed their progress to France as the best runners-up.

Over 4,000 England fans had made the trip into Poland's inhospitable industrial heartland of Silesia, and they were given the best possible welcome as England took the lead with a goal of the highest quality after five minutes. Lee played a simple ball to Paul Ince, who burst into the Polish half and released Shearer with a pass of snooker-standard precision. The England captain needed just one touch to keep ahead of his marker before firing a low shot into the left-hand corner of the net from the edge of the area. Shearer missed a penalty on the stroke of half-time, but even that failed to take the gloss of his best performance in an England shirt.

Teddy Sheringham sealed three vital points in the dying seconds of a brutally physical match which saw Gascoigne stretchered off with a gashed thigh. Victory more or less guaranteed a place in the play-offs and stepped up the pressure on Italy who they faced in the final group game. "That'll have the Italians choking on their spaghetti," said Ince.

# ENGLAND

## THE
## OFFICIAL
## F.A. HISTORY

## *Statistics*
### (May 31st 1997 inclusive)

### TOP 20 GOALSCORERS

(Goals/games)

| | |
|---|---|
| Bobby Charlton | 49/106 |
| Gary Lineker | 48/80 |
| Jimmy Greaves | 44/57 |
| Tom Finney | 30/76 |
| Nat Lofthouse | 30/33 |
| Vivian Woodward | 29/23 |
| Steve Bloomer | 28/23 |
| David Platt | 27/62 |
| Bryan Robson | 26/90 |
| Geoff Hurst | 24/49 |
| Stan Mortensen | 23/25 |
| Tommy Lawton | 22/23 |
| Mick Channon | 21/46 |
| Kevin Keegan | 21/63 |
| Martin Peters | 20/67 |
| George Camsell | 18/9 |
| Dixie Dean | 18/16 |
| Johnny Haynes | 18/56 |
| Roger Hunt | 18/34 |
| Tommy Taylor | 16/19 |

### TOP 20 APPEARANCES

| | |
|---|---|
| Peter Shilton | 125 |
| Bobby Moore | 108 |
| Bobby Charlton | 106 |
| Billy Wright | 105 |
| Bryan Robson | 90 |
| Kenny Sansom | 86 |
| Ray Wilkins | 84 |
| Gary Lineker | 80 |
| John Barnes | 79 |
| Terry Butcher | 77 |
| Tom Finney | 76 |
| Stuart Pearce | 76 |
| Gordon Banks | 73 |
| Alan Ball | 72 |
| Martin Peters | 67 |
| Dave Watson | 65 |
| Kevin Keegan | 63 |
| Ray Wilson | 63 |
| Emlyn Hughes | 62 |
| Chris Waddle | 62 |

### CHRONOLOGICAL

W = won    D = drawn    A = abandoned    L = lost
WCQ  World Cup qualifier
WCF  World Cup finals
ECQ  European Championship qualifier
ECF  European Championship finals

| year date | v | opposition, venue | result | score |
|---|---|---|---|---|
| 1872 30/11 | v | Scotland Glasgow | D | 0–0 |
| 1873 8/3 | v | Scotland Kennington | W | 4–2 |
| 1874 7/3 | v | Scotland Glasgow | L | 1–2 |
| 1875 6/3 | v | Scotland Kennington | D | 2–2 |
| 1876 4/3 | v | Scotland Glasgow | L | 0–3 |
| 1877 3/3 | v | Scotland Kennington | L | 1–3 |
| 1878 2/3 | v | Scotland Glasgow | L | 2–7 |
| 1879 18/1 | v | Wales Kennington | W | 2–1 |
| 1879 5/4 | v | Scotland Kennington | W | 5–4 |
| 1880 13/3 | v | Scotland Glasgow | L | 4–5 |
| 1880 15/3 | v | Wales Wrexham | W | 3–2 |
| 1881 26/2 | v | Wales Blackburn | L | 0–1 |
| 1881 12/3 | v | Scotland Kennington | L | 1–6 |
| 1882 18/2 | v | Ireland Belfast | W | 13–0 |
| 1882 11/3 | v | Scotland Glasgow | L | 1–5 |
| 1882 13/3 | v | Wales Wrexham | L | 3–5 |
| 1883 3/2 | v | Wales Kennington | W | 5–0 |
| 1883 24/2 | v | Ireland Liverpool | W | 7–0 |
| 1883 10/3 | v | Scotland Sheffield | L | 2–3 |
| 1884 23/2 | v | Ireland Belfast | W | 8–1 |
| 1884 15/3 | v | Scotland Glasgow | L | 0–1 |
| 1884 17/3 | v | Wales Wrexham | W | 4–0 |
| 1885 28/2 | v | Ireland Manchester | W | 4–0 |
| 1885 14/3 | v | Wales Blackburn | D | 1–1 |
| 1885 21/3 | v | Scotland Kennington | D | 1–1 |
| 1886 13/3 | v | Ireland Belfast | W | 6–1 |
| 1886 29/3 | v | Wales Wrexham | W | 3–1 |
| 1886 31/3 | v | Scotland Glasgow | D | 1–1 |
| 1887 5/2 | v | Ireland Sheffield | W | 7–0 |
| 1887 26/2 | v | Wales Kennington | W | 4–0 |
| 1887 19/3 | v | Scotland Blackburn | L | 2–3 |
| 1888 4/2 | v | Wales Crewe | W | 5–1 |
| 1888 17/3 | v | Scotland Glasgow | W | 5–0 |
| 1888 31/3 | v | Ireland Belfast | W | 5–1 |
| 1889 23/2 | v | Wales Stoke | W | 4–1 |
| 1889 2/3 | v | Ireland Everton | W | 6–1 |
| 1889 13/3 | v | Scotland Kennington | L | 2–3 |
| 1890 15/3 | v | Ireland Belfast | W | 9–1 |
| 1890 15/3 | v | Wales Wrexham | W | 3–1 |
| 1890 5/4 | v | Scotland Glasgow | D | 1–1 |
| 1891 7/5 | v | Wales Sunderland | W | 4–1 |
| 1891 7/3 | v | Ireland Wolverhampton | W | 6–1 |
| 1891 6/4 | v | Scotland Blackburn | W | 2–1 |
| 1892 5/3 | v | Wales Wrexham | W | 2–0 |
| 1892 5/3 | v | Ireland Belfast | W | 2–0 |
| 1892 2/4 | v | Scotland Glasgow | W | 4–1 |
| 1893 25/2 | v | Ireland Birmingham | W | 6–1 |
| 1893 13/3 | v | Wales Stoke | W | 6–0 |
| 1893 1/4 | v | Scotland Richmond | W | 5–2 |
| 1894 3/3 | v | Ireland Belfast | D | 2–2 |

| Year | Date | | Opponent Venue | Result | Score |
|---|---|---|---|---|---|
| 1894 | 12/3 | v | Wales Wrexham | W | 5–1 |
| 1894 | 7/4 | v | Scotland Glasgow | D | 2–2 |
| 1895 | 9/3 | v | Ireland Derby | W | 9–0 |
| 1895 | 18/3 | v | Wales Kennington | D | 1–1 |
| 1895 | 6/4 | v | Scotland Everton | W | 3–0 |
| 1896 | 7/3 | v | Ireland Belfast | W | 2–0 |
| 1896 | 16/3 | v | Wales Cardiff | W | 9–1 |
| 1896 | 4/4 | v | Scotland Glasgow | L | 1–2 |
| 1897 | 20/2 | v | Ireland Nottingham | W | 6–0 |
| 1897 | 29/3 | v | Wales Sheffield | W | 4–0 |
| 1897 | 3/4 | v | Scotland Crystal Palace | L | 1–2 |
| 1898 | 5/3 | v | Ireland Belfast | W | 3–2 |
| 1898 | 28/3 | v | Wales Wrexham | W | 3–0 |
| 1898 | 2/4 | v | Scotland Glasgow | W | 3–1 |
| 1899 | 18/2 | v | Ireland Sunderland | W | 13–2 |
| 1899 | 20/3 | v | Wales Bristol | W | 4–0 |
| 1899 | 8/4 | v | Scotland Birmingham | W | 2–1 |
| 1900 | 17/3 | v | Ireland Dublin | W | 2–0 |
| 1900 | 26/3 | v | Wales Cardiff | D | 1–1 |
| 1900 | 7/4 | v | Scotland Glasgow | L | 1–4 |
| 1901 | 9/3 | v | Ireland Southampton | W | 3–0 |
| 1901 | 18/3 | v | Wales Newcastle | W | 6–0 |
| 1901 | 30/3 | v | Scotland Crystal Palace | D | 2–2 |
| 1902 | 3/3 | v | Wales Wrexham | D | 0–0 |
| 1902 | 22/3 | v | Ireland Belfast | W | 1–0 |
| 1902 | 5/4 | v | Scotland Glasgow | A | 1–1 |
| 1902 | 3/5 | v | Scotland Birmingham | D | 2–2 |
| 1903 | 14/2 | v | Ireland Wolverhampton | W | 4–0 |
| 1903 | 2/3 | v | Wales Portsmouth | W | 2–0 |
| 1903 | 4/4 | v | Scotland Sheffield | L | 1–2 |
| 1904 | 29/2 | v | Wales Wrexham | D | 2–2 |
| 1904 | 12/3 | v | Ireland Belfast | W | 3–1 |
| 1904 | 9/4 | v | Scotland Glasgow | W | 1–0 |
| 1905 | 25/2 | v | Ireland Middlesbrough | D | 1–1 |
| 1905 | 27/3 | v | Wales Liverpool | W | 3–1 |
| 1905 | 1/4 | v | Scotland Crystal Palace | W | 1–0 |
| 1906 | 17/2 | v | Ireland Belfast | W | 5–0 |
| 1906 | 19/3 | v | Wales Cardiff | W | 1–0 |
| 1906 | 7/4 | v | Scotland Glasgow | L | 1–2 |
| 1907 | 16/2 | v | Ireland Everton | W | 1–0 |
| 1907 | 18/3 | v | Wales Fulham | D | 1–1 |
| 1907 | 6/4 | v | Scotland Newcastle | D | 1–1 |
| 1908 | 15/2 | v | Ireland Belfast | W | 3–1 |
| 1908 | 16/3 | v | Wales Wrexham | W | 7–1 |
| 1908 | 4/4 | v | Scotland Glasgow | D | 1–1 |
| 1908 | 6/6 | v | Austria Vienna | W | 6–1 |
| 1908 | 8/6 | v | Austria Vienna | W | 11–1 |
| 1908 | 10/6 | v | Hungary Budapest | W | 7–0 |
| 1908 | 13/6 | v | Bohemia Prague | W | 4–0 |
| 1909 | 13/2 | v | Ireland Bradford | W | 4–0 |
| 1909 | 15/3 | v | Wales Nottingham | W | 2–0 |
| 1909 | 3/4 | v | Scotland Crystal Palace | W | 2–0 |
| 1909 | 29/5 | v | Hungary Budapest | W | 4–2 |
| 1909 | 31/5 | v | Hungary Budapest | W | 8–2 |
| 1909 | 1/6 | v | Austria Vienna | W | 8–1 |
| 1910 | 12/2 | v | Ireland Belfast | D | 1–1 |
| 1910 | 14/3 | v | Wales Cardiff | W | 1–0 |
| 1910 | 2/4 | v | Scotland Glasgow | L | 0–2 |
| 1911 | 11/2 | v | Ireland Derby | W | 2–1 |
| 1911 | 13/3 | v | Wales Millwall | W | 3–0 |
| 1911 | 1/4 | v | Scotland Everton | D | 1–1 |
| 1912 | 10/2 | v | Ireland Dublin | W | 6–1 |
| 1912 | 11/3 | v | Wales Wrexham | W | 2–0 |
| 1912 | 23/3 | v | Scotland Glasgow | D | 1–1 |
| 1913 | 15/2 | v | Ireland Belfast | L | 1–2 |
| 1913 | 17/3 | v | Wales Bristol | W | 4–3 |
| 1913 | 5/4 | v | Scotland Chelsea | W | 1–0 |
| 1914 | 14/2 | v | Ireland Middlesbrough | L | 0–3 |
| 1914 | 16/3 | v | Wales Cardiff | W | 2–0 |
| 1914 | 14/4 | v | Scotland Glasgow | L | 1–3 |
| 1919 | 25/10 | v | Ireland Belfast | D | 1–1 |
| 1920 | 15/3 | v | Wales Highbury | W | 1–2 |
| 1920 | 10/4 | v | Scotland Sheffield | W | 5–4 |
| 1920 | 23/10 | v | Ireland Sunderland | W | 2–0 |
| 1921 | 14/3 | v | Wales Cardiff | D | 0–0 |
| 1921 | 9/4 | v | Scotland Glasgow | L | 0–3 |
| 1921 | 21/5 | v | Belgium Brussels | W | 2–0 |
| 1921 | 22/10 | v | N Ireland Belfast | D | 1–1 |
| 1922 | 13/3 | v | Wales Liverpool | W | 1–0 |
| 1922 | 8/4 | v | Scotland Villa Park | L | 0–1 |
| 1922 | 21/10 | v | N Ireland West Bromwich | W | 2–0 |
| 1923 | 5/3 | v | Wales Cardiff | D | 2–2 |
| 1923 | 19/3 | v | Belgium Highbury | W | 6–1 |
| 1923 | 14/4 | v | Scotland Glasgow | D | 2–2 |
| 1923 | 10/5 | v | France Paris | W | 4–1 |
| 1923 | 21/5 | v | Sweden Stockholm | W | 4–2 |
| 1923 | 24/5 | v | Sweden Stockholm | W | 3–1 |
| 1923 | 20/10 | v | N Ireland Belfast | L | 1–2 |
| 1923 | 1/11 | v | Belgium Antwerp | D | 2–2 |
| 1924 | 3/3 | v | Wales Blackburn | L | 1–2 |
| 1924 | 12/4 | v | Scotland Wembley | D | 1–1 |
| 1924 | 17/5 | v | France Paris | W | 3–1 |
| 1924 | 22/10 | v | N Ireland Everton | W | 3–1 |
| 1924 | 8/12 | v | Belgium West Bromwich | W | 4–0 |
| 1925 | 28/2 | v | Wales Swansea | W | 2–1 |
| 1925 | 4/4 | v | Scotland Glasgow | L | 0–2 |
| 1925 | 21/5 | v | France Paris | W | 3–2 |
| 1925 | 24/10 | v | N Ireland Belfast | D | 0–0 |
| 1926 | 1/3 | v | Wales Crystal Palace | L | 1–3 |
| 1926 | 17/4 | v | Scotland Manchester | L | 0–1 |
| 1926 | 24/5 | v | Belgium Antwerp | W | 5–3 |
| 1926 | 20/10 | v | N Ireland Liverpool | D | 3–3 |
| 1927 | 12/2 | v | Wales Wrexham | D | 3–3 |
| 1927 | 2/4 | v | Scotland Glasgow | W | 2–1 |
| 1927 | 11/5 | v | Belgium Brussels | W | 9–1 |
| 1927 | 21/5 | v | Luxembourg Luxembourg | W | 5–2 |
| 1927 | 26/5 | v | France Paris | W | 6–0 |
| 1927 | 22/10 | v | N Ireland Belfast | L | 0–2 |
| 1927 | 28/11 | v | Wales Burnley | L | 1–2 |
| 1928 | 31/3 | v | Scotland Wembley | L | 1–5 |
| 1928 | 17/5 | v | France Paris | W | 5–1 |
| 1928 | 19/5 | v | Belgium Antwerp | W | 3–1 |
| 1928 | 22/10 | v | N Ireland Everton | W | 2–1 |
| 1928 | 17/11 | v | Wales Swansea | W | 3–2 |
| 1929 | 13/4 | v | Scotland Glasgow | L | 0–1 |
| 1929 | 9/5 | v | France Paris | W | 4–1 |
| 1929 | 11/5 | v | Belgium Brussels | W | 5–1 |
| 1929 | 15/5 | v | Spain Madrid | L | 3–4 |
| 1929 | 19/10 | v | N Ireland Belfast | W | 3–0 |
| 1929 | 20/11 | v | Wales Chelsea | W | 6–0 |
| 1930 | 5/4 | v | Scotland Wembley | W | 5–2 |
| 1930 | 10/5 | v | Germany Berlin | D | 3–3 |
| 1930 | 14/5 | v | Austria Vienna | D | 0–0 |
| 1930 | 20/10 | v | N Ireland Sheffield | W | 5–1 |

| | | | | | |
|---|---|---|---|---|---|
| 1930 22/11 | v | Wales Wrexham | W | 4–0 |
| 1931 5/4 | v | Scotland Glasgow | L | 0–2 |
| 1931 14/5 | v | France Paris | L | 2–5 |
| 1931 16/5 | v | Belgium Brussels | W | 4–1 |
| 1931 17/10 | v | N Ireland Belfast | W | 6–2 |
| 1931 18/11 | v | Wales Liverpool | W | 3–1 |
| 1931 9/12 | v | Spain Arsenal | W | 7–1 |
| 1932 9/4 | v | Scotland Wembley | W | 3–0 |
| 1932 17/10 | v | N Ireland Blackpool | W | 1–0 |
| 1932 16/11 | v | Wales Wrexham | D | 0–0 |
| 1932 7/12 | v | Austria Chelsea | W | 4–3 |
| 1933 1/4 | v | Scotland Glasgow | L | 1–2 |
| 1933 13/5 | v | Italy Rome | D | 1–1 |
| 1933 29/5 | v | Switzerland Berne | W | 4–0 |
| 1933 14/10 | v | N Ireland Belfast | W | 3–0 |
| 1933 15/11 | v | Wales Newcastle | L | 1–2 |
| 1933 6/12 | v | France Tottenham | W | 4–1 |
| 1934 14/4 | v | Scotland Wembley | W | 3–0 |
| 1934 10/5 | v | Hungary Budapest | L | 1–2 |
| 1934 16/5 | v | Czechoslovakia Prague | L | 1–2 |
| 1934 29/9 | v | Wales Cardiff | W | 4–0 |
| 1934 14/11 | v | Italy Arsenal | W | 3–2 |
| 1935 6/2 | v | N Ireland Everton | W | 2–1 |
| 1935 6/4 | v | Scotland Glasgow | L | 0–2 |
| 1935 18/5 | v | Holland Amsterdam | W | 1–0 |
| 1935 19/10 | v | N Ireland Belfast | W | 3–1 |
| 1935 4/12 | v | Germany Tottenham | W | 3–0 |
| 1936 5/2 | v | Wales Wolverhampton | L | 1–2 |
| 1936 4/4 | v | Scotland Wembley | D | 1–1 |
| 1936 6/5 | v | Austria Vienna | L | 1–2 |
| 1936 9/5 | v | Belgium Brussels | L | 2–3 |
| 1936 17/10 | v | Wales Cardiff | L | 1–2 |
| 1936 18/11 | v | N Ireland Stoke | W | 3–1 |
| 1936 2/12 | v | Hungary Arsenal | W | 6–2 |
| 1937 17/4 | v | Scotland Glasgow | L | 1–3 |
| 1937 14/5 | v | Norway Oslo | W | 6–0 |
| 1937 17/5 | v | Sweden Stockholm | W | 4–0 |
| 1937 20/5 | v | Finland Helsinki | W | 8–0 |
| 1937 23/10 | v | N Ireland Belfast | W | 5–1 |
| 1937 17/11 | v | Wales Middlesbrough | W | 2–1 |
| 1937 1/12 | v | Czechoslovakia Tottenham | W | 5–4 |
| 1938 9/4 | v | Scotland Wembley | L | 0–1 |
| 1938 14/5 | v | Germany Berlin | W | 6–3 |
| 1938 21/5 | v | Switzerland Zurich | L | 1–2 |
| 1938 26/5 | v | France Paris | W | 4–2 |
| 1938 22/10 | v | Wales Cardiff | L | 2–4 |
| 1938 9/11 | v | Norway Newcastle | W | 4–0 |
| 1938 16/11 | v | N Ireland Manchester | W | 7–0 |
| 1939 15/4 | v | Scotland Glasgow | W | 2–1 |
| 1939 13/5 | v | Italy Milan | D | 2–2 |
| 1939 18/5 | v | Yugoslavia Belgrade | L | 1–2 |
| 1939 24/5 | v | Romania Bucharest | W | 2–0 |
| 1946 28/9 | v | N Ireland Belfast | W | 7–2 |
| 1946 30/9 | v | Republic of Ireland Dublin | W | 1–0 |
| 1946 13/11 | v | Wales Manchester | W | 3–0 |
| 1946 27/11 | v | Holland Huddersfield | W | 8–2 |
| 1947 12/4 | v | Scotland Wembley | D | 1–1 |
| 1947 3/5 | v | France Arsenal | W | 3–0 |
| 1947 18/5 | v | Switzerland Zurich | L | 0–1 |
| 1947 25/5 | v | Portugal Lisbon | W | 10–0 |
| 1947 21/9 | v | Belgium Brussels | W | 5–2 |
| 1947 18/10 | v | Wales Cardiff | W | 3–0 |

| | | | | | |
|---|---|---|---|---|---|
| 1947 5/11 | v | N Ireland Everton | D | 2–2 |
| 1947 19/11 | v | Sweden Arsenal | W | 4–2 |
| 1948 10/4 | v | Scotland Glasgow | W | 2–0 |
| 1948 16/5 | v | Italy Turin | W | 4–0 |
| 1948 26/9 | v | Denmark Copenhagen | D | 0–0 |
| 1948 9/10 | v | N Ireland Belfast | W | 6–2 |
| 1948 10/11 | v | Wales Aston Villa | W | 1–0 |
| 1948 2/12 | v | Switzerland Arsenal | W | 6–0 |
| 1949 9/4 | v | Scotland Wembley | L | 1–3 |
| 1949 13/5 | v | Sweden Stockholm | L | 1–3 |
| 1949 18/5 | v | Norway Oslo | W | 4–1 |
| 1949 22/5 | v | France Paris | W | 3–1 |
| 1949 21/9 | v | Republic of Ireland Everton | L | 0–2 |
| 1949 15/10 | v | Wales Cardiff *wcq* | W | 4–1 |
| 1949 16/11 | v | N Ireland Manchester *wcq* | W | 9–2 |
| 1949 30/11 | v | Italy Tottenham | W | 2–0 |
| 1950 15/4 | v | Scotland Glasgow *wcq* | W | 1–0= |
| 1950 14/5 | v | Portugal Lisbon | W | 5–3 |
| 1950 18/5 | v | Belgium Brussels | W | 4–1 |
| 1950 25/6 | v | Chile Rio de Janeiro *wcf* | W | 2–0 |
| 1950 29/6 | v | USA Belo Horizonte *wcf* | L | 0–1 |
| 1950 2/7 | v | Spain Rio De Janeiro *wcf* | L | 1–0 |
| 1950 7/10 | v | N Ireland Belfast | W | 4–1 |
| 1950 15/11 | v | Wales Sunderland | W | 4–2 |
| 1950 22/11 | v | Yugoslavia Highbury | D | 2–2 |
| 1951 14/4 | v | Scotland Wembley | L | 2–3 |
| 1951 9/5 | v | Argentina Wembley | W | 2–1 |
| 1951 19/5 | v | Portugal Everton | W | 5–3 |
| 1951 3/10 | v | France Arsenal | D | 2–2 |
| 1951 20/10 | v | Wales Cardiff | D | 1–1 |
| 1951 14/11 | v | N Ireland Aston Villa | W | 2–0 |
| 1951 28/11 | v | Austria Wembley | D | 2–2 |
| 1952 5/4 | v | Scotland Glasgow | W | 2–1 |
| 1952 18/5 | v | Italy Florence | D | 1–1 |
| 1952 25/5 | v | Austria Vienna | W | 3–2 |
| 1952 28/5 | v | Switzerland Zurich | W | 3–0 |
| 1952 4/10 | v | N Ireland Belfast | D | 2–2 |
| 1952 12/11 | v | Wales Wembley | W | 5–2 |
| 1952 26/11 | v | Belgium Wembley | W | 5–0 |
| 1953 18/4 | v | Scotland Wembley | D | 2–2 |
| 1953 17/5 | v | Argentina Buenos Aires | †A | 0–0 |
| 1953 24/5 | v | Chile Santiago | W | 2–1 |
| 1953 31/5 | v | Uruguay Montevideo | L | 1–2 |
| 1953 8/6 | v | USA New York | W | 6–3 |
| 1953 10/10 | v | Wales Cardiff *wcq* | W | 4–1 |
| 1953 11/11 | v | N Ireland Everton *wcq* | W | 3–1 |
| 1953 25/11 | v | Hungary Wembley | L | 3–6 |
| 1954 3/4 | v | Scotland Glasgow *wcq* | W | 4–2 |
| 1954 16/5 | v | Yugoslavia Belgrade | L | 0–1 |
| 1954 23/5 | v | Hungary Budapest | L | 1–7 |
| 1954 17/6 | v | Belgium Basle *wcf* | D | 4–4 |
| 1954 20/6 | v | Switzerland Berne *wcf* | W | 2–0 |
| 1954 26/6 | v | Uruguay Basle *wcf* | L | 2–4 |
| 1954 2/10 | v | N Ireland Belfast | W | 2–0 |
| 1954 10/11 | v | Wales Wembley | W | 3–2 |
| 1954 1/12 | v | West Germany Wembley | W | 3–1 |
| 1955 2/4 | v | Scotland Wembley | W | 7–2 |
| 1955 15/5 | v | France Paris | L | 0–1 |
| 1955 18/5 | v | Spain Madrid | D | 1–1 |
| 1955 22/5 | v | Portugal Oporto | L | 1–3 |
| 1955 2/10 | v | Denmark Copenhagen | W | 5–1 |
| 1955 22/10 | v | Wales Cardiff | L | 1–2 |

*† abandoned after 23 minutes due to rain*

**ENGLAND: The Official F.A. History**

| Date | | Opponent & Venue | Result | Score |
|---|---|---|---|---|
| 1955 2/11 | v | N Ireland Wembley | W | 3–0 |
| 1955 30/11 | v | Spain Wembley | W | 4–1 |
| 1956 14/4 | v | Scotland Glasgow | D | 1–1 |
| 1956 9/5 | v | Brazil Wembley | W | 4–2 |
| 1956 16/5 | v | Sweden Stockholm | D | 0–0 |
| 1956 20/5 | v | Finland Helsinki | W | 5–1 |
| 1956 26/5 | v | West Germany Berlin | W | 3–1 |
| 1956 6/10 | v | N Ireland Belfast | D | 1–1 |
| 1956 14/11 | v | Wales Wembley | W | 3–1 |
| 1956 28/11 | v | Yugoslavia Wembley | W | 3–0 |
| 1956 5/12 | v | Denmark Wolverhampton *WCQ* | W | 5–2 |
| 1957 16/4 | v | Scotland Wembley | W | 2–1 |
| 1957 8/5 | v | Rep of Ireland Wembley *WCQ* | W | 5–1 |
| 1957 15/5 | v | Denmark Copenhagen *WCQ* | W | 4–1 |
| 1957 19/5 | v | Rep of Ireland Dublin *WCQ* | D | 1–1 |
| 1957 19/10 | v | Wales Cardiff | W | 4–0 |
| 1957 6/11 | v | N Ireland Wembley | L | 2–3 |
| 1957 27/11 | v | France Wembley | W | 4–0 |
| 1958 19/4 | v | Scotland Glasgow | W | 4–0 |
| 1958 7/5 | v | Portugal Wembley | W | 2–1 |
| 1958 11/5 | v | Yugoslavia Belgrade | L | 0–5 |
| 1958 18/5 | v | USSR Moscow | D | 1–1 |
| 1958 8/6 | v | USSR Gothenburg *WCF* | D | 2–2 |
| 1958 11/6 | v | Brazil Gothenburg *WCF* | D | 0–0 |
| 1958 15/6 | v | Austria Boras *WCF* | D | 2–2 |
| 1958 17/6 | v | USSR Gothenburg *WCF* | L | 0–1 |
| 1958 4/10 | v | N Ireland Belfast | D | 3–3 |
| 1958 22/10 | v | USSR Wembley | W | 5–0 |
| 1958 26/11 | v | Wales Aston Villa | D | 2–2 |
| 1959 11/4 | v | Scotland Wembley | W | 1–0 |
| 1959 6/5 | v | Italy Wembley | D | 2–2 |
| 1959 13/5 | v | Brazil Rio de Janeiro | L | 0–2 |
| 1959 17/5 | v | Peru Lima | L | 1–4 |
| 1959 24/5 | v | Mexico Mexico City | L | 1–2 |
| 1959 28/5 | v | USA Los Angeles | W | 8–1 |
| 1959 17/10 | v | Wales Cardiff | D | 1–1 |
| 1959 28/10 | v | Sweden Wembley | L | 2–3 |
| 1959 18/11 | v | N Ireland Wembley | W | 2–1 |
| 1960 19/4 | v | Scotland Glasgow | D | 1–1 |
| 1960 11/5 | v | Yugoslavia Wembley | D | 3–3 |
| 1960 15/5 | v | Spain Madrid | L | 0–3 |
| 1960 22/5 | v | Hungary Budapest | L | 0–2 |
| 1960 8/10 | v | N Ireland Belfast | W | 5–2 |
| 1960 19/10 | v | Luxembourg Luxembourg *WCF* | W | 9–0 |
| 1960 26/10 | v | Spain Wembley | W | 4–2 |
| 1960 23/11 | v | Wales Wembley | W | 5–1 |
| 1961 15/4 | v | Scotland Wembley | W | 9–3 |
| 1961 10/5 | v | Mexico Wembley | W | 8–0 |
| 1961 21/5 | v | Portugal Lisbon *WCQ* | D | 1–1 |
| 1961 24/5 | v | Italy Rome | W | 3–2 |
| 1961 27/5 | v | Austria Vienna | L | 1–3 |
| 1961 28/9 | v | Luxembourg Arsenal *WCQ* | W | 4–1 |
| 1961 14/10 | v | Wales Cardiff | D | 1–1 |
| 1961 25/10 | v | Portugal Wembley *WCQ* | W | 2–0 |
| 1961 22/11 | v | N Ireland Wembley | D | 1–1 |
| 1962 4/4 | v | Austria Wembley | W | 3–1 |
| 1962 14/4 | v | Scotland Glasgow | L | 0–2 |
| 1962 9/5 | v | Switzerland Wembley | W | 3–1 |
| 1962 20/5 | v | Peru Lima | W | 4–0 |
| 1962 31/5 | v | Hungary Rancagua *WCF* | L | 1–2 |
| 1962 2/6 | v | Argentina Rancagua *WCF* | W | 3–1 |
| 1962 7/6 | v | Bulgaria Rancagua *WCF* | D | 0–0 |
| 1962 10/6 | v | Brazil Vina del Mar *WCF* | L | 1–3 |
| 1962 3/10 | v | France Sheffield *ECQ* | D | 1–1 |
| 1962 20/10 | v | N Ireland Belfast | W | 3–1 |
| 1962 21/11 | v | Wales Wembley | W | 4–0 |
| 1963 27/2 | v | France Paris *ECQ* | L | 2–5 |
| 1963 6/4 | v | Scotland Wembley | L | 1–2 |
| 1963 8/5 | v | Brazil Wembley | D | 1–1 |
| 1963 29/5 | v | Czechoslovakia Bratislava | W | 4–2 |
| 1963 2/6 | v | East Germany Leipzig | W | 2–1 |
| 1963 5/6 | v | Switzerland Basle | W | 8–1 |
| 1963 12/10 | v | Wales Cardiff | W | 4–0 |
| 1963 20/11 | v | N Ireland Wembley | W | 8–3 |
| 1964 11/4 | v | Scotland Glasgow | L | 0–1 |
| 1964 6/5 | v | Uruguay Wembley | W | 2–1 |
| 1964 17/5 | v | Portugal Lisbon | W | 4–3 |
| 1964 24/5 | v | Republic of Ireland Dublin | W | 3–1 |
| 1964 27/5 | v | USA New York | W | 10–0 |
| 1964 30/5 | v | Brazil Rio de Janeiro | L | 1–5 |
| 1964 4/6 | v | Portugal São Paolo | D | 1–1 |
| 1964 6/6 | v | Argentina Rio de Janeiro | L | 0–1 |
| 1964 3/10 | v | N Ireland Belfast | W | 4–3 |
| 1964 21/10 | v | Belgium Wembley | D | 2–2 |
| 1964 18/11 | v | Wales Wembley | W | 2–1 |
| 1964 9/12 | v | Holland Amsterdam | D | 1–1 |
| 1965 10/4 | v | Scotland Wembley | D | 2–2 |
| 1965 5/5 | v | Hungary Wembley | W | 1–0 |
| 1965 9/5 | v | Yugoslavia Belgrade | D | 1–1 |
| 1965 12/5 | v | West Germany Nuremberg | W | 1–0 |
| 1965 16/5 | v | Sweden Gothenburg | W | 2–1 |
| 1965 2/10 | v | Wales Cardiff | D | 0–0 |
| 1965 20/10 | v | Austria Wembley | L | 2–3 |
| 1965 10/11 | v | N Ireland Wembley | W | 2–1 |
| 1965 8/12 | v | Spain Madrid | W | 2–0 |
| 1966 5/1 | v | Poland Everton | D | 1–1 |
| 1966 23/2 | v | West Germany Wembley | W | 1–0 |
| 1966 2/4 | v | Scotland Glasgow | W | 4–3 |
| 1966 4/5 | v | Yugoslavia Wembley | W | 2–0 |
| 1966 26/6 | v | Finland Helsinki | W | 3–0 |
| 1966 29/6 | v | Norway Oslo | W | 6–1 |
| 1966 3/7 | v | Denmark Copenhagen | W | 2–0 |
| 1966 5/7 | v | Poland Chorzow | W | 1–0 |
| 1966 11/7 | v | Uruguay Wembley *WCF* | D | 0–0 |
| 1966 16/7 | v | Mexico Wembley *WCF* | W | 2–0 |
| 1966 20/7 | v | France Wembley *WCF* | W | 2–0 |
| 1966 23/7 | v | Argentina Wembley *WCF* | W | 1–0 |
| 1966 26/7 | v | Portugal Wembley *WCF* | W | 2–1 |
| 1966 30/7 | v | West Germany Wembley *WCF* | W | 4–2 |
| 1966 20/10 | v | N Ireland Belfast *ECQ* | W | 2–0 |
| 1966 2/11 | v | Czechoslovakia Wembley | D | 0–0 |
| 1966 16/11 | v | Wales Wembley *ECQ* | W | 5–1 |
| 1967 15/4 | v | Scotland Wembley *ECQ* | L | 2–3 |
| 1967 24/5 | v | Spain Wembley | W | 2–0 |
| 1967 27/5 | v | Austria Vienna | W | 1–0 |
| 1967 21/10 | v | Wales Cardiff *ECQ* | W | 3–0 |
| 1967 22/11 | v | N Ireland Wembley *ECQ* | W | 2–0 |
| 1967 6/12 | v | USSR Wembley | D | 2–2 |
| 1968 24/2 | v | Scotland Glasgow *ECQ* | D | 1–1 |
| 1968 3/4 | v | Spain Wembley *ECQ* | W | 1–0 |
| 1968 8/5 | v | Spain Madrid *ECQ* | W | 2–1 |
| 1968 22/5 | v | Sweden Wembley | W | 3–1 |
| 1968 1/6 | v | West Germany Hanover | L | 0–1 |
| 1968 5/6 | v | Yugoslavia Florence *ECF* | L | 0–1 |

| Year | Date | | Opponent / Venue | | Result | Score |
|---|---|---|---|---|---|---|
| 1968 | 8/6 | v | USSR Rome *ECF* | | W | 2–0 |
| 1968 | 6/11 | v | Romania Bucharest | | D | 0–0 |
| 1968 | 11/12 | v | Bulgaria Wembley | | D | 1–1 |
| 1969 | 15/1 | v | Romania Wembley | | D | 1–1 |
| 1969 | 12/3 | v | France Wembley | | W | 5–0 |
| 1969 | 3/5 | v | N Ireland Belfast | | W | 3–1 |
| 1969 | 7/5 | v | Wales Wembley | | W | 2–1 |
| 1969 | 10/5 | v | Scotland Wembley | | W | 4–1 |
| 1969 | 1/6 | v | Mexico Mexico City | | D | 0–0 |
| 1969 | 8/6 | v | Uruguay Montevideo | | W | 2–1 |
| 1969 | 12/6 | v | Brazil Rio de Janeiro | | L | 1–2 |
| 1969 | 5/11 | v | Holland Amsterdam | | W | 1–0 |
| 1969 | 10/12 | v | Portugal Wembley | | W | 1–0 |
| 1970 | 14/1 | v | Holland Wembley | | D | 0–0 |
| 1970 | 25/2 | v | Belgium Brussels | | W | 3–1 |
| 1970 | 8/4 | v | Wales Cardiff | | D | 1–1 |
| 1970 | 21/4 | v | N Ireland Wembley | | W | 3–1 |
| 1970 | 25/4 | v | Scotland Glasgow | | D | 0–0 |
| 1970 | 20/5 | v | Colombia Bogota | | W | 4–0 |
| 1970 | 24/5 | v | Ecuador Quito | | W | 2–0 |
| 1970 | 2/6 | v | Romania Guadalajara *WCF* | | W | 1–0 |
| 1970 | 7/6 | v | Brazil Guadalajara *WCF* | | L | 0–1 |
| 1970 | 11/6 | v | Czechoslovakia Guadalajara *WCF* | | W | 1–0 |
| 1970 | 14/6 | v | West Germany Leon *WCF* | | L | 2–3 |
| 1970 | 25/11 | v | East Germany Wembley | | W | 3–1 |
| 1971 | 3/2 | v | Malta Valletta *ECQ* | | W | 1–0 |
| 1971 | 21/4 | v | Greece Wembley *ECQ* | | W | 3–0 |
| 1971 | 12/5 | v | Malta Wembley *ECQ* | | W | 5–0 |
| 1971 | 15/5 | v | N Ireland Belfast | | W | 1–0 |
| 1971 | 19/5 | v | Wales Wembley | | D | 0–0 |
| 1971 | 22/5 | v | Scotland Wembley | | W | 3–1 |
| 1971 | 13/10 | v | Switzerland Basle *ECQ* | | W | 3–2 |
| 1971 | 10/11 | v | Switzerland Wembley *ECQ* | | D | 1–1 |
| 1971 | 1/12 | v | Greece Athens *ECQ* | | W | 2–0 |
| 1972 | 29/4 | v | West Germany Wembley *ECQ* | | L | 1–3 |
| 1972 | 13/5 | v | West Germany Berlin *ECQ* | | D | 0–0 |
| 1972 | 20/5 | v | Wales Cardiff | | W | 3–0 |
| 1972 | 23/5 | v | N Ireland Wembley | | L | 0–1 |
| 1972 | 27/5 | v | Scotland Glasgow | | W | 1–0 |
| 1972 | 11/10 | v | Yugoslavia Wembley | | D | 1–1 |
| 1972 | 15/11 | v | Wales Cardiff *WCQ* | | W | 1–0 |
| 1973 | 24/1 | v | Wales Wembley *WCQ* | | W | 1–1 |
| 1973 | 14/2 | v | Scotland Glasgow | | W | 5–0 |
| 1973 | 12/5 | v | N Ireland Everton | | W | 2–1 |
| 1973 | 15/5 | v | Wales Wembley | | W | 3–0 |
| 1973 | 19/5 | v | Scotland Wembley | | W | 1–0 |
| 1973 | 27/5 | v | Czechoslovakia Prague | | D | 1–1 |
| 1973 | 6/6 | v | Poland Chorzow *WCQ* | | L | 0–2 |
| 1973 | 10/6 | v | USSR Moscow | | W | 2–1 |
| 1973 | 14/6 | v | Italy Turin | | L | 0 2 |
| 1973 | 26/9 | v | Austria Wembley | | W | 7–0 |
| 1973 | 17/10 | v | Poland Wembley *WCQ* | | D | 1–1 |
| 1973 | 14/11 | v | Italy Wembley | | L | 0–1 |
| 1974 | 3/4 | v | Portugal Lisbon | | D | 0–0 |
| 1974 | 11/5 | v | Wales Cardiff | | W | 2–0 |
| 1974 | 15/5 | v | N Ireland Wembley | | W | 1–0 |
| 1974 | 18/5 | v | Scotland Glasgow | | L | 0–2 |
| 1974 | 22/5 | v | Argentina Wembley | | D | 2–2 |
| 1974 | 29/5 | v | East Germany Leipzig | | D | 1–1 |
| 1974 | 1/6 | v | Bulgaria Sofia | | W | 1–0 |
| 1974 | 5/6 | v | Yugoslavia Belgrade | | D | 2–2 |
| 1974 | 30/10 | v | Czechoslovakia Wembley *ECQ* | | W | 3–0 |
| 1974 | 20/11 | v | Portugal Wembley *ECQ* | | D | 0–0 |
| 1975 | 12/3 | v | West Germany Wembley | | W | 2–0 |
| 1975 | 16/4 | v | Cyprus Wembley *ECQ* | | W | 5–0 |
| 1975 | 11/5 | v | Cyprus Limassol *ECQ* | | W | 1–0 |
| 1975 | 17/5 | v | N Ireland Belfast | | D | 0–0 |
| 1975 | 21/5 | v | Wales Wembley | | D | 2–2 |
| 1975 | 24/5 | v | Scotland Wembley | | W | 5–1 |
| 1975 | 3/9 | v | Switzerland Basle | | W | 2–1 |
| 1975 | 30/10 | v | Czechoslovakia Bratislava *ECQ* | | L | 1–2 |
| 1975 | 19/11 | v | Portugal Lisbon *ECQ* | | D | 1–1 |
| 1976 | 24/3 | v | Wales Wrexham | | W | 2–1 |
| 1976 | 8/5 | v | Wales Cardiff | | W | 1–0 |
| 1976 | 11/5 | v | N Ireland Wembley | | W | 4–0 |
| 1976 | 15/5 | v | Scotland Glasgow | | L | 1–2 |
| 1976 | 23/5 | v | Brazil Los Angeles | | L | 0–1 |
| 1976 | 28/5 | v | Italy New York | | W | 3–2 |
| 1976 | 13/6 | v | Finland Helsinki *WCQ* | | W | 4–1 |
| 1976 | 8/9 | v | Republic of Ireland Wembley | | D | 1–1 |
| 1976 | 13/10 | v | Finland Wembley *WCQ* | | W | 2–1 |
| 1976 | 17/11 | v | Italy Rome *WCQ* | | L | 0–2 |
| 1977 | 9/2 | v | Holland Wembley | | L | 0–2 |
| 1977 | 30/3 | v | Luxembourg Wembley *WCQ* | | W | 5–0 |
| 1977 | 28/5 | v | N Ireland Belfast | | W | 2–1 |
| 1977 | 31/5 | v | Wales Wembley | | L | 0–1 |
| 1977 | 4/6 | v | Scotland Wembley | | L | 1–2 |
| 1977 | 8/6 | v | Brazil Rio de Janeiro | | D | 0–0 |
| 1977 | 12/6 | v | Argentina Buenos Aires | | D | 1–1 |
| 1977 | 15/6 | v | Uruguay Montevideo | | D | 0–0 |
| 1977 | 7/9 | v | Switzerland Wembley | | D | 0–0 |
| 1977 | 12/10 | v | Luxembourg Luxembourg *WCQ* | | W | 2–0 |
| 1977 | 16/11 | v | Italy Wembley *WCQ* | | W | 2–0 |
| 1978 | 22/2 | v | West Germany Munich | | L | 1–2 |
| 1978 | 19/4 | v | Brazil Wembley | | D | 1–1 |
| 1978 | 3/5 | v | Wales Cardiff | | W | 3–1 |
| 1978 | 16/5 | v | N Ireland Wembley | | W | 1–0 |
| 1978 | 20/5 | v | Scotland Glasgow | | W | 1–0 |
| 1978 | 24/5 | v | Hungary Wembley | | W | 4–1 |
| 1978 | 20/9 | v | Denmark Copenhagen *ECQ* | | W | 4–3 |
| 1978 | 25/10 | v | Republic of Ireland Dublin *ECQ* | | D | 1–1 |
| 1978 | 29/11 | v | Czechoslovakia Wembley | | W | 1–0 |
| 1979 | 7/2 | v | N Ireland Wembley *ECQ* | | W | 4–0 |
| 1979 | 19/5 | v | N Ireland Belfast | | W | 2–0 |
| 1979 | 23/5 | v | Wales Wembley | | D | 0–0 |
| 1979 | 26/5 | v | Scotland Wembley | | W | 3–1 |
| 1979 | 6/6 | v | Bulgaria Sofia *ECQ* | | W | 3–0 |
| 1979 | 10/6 | v | Sweden Stockholm | | D | 0–0 |
| 1979 | 13/6 | v | Austria Vienna | | L | 3–4 |
| 1979 | 12/9 | v | Denmark Wembley *ECQ* | | W | 1–0 |
| 1979 | 17/10 | v | N Ireland Belfast *ECQ* | | W | 5–1 |
| 1979 | 22/11 | v | Bulgaria Wembley *ECQ* | | W | 2–0 |
| 1980 | 6/2 | v | Rep of Ireland Wembley *ECQ* | | W | 2–0 |
| 1980 | 26/3 | v | Spain Barcelona | | W | 2–0 |
| 1980 | 13/5 | v | Argentina Wembley | | W | 3–1 |
| 1980 | 17/5 | v | Wales Wrexham | | L | 1–4 |
| 1980 | 20/5 | v | N Ireland Wembley | | D | 1–1 |
| 1980 | 24/5 | v | Scotland Glasgow | | W | 2–0 |
| 1980 | 31/5 | v | Australia Sydney | | W | 2–1 |
| 1980 | 12/6 | v | Belgium Turin *ECF* | | D | 1–1 |
| 1980 | 15/6 | v | Italy Turin *ECF* | | L | 0–1 |
| 1980 | 18/6 | v | Spain Naples *ECF* | | W | 2–1 |
| 1980 | 10/9 | v | Norway Wembley *WCQ* | | W | 4–0 |
| 1980 | 15/10 | v | Romania Bucharest *WCQ* | | L | 1–2 |

| | | | | | | |
|---|---|---|---|---|---|---|
| 1980 19/11 | v | Switzerland Wembley *WCQ* | W | 2–1 | | |
| 1981 25/3 | v | Spain Wembley | L | 1–2 | | |
| 1981 29/4 | v | Romania Wembley *WCQ* | D | 0–0 | | |
| 1981 12/5 | v | Brazil Wembley | L | 0–1 | | |
| 1981 20/5 | v | Wales Wembley | D | 0–0 | | |
| 1981 23/5 | v | Scotland Wembley | L | 0–1 | | |
| 1981 30/5 | v | Switzerland Basle *WCQ* | L | 1–2 | | |
| 1981 6/6 | v | Hungary Budapest *WCQ* | W | 3–1 | | |
| 1981 9/9 | v | Norway Oslo *WCQ* | L | 1–2 | | |
| 1981 18/11 | v | Hungary Wembley *WCQ* | W | 1–0 | | |
| 1982 23/2 | v | N Ireland Wembley | W | 4–0 | | |
| 1982 27/4 | v | Wales Cardiff | W | 1–0 | | |
| 1982 25/5 | v | Holland Wembley | W | 2–0 | | |
| 1982 29/5 | v | Scotland Glasgow | W | 1–0 | | |
| 1982 2/6 | v | Iceland Reykjavik | D | 1–1 | | |
| 1982 3/6 | v | Finland Helsinki | W | 4–1 | | |
| 1982 16/6 | v | France Bilbao *WCF* | W | 3–1 | | |
| 1982 20/6 | v | Czechoslovakia Bilbao *WCF* | W | 2–0 | | |
| 1982 25/6 | v | Kuwait Bilbao *WCF* | W | 1–0 | | |
| 1982 29/6 | v | West Germany Madrid *WCF* | D | 0–0 | | |
| 1982 5/7 | v | Spain Madrid *WCF* | D | 0–0 | | |
| 1982 22/9 | v | Denmark Copenhagen *ECQ* | D | 2–2 | | |
| 1982 13/10 | v | West Germany Wembley | L | 1–2 | | |
| 1982 17/11 | v | Greece Salonika *ECQ* | W | 3–0 | | |
| 1982 15/12 | v | Luxembourg Wembley *ECQ* | W | 9–0 | | |
| 1983 23/2 | v | Wales Wembley | W | 2–1 | | |
| 1983 30/3 | v | Greece Wembley *ECQ* | D | 0–0 | | |
| 1983 27/4 | v | Hungary Wembley *ECQ* | W | 2–0 | | |
| 1983 28/5 | v | N Ireland Belfast | D | 0–0 | | |
| 1983 1/6 | v | Scotland Wembley | W | 2–0 | | |
| 1983 12/6 | v | Australia Sydney | D | 0–0 | | |
| 1983 15/6 | v | Australia Brisbane | W | 1–0 | | |
| 1983 19/6 | v | Australia Melbourne | D | 1–1 | | |
| 1983 21/9 | v | Denmark Wembley *ECQ* | L | 0–1 | | |
| 1983 12/10 | v | Hungary Budapest *ECQ* | W | 3–0 | | |
| 1983 16/11 | v | Luxembourg Luxembourg *ECQ* | W | 4–0 | | |
| 1984 29/2 | v | France Paris | L | 0–2 | | |
| 1984 4/4 | v | N Ireland Wembley | W | 1–0 | | |
| 1984 2/5 | v | Wales Wrexham | L | 0–1 | | |
| 1984 26/5 | v | Scotland Glasgow | D | 1–1 | | |
| 1984 2/6 | v | USSR Wembley | L | 0–2 | | |
| 1984 10/6 | v | Brazil Rio de Janeiro | W | 2–0 | | |
| 1984 13/6 | v | Uruguay Montevideo | L | 0–2 | | |
| 1984 17/6 | v | Chile Santiago | D | 0–0 | | |
| 1984 12/9 | v | East Germany Wembley | W | 1–0 | | |
| 1984 17/10 | v | Finland Wembley *WCQ* | W | 5–0 | | |
| 1984 14/11 | v | Turkey Istanbul *WCQ* | W | 8–0 | | |
| 1985 27/2 | v | N Ireland Belfast *WCQ* | W | 1–0 | | |
| 1985 26/3 | v | Rep of Ireland Wembley | W | 2–1 | | |
| 1985 1/5 | v | Romania Bucharest *WCQ* | D | 0–0 | | |
| 1985 22/5 | v | Finland Helsinki *WCQ* | D | 1–1 | | |
| 1985 25/5 | v | Scotland Glasgow | L | 0–1 | | |
| 1985 6/6 | v | Italy Mexico City | L | 1–2 | | |
| 1985 9/6 | v | Mexico Mexico City | L | 0–1 | | |
| 1985 12/6 | v | West Germany Mexico City | W | 3–0 | | |
| 1985 16/6 | v | USA Los Angeles | W | 5–0 | | |
| 1985 11/9 | v | Romania Wembley *WCQ* | D | 1–1 | | |
| 1985 16/10 | v | Turkey Wembley *WCQ* | W | 5–0 | | |
| 1985 13/11 | v | N Ireland Wembley *WCQ* | D | 0–0 | | |
| 1986 29/1 | v | Egypt Cairo | W | 4–0 | | |
| 1986 26/2 | v | Israel Tel Aviv | W | 2–1 | | |
| 1986 26/3 | v | USSR Tbilisi | W | 1–0 | | |
| 1986 23/4 | v | Scotland Wembley | W | 2–1 | | |
| 1986 17/5 | v | Mexico Los Angeles | W | 3–0 | | |
| 1986 24/5 | v | Canada Vancouver | W | 1–0 | | |
| 1986 3/6 | v | Portugal Monterrey *WCF* | L | 0–1 | | |
| 1986 6/6 | v | Morocco Monterrey *WCF* | D | 0–0 | | |
| 1986 11/6 | v | Poland Monterrey *WCF* | W | 3–0 | | |
| 1986 18/6 | v | Paraguay Mexico City *WCF* | W | 3–0 | | |
| 1986 22/6 | v | Argentina Mexico City *WCF* | L | 1–2 | | |
| 1986 10/9 | v | Sweden Stockholm | L | 0–1 | | |
| 1986 15/10 | v | N Ireland Wembley *ECQ* | W | 3–0 | | |
| 1986 12/11 | v | Yugoslavia Wembley *ECQ* | W | 2–0 | | |
| 1987 18/2 | v | Spain Madrid | W | 4–2 | | |
| 1987 1/4 | v | N Ireland Belfast *ECQ* | W | 2–0 | | |
| 1987 29/4 | v | Turkey Izmir *ECQ* | D | 0–0 | | |
| 1987 19/5 | v | Brazil Wembley | D | 1–1 | | |
| 1987 23/5 | v | Scotland Glasgow | D | 0–0 | | |
| 1987 9/9 | v | West Germany Dusseldorf | L | 1–3 | | |
| 1987 14/10 | v | Turkey Wembley *ECQ* | W | 8–0 | | |
| 1987 11/11 | v | Yugoslavia Belgrade *ECQ* | W | 4–1 | | |
| 1988 17/2 | v | Israel Tel Aviv | D | 0–0 | | |
| 1988 23/3 | v | Holland Wembley | D | 2–2 | | |
| 1988 27/4 | v | Hungary Budapest | D | 0–0 | | |
| 1988 21/5 | v | Scotland Wembley | W | 1–0 | | |
| 1988 24/5 | v | Colombia Wembley | D | 1–1 | | |
| 1988 28/5 | v | Switzerland Lausanne | W | 1–0 | | |
| 1988 12/6 | v | Rep of Ireland Stuttgart *ECF* | L | 0–1 | | |
| 1988 15/6 | v | Holland Dusseldorf *ECF* | L | 1–3 | | |
| 1988 18/6 | v | USSR Frankfurt *ECF* | L | 1–3 | | |
| 1988 14/9 | v | Denmark Wembley | W | 1–0 | | |
| 1988 19/10 | v | Sweden Wembley *WCQ* | D | 0–0 | | |
| 1988 16/11 | v | Saudi Arabia Riyadh | D | 1–1 | | |
| 1989 8/2 | v | Greece Athens | W | 2–1 | | |
| 1989 8/3 | v | Albania Tirana *WCQ* | W | 2–0 | | |
| 1989 26/4 | v | Albania Wembley *WCQ* | W | 5–0 | | |
| 1989 23/5 | v | Chile Wembley | D | 0–0 | | |
| 1989 27/5 | v | Scotland Glasgow | W | 2–0 | | |
| 1989 3/6 | v | Poland Wembley *WCQ* | W | 3–0 | | |
| 1989 7/6 | v | Denmark Copenhagen | D | 1–1 | | |
| 1989 6/9 | v | Sweden Stockholm *WCQ* | D | 0–0 | | |
| 1989 11/10 | v | Poland Katowice *WCQ* | D | 0–0 | | |
| 1989 15/11 | v | Italy Wembley | D | 0–0 | | |
| 1989 13/12 | v | Yugoslavia Wembley | W | 2–1 | | |
| 1990 28/3 | v | Brazil Wembley | W | 1–0 | | |
| 1990 25/4 | v | Czechoslovakia Wembley | W | 4–2 | | |
| 1990 15/5 | v | Denmark Wembley | W | 1–0 | | |
| 1990 22/5 | v | Uruguay Wembley | L | 1–2 | | |
| 1990 2/6 | v | Tunisia Tunis | D | 1–1 | | |
| 1990 11/6 | v | Rep of Ireland Cagliari *WCF* | D | 1–1 | | |
| 1990 16/6 | v | Holland Cagliari *WCF* | D | 0–0 | | |
| 1990 21/6 | v | Egypt Cagliari *WCF* | W | 1–0 | | |
| 1990 26/6 | v | Belgium Bologna *WCF* | W | 1–0 | | |
| 1990 1/7 | v | Cameroon Naples *WCF* | W | 3–2 | | |
| 1990 4/7 | v | West Germany Turin *WCF* | †D | 1–1 | | |
| 1990 7/7 | v | Italy Bari *WCF* | L | 1–2 | | |
| 1990 12/9 | v | Hungary Wembley | W | 1–0 | | |
| 1990 17/10 | v | Poland Wembley *ECQ* | W | 2–0 | | |
| 1990 14/11 | v | Rep of Ireland Dublin *ECQ* | D | 1–1 | | |
| 1991 6/2 | v | Cameroon Wembley | W | 2–0 | | |
| 1991 27/3 | v | Rep of Ireland Wembley *ECQ* | D | 1–1 | | |
| 1991 1/5 | v | Turkey Izmir *ECQ* | W | 1–0 | | |
| 1991 21/5 | v | USSR Wembley | W | 3–1 | | |
| 1991 25/5 | v | Argentina Wembley | D | 2–2 | | |

*† aet Eng lost 4–3 on penalties*

| | | | | | |
|---|---|---|---|---|---|
| 1991 1/6 | v | Australia Sydney | | W | 1–0 |
| 1991 3/6 | v | New Zealand Auckland | | W | 1–0 |
| 1991 8/6 | v | New Zealand Wellington | | W | 2–0 |
| 1991 12/6 | v | Malaysia Kuala Lumpur | | W | 4–2 |
| 1991 11/9 | v | Germany Wembley | | L | 0–1 |
| 1991 16/10 | v | Turkey Wembley *ECQ* | | W | 1–0 |
| 1991 13/11 | v | Poland Poznan *ECQ* | | D | 1–1 |
| 1992 19/2 | v | France Wembley | | W | 2–0 |
| 1992 25/3 | v | Czechoslovakia Prague | | D | 2–2 |
| 1992 29/4 | v | CIS Moscow | | D | 2–2 |
| 1992 12/5 | v | Hungary Budapest | | W | 1–0 |
| 1992 17/5 | v | Brazil Wembley | | D | 1–1 |
| 1992 3/6 | v | Finland Helsinki | | W | 2–1 |
| 1992 11/6 | v | Denmark Malmo *ECF* | | D | 0–0 |
| 1992 14/6 | v | France Malmo *ECF* | | D | 0–0 |
| 1992 17/6 | v | Sweden Stockholm *ECF* | | L | 1–2 |
| 1992 9/9 | v | Spain Santander | | L | 0–1 |
| 1992 14/10 | v | Norway Wembley *WCQ* | | D | 1–1 |
| 1992 18/11 | v | Turkey Wembley *WCQ* | | W | 4–0 |
| 1993 17/2 | v | San Marino Wembley *WCQ* | | W | 6–0 |
| 1993 31/3 | v | Turkey Izmir *WCQ* | | W | 2–0 |
| 1993 28/4 | v | Holland Wembley *WCQ* | | D | 2–2 |
| 1993 29/5 | v | Poland Katowice *WCQ* | | D | 1–1 |
| 1993 2/6 | v | Norway Oslo *WCQ* | | L | 0–2 |
| 1993 9/6 | v | USA Boston | | L | 0–2 |
| 1993 13/6 | v | Brazil Washington | | D | 1–1 |
| 1993 19/6 | v | Germany Detroit | | L | 1–2 |
| 1993 8/9 | v | Poland Wembley *WCQ* | | W | 3–0 |
| 1993 13/10 | v | Holland Rotterdam *WCQ* | | L | 0–2 |
| 1993 17/11 | v | San Marino Bologna *WCQ* | | W | 7–1 |
| 1994 9/3 | v | Denmark Wembley | | W | 1–0 |
| 1994 17/5 | v | Greece Wembley | | W | 5–0 |
| 1994 22/5 | v | Norway Wembley | | D | 0–0 |
| 1994 7/9 | v | USA Wembley | | W | 2–0 |
| 1994 12/10 | v | Romania Wembley | | D | 1–1 |
| 1994 16/11 | v | Nigeria Wembley | | W | 1–0 |
| 1995 15/2 | v | Republic of Ireland Wembley | †A | | 1–1 |
| 1995 29/3 | v | Uruguay Wembley | | D | 0–0 |
| 1995 3/6 | v | Japan Wembley | | W | 2–1 |
| 1995 8/6 | v | Sweden Leeds | | D | 3–3 |
| 1995 11/6 | v | Brazil Wembley | | L | 1–3 |
| 1995 6/9 | v | Colombia Wembley | | D | 0–0 |
| 1995 11/10 | v | Norway Oslo | | D | 0–0 |
| 1995 15/11 | v | Switzerland Wembley | | W | 3–1 |
| 1995 12/12 | v | Portugal Wembley | | D | 1–1 |
| 1996 27/3 | v | Bulgaria Wembley | | W | 1–0 |
| 1996 24/4 | v | Croatia Wembley | | D | 0–0 |
| 1996 18/5 | v | Hungary Wembley | | W | 3–0 |
| 1996 23/5 | v | China Beijing | | W | 3–0 |
| 1996 8/6 | v | Switzerland Wembley *ECF* | | D | 1–1 |
| 1996 15/6 | v | Scotland Wembley *ECF* | | W | 2–0 |
| 1996 18/6 | v | Holland Wembley *ECF* | | W | 4–1 |
| 1996 22/6 | v | Spain Wembley *ECF* | *D | | 0–0 |
| 1996 26/6 | v | Germany Wembley *ECF* | ≠D | | 1–1 |
| 1996 1/9 | v | Moldova Chisinau *WCQ* | | W | 3–0 |
| 1996 9/10 | v | Poland Wembley *WCQ* | | W | 2–1 |
| 1996 9/11 | v | Georgia Tbilisi *WCQ* | | W | 2–0 |
| 1997 12/2 | v | Italy Wembley *WCQ* | | L | 1–0 |
| 1997 29/3 | v | Mexico Wembley | | W | 2–0 |
| 1997 30/4 | v | Georgia Wembley *WCQ* | | W | 2–0 |
| 1997 24/5 | v | South Africa Old Trafford | | W | 2–1 |
| 1997 31/5 | v | Poland Katowice *WCQ* | | W | 2–0 |

**v Albania**

| | | | | |
|---|---|---|---|---|
| 1989 8/3 | Tirana *WCQ* | | W | 2–0 |
| 1989 26/4 | Wembley *WCQ* | | W | 5–0 |

**P2 W2 D0 L0 F7 A0**

**v Argentina**

| | | | | |
|---|---|---|---|---|
| 1951 9/5 | Wembley | | W | 2–1 |
| 1953 17/5 | Buenos Aires | **A | | 0–0 |
| 1962 2/6 | Rancagua *WCF* | | W | 3–1 |
| 1964 6/6 | Rio de Janeiro | | L | 0–1 |
| 1966 23/7 | Wembley *WCF* | | W | 1–0 |
| 1974 22/5 | Wembley | | D | 2–2 |
| 1977 12/6 | Buenos Aires | | D | 1–1 |
| 1980 13/5 | Wembley | | W | 3–1 |
| 1986 22/6 | Mexico City *WCF* | | L | 1–2 |
| 1991 25/5 | Wembley | | D | 2–2 |

**P10 W4 D4 L2 F15 A11**

**v Australia**

| | | | | |
|---|---|---|---|---|
| 1980 31/5 | Sydney | | W | 2–1 |
| 1983 12/6 | Sydney | | D | 0–0 |
| 1983 15/6 | Brisbane | | W | 1–0 |
| 1983 19/6 | Melbourne | | D | 1–1 |
| 1991 1/6 | Sydney | | W | 1–0 |

**P5 W3 D2 L0 F5 A2**

**v Austria**

| | | | | |
|---|---|---|---|---|
| 1908 6/6 | Vienna | | W | 6–1 |
| 1908 8/6 | Vienna | | W | 11–1 |
| 1909 1/6 | Vienna | | W | 8–1 |
| 1930 14/5 | Vienna | | D | 0–0 |
| 1932 7/12 | Chelsea | | W | 4–3 |
| 1936 6/5 | Vienna | | L | 1–2 |
| 1951 28/11 | Wembley | | D | 2–2 |
| 1952 25/5 | Vienna | | W | 3–2 |
| 1958 15/6 | Boras *WCF* | | D | 2–2 |
| 1961 27/5 | Vienna | | L | 3–1 |
| 1962 4/4 | Wembley | | W | 3–1 |
| 1965 20/10 | Wembley | | L | 2–3 |
| 1967 27/5 | Vienna | | W | 1–0 |
| 1973 26/9 | Wembley | | W | 7–0 |
| 1979 13/6 | Vienna | | L | 3–4 |

**P15 W8 D3 L4 F54 A25**

**v Belgium**

| | | | | |
|---|---|---|---|---|
| 1921 21/5 | Brussels | | W | 2–0 |
| 1923 19/3 | Arsenal | | W | 6–1 |
| 1923 1/11 | Antwerp | | D | 2–2 |
| 1924 8/12 | West Bromwich | | W | 4–0 |
| 1926 24/5 | Antwerp | | W | 5–3 |
| 1927 11/5 | Brussels | | W | 9–1 |
| 1928 19/5 | Antwerp | | W | 3–1 |
| 1929 11/5 | Brussels | | W | 5–1 |
| 1931 16/5 | Brussels | | W | 4–1 |
| 1936 9/5 | Brussels | | L | 2–3 |
| 1947 21/9 | Brussels | | W | 5–2 |
| 1950 18/5 | Brussels | | W | 4–1 |
| 1952 26/11 | Wembley | | W | 5–0 |
| 1954 17/6 | Basle *WCF* | | D | 4–4 |
| 1964 21/10 | Wembley | | D | 2–2 |

*† abandoned due to crowd trouble    * aet won 4–2 on penalties    ** abandoned after 23 minutes*
*≠ aet lost 6–5 on penalties*

| | | | | |
|---|---|---|---|---|
| 1970 25/2 | Brussels | | W | 3–1 |
| 1980 12/6 | Turin *ECF* | | D | 1–1 |
| 1990 26/6 | Bologna *WCF* | | W | 1–0 |

**P18 W13 D4 L1 F67 A24**

### v Bohemia

| | | | | |
|---|---|---|---|---|
| 1908 13/6 | Prague | | W | 4–0 |

**P1 W1 D0 L0 F4 A0**

### v Brazil

| | | | | |
|---|---|---|---|---|
| 1956 9/5 | Wembley | | W | 4–2 |
| 1958 11/6 | Gothenburg *WCF* | | D | 0–0 |
| 1959 13/5 | Rio de Janeiro | | L | 0–2 |
| 1962 10/6 | Vina del Mar *WCF* | | L | 1–3 |
| 1963 8/5 | Wembley | | D | 1–1 |
| 1964 30/5 | Rio de Janeiro | | L | 1–5 |
| 1969 12/6 | Rio de Janeiro | | L | 1–2 |
| 1970 7/6 | Guadalajara *WCF* | | L | 0–1 |
| 1976 23/5 | Los Angeles | | L | 0–1 |
| 1977 8/6 | Rio de Janeiro | | D | 0–0 |
| 1978 19/4 | Wembley | | D | 1–1 |
| 1981 12/5 | Wembley | | L | 0–1 |
| 1984 10/6 | Rio de Janeiro | | W | 2–0 |
| 1987 19/5 | Wembley | | D | 1–1 |
| 1990 28/3 | Wembley | | W | 1–0 |
| 1992 17/5 | Wembley | | D | 1–1 |
| 1993 13/6 | Washington | | D | 1–1 |
| 1995 11/6 | Wembley | | L | 1–3 |

**P18 W3 D7 L8 F16 A25**

### v Bulgaria

| | | | | |
|---|---|---|---|---|
| 1962 7/6 | Rancagua *WCF* | | D | 0–0 |
| 1968 11/12 | Wembley | | D | 1–1 |
| 1974 1/6 | Sofia | | W | 1–0 |
| 1979 6/6 | Sofia *ECQ* | | W | 3–0 |
| 1979 22/11 | Wembley *ECQ* | | W | 2–0 |
| 1996 27/3 | Wembley | | W | 1–0 |

**P6 W4 D2 L0 F8 A1**

### v Cameroon

| | | | | |
|---|---|---|---|---|
| 1990 1/7 | Naples *WCF* | | W | 3–2 |
| 1991 6/2 | Wembley | | W | 2–0 |

**P2 W2 D0 L0 F5 A2**

### v Canada

| | | | | |
|---|---|---|---|---|
| 1986 24/5 | Vancouver | | W | 1–0 |

**P1 W1 D0 L0 F1 A0**

### v Chile

| | | | | |
|---|---|---|---|---|
| 1950 25/6 | Rio de Janeiro *WCF* | | W | 2–0 |
| 1953 24/5 | Santiago | | W | 2–1 |
| 1984 17/6 | Santiago | | D | 0–0 |
| 1989 23/5 | Wembley | | D | 0–0 |

**P4 W2 D2 L0 F4 A1**

### v China

| | | | | |
|---|---|---|---|---|
| 1996 23/5 | Beijing | | W | 3–0 |

**P1 W1 D0 L0 F3 A0**

### v CIS

| | | | | |
|---|---|---|---|---|
| 1992 29/4 | Moscow | | D | 2–2 |

**P1 W0 D1 L0 F2 A2**

### v Colombia

| | | | | |
|---|---|---|---|---|
| 1970 20/5 | Bogota | | W | 4–0 |
| 1988 24/5 | Wembley | | D | 1–1 |
| 1995 6/9 | Wembley | | D | 0–0 |

**P3 W1 D2 L0 F5 A1**

### v Croatia

| | | |
|---|---|---|
| 1996 24/4 | Wembley | 0–0 |

**P1 W0 D1 L0 F0 A0**

### v Cyprus

| | | | | |
|---|---|---|---|---|
| 1975 16/4 | Wembley *ECQ* | | W | 5–0 |
| 1975 11/5 | Limassol *ECQ* | | W | 1–0 |

**P2 W2 D0 L0 F6 A0**

### v Czechoslovakia

| | | | | |
|---|---|---|---|---|
| 1934 16/5 | Prague | | L | 1–2 |
| 1937 1/12 | Tottenham | | W | 5–4 |
| 1963 29/5 | Bratislava | | W | 4–2 |
| 1966 2/11 | Wembley | | D | 0–0 |
| 1970 11/6 | Guadalajara *WCF* | | W | 1–0 |
| 1973 27/5 | Prague | | D | 1–1 |
| 1974 30/10 | Wembley *ECQ* | | W | 3–0 |
| 1975 30/10 | Bratislava *ECQ* | | L | 1–2 |
| 1978 29/11 | Wembley | | W | 1–0 |
| 1982 20/6 | Bilbao *WCF* | | W | 2–0 |
| 1990 25/4 | Wembley | | W | 4–2 |
| 1992 25/3 | Prague | | D | 2–2 |

**P12 W7 D3 L2 F25 A15**

### v Denmark

| | | | | |
|---|---|---|---|---|
| 1948 26/9 | Copenhagen | | D | 0–0 |
| 1955 2/10 | Copenhagen | | W | 5–1 |
| 1956 5/12 | Wolverhampton *WCQ* | | W | 5–2 |
| 1957 15/5 | Copenhagen *WCQ* | | W | 4–1 |
| 1966 3/7 | Copenhagen | | W | 2–0 |
| 1978 20/9 | Copenhagen *ECQ* | | W | 4–3 |
| 1979 12/9 | Wembley *ECQ* | | W | 1–0 |
| 1982 22/9 | Copenhagen *ECQ* | | D | 2–2 |
| 1983 21/9 | Wembley *ECQ* | | L | 0–1 |
| 1988 14/9 | Wembley | | W | 1–0 |
| 1989 7/6 | Copenhagen | | D | 1–1 |
| 1990 15/5 | Wembley | | W | 1–0 |
| 1992 11/6 | Malmo *ECF* | | D | 0–0 |
| 1994 9/3 | Wembley | | W | 1–0 |

**P14 W9 D4 L1 F27 A11**

### v Ecuador

| | | | | |
|---|---|---|---|---|
| 1970 24/5 | Quito | | W | 2–0 |

**P1 W1 D0 L0 F2 A0**

### v Egypt

| | | | | |
|---|---|---|---|---|
| 1986 29/1 | Cairo | | W | 4–0 |
| 1990 21/6 | Cagliari *WCF* | | W | 1–0 |

**P2 W2 D0 L0 F5 A0**

### v Finland

| | | | | |
|---|---|---|---|---|
| 1937 20/5 | Helsinki | | W | 8–0 |
| 1956 20/5 | Helsinki | | W | 5–1 |
| 1966 26/6 | Helsinki | | W | 3–0 |
| 1976 13/6 | Helsinki *WCQ* | | W | 4–1 |
| 1976 13/10 | Wembley *WCQ* | | W | 2–1 |

| 1982 | 3/6 | Helsinki | | W | 4–1 |
|---|---|---|---|---|---|
| 1984 | 17/10 | Wembley *WCQ* | | W | 5–0 |
| 1985 | 22/5 | Helsinki *WCQ* | | D | 1–1 |
| 1992 | 3/6 | Helsinki | | W | 2–1 |

**P9 W8 D1 L0 F34 A6**

### v France

| 1923 | 10/5 | Paris | | W | 4–1 |
|---|---|---|---|---|---|
| 1924 | 17/5 | Paris | | W | 3–1 |
| 1925 | 21/5 | Paris | | W | 3–2 |
| 1927 | 26/5 | Paris | | W | 6–0 |
| 1928 | 17/5 | Paris | | W | 5–1 |
| 1929 | 9/5 | Paris | | W | 4–1 |
| 1931 | 14/5 | Paris | | L | 2–5 |
| 1933 | 6/12 | Tottenham | | W | 4–1 |
| 1938 | 26/5 | Paris | | W | 4–2 |
| 1947 | 3/5 | Arsenal | | W | 3–0 |
| 1949 | 22/5 | Paris | | W | 3–1 |
| 1951 | 3/10 | Arsenal | | D | 2–2 |
| 1955 | 15/5 | Paris | | L | 0–1 |
| 1957 | 27/11 | Wembley | | W | 4–0 |
| 1962 | 3/10 | Sheffield *ECQ* | | D | 1–1 |
| 1963 | 27/2 | Paris *ECQ* | | L | 2–5 |
| 1966 | 20/7 | Wembley *WCF* | | W | 2–0 |
| 1969 | 12/3 | Wembley | | W | 5–0 |
| 1982 | 16/6 | Bilbao *WCF* | | W | 3–1 |
| 1984 | 29/2 | Paris | | L | 0–2 |
| 1992 | 19/2 | Wembley | | W | 2–0 |
| 1992 | 14/6 | Malmo *ECF* | | D | 0–0 |

**P22 W15 D3 L4 F62 A27**

### v Georgia

| 1996 | 9/10 | Tbilisi | | W | 2–0 |
|---|---|---|---|---|---|
| 1997 | 30/4 | Wembley | | W | 2–0 |

**P2 W2 D0 L0 F4 A0**

### v East Germany

| 1963 | 2/6 | Leipzig | | W | 2–1 |
|---|---|---|---|---|---|
| 1970 | 25/11 | Wembley | | W | 3–1 |
| 1974 | 29/5 | Leipzig | | D | 1–1 |
| 1984 | 12/9 | Wembley | | W | 1–0 |

**P4 W3 D1 L0 F7 A3**

### v West Germany

| 1930 | 10/5 | Berlin | | D | 3–3 |
|---|---|---|---|---|---|
| 1935 | 4/12 | Tottenham | | W | 3–0 |
| 1938 | 14/5 | Berlin | | W | 6–3 |
| 1954 | 1/12 | Wembley | | W | 3–1 |
| 1956 | 26/5 | Berlin | | W | 3–1 |
| 1965 | 12/5 | Nuremberg | | W | 1–0 |
| 1966 | 23/2 | Wembley | | W | 1–0 |
| 1966 | 30/7 | Wembley *WCF* | | W | 4–2 |
| 1968 | 1/6 | Hanover | | L | 0–1 |
| 1970 | 14/6 | Leon *WCF* | | L | 2–3 |
| 1972 | 29/4 | Wembley *ECQ* | | L | 1–3 |
| 1972 | 13/5 | Berlin *ECQ* | | D | 0–0 |
| 1975 | 12/3 | Wembley | | W | 2–0 |
| 1978 | 22/2 | Munich | | L | 1–2 |
| 1982 | 29/6 | Madrid *WCF* | | D | 0–0 |
| 1982 | 13/10 | Wembley | | L | 1–2 |
| 1985 | 12/6 | Mexico City | | W | 3–0 |
| 1987 | 9/9 | Dusseldorf | | L | 1–3 |

| 1990 | 4/7 | Turin *WCF* | *D | 1–1 |
|---|---|---|---|---|

**P19 W9 D4 L6 F36 A25**

### v Germany

| 1991 | 11/9 | Wembley | | L | 0–1 |
|---|---|---|---|---|---|
| 1993 | 19/6 | Detroit | | L | 1–2 |
| 1996 | 26/6 | Wembley *ECF* | | †D | 1–1 |

**P3 W0 D1 L2 F2 A4**

### v Greece

| 1971 | 21/4 | Wembley *ECQ* | | W | 3–0 |
|---|---|---|---|---|---|
| 1971 | 1/12 | Athens *ECQ* | | W | 2–0 |
| 1982 | 17/11 | Salonika *ECQ* | | W | 3–0 |
| 1983 | 30/3 | Wembley *ECQ* | | D | 0–0 |
| 1989 | 8/2 | Athens | | W | 2–1 |
| 1994 | 17/5 | Wembley | | W | 5–0 |

**P6 W5 D1 L0 F15 A1**

### v Holland

| 1935 | 18/5 | Amsterdam | | W | 1–0 |
|---|---|---|---|---|---|
| 1946 | 27/11 | Huddersfield | | W | 8–2 |
| 1964 | 9/12 | Amsterdam | | D | 1–1 |
| 1969 | 5/11 | Amsterdam | | W | 1–0 |
| 1970 | 14/1 | Wembley | | D | 0–0 |
| 1977 | 9/2 | Wembley | | L | 0–2 |
| 1982 | 25/5 | Wembley | | W | 2–0 |
| 1988 | 23/3 | Wembley | | D | 2–2 |
| 1988 | 15/6 | Dusseldorf *ECF* | | L | 1–3 |
| 1990 | 16/6 | Cagliari *WCF* | | D | 0–0 |
| 1993 | 28/4 | Wembley *WCQ* | | D | 2–2 |
| 1993 | 13/10 | Rotterdam *WCQ* | | L | 0–2 |
| 1996 | 18/6 | Wembley *ECF* | | W | 4–1 |

**P13 W5 D5 L3 F22 A15**

### v Hungary

| 1908 | 10/6 | Budapest | | W | 7–0 |
|---|---|---|---|---|---|
| 1909 | 29/5 | Budapest | | W | 4–2 |
| 1909 | 31/5 | Budapest | | W | 8–2 |
| 1934 | 10/5 | Budapest | | L | 1–2 |
| 1936 | 2/12 | Arsenal | | W | 6–2 |
| 1953 | 25/11 | Wembley | | L | 3–6 |
| 1954 | 23/5 | Budapest | | L | 1–7 |
| 1960 | 22/5 | Budapest | | L | 0–2 |
| 1962 | 31/5 | Rancagua *WCF* | | L | 1–2 |
| 1965 | 5/5 | Wembley | | W | 1–0 |
| 1978 | 24/5 | Wembley | | W | 4–1 |
| 1981 | 6/6 | Budapest *WCQ* | | W | 3–1 |
| 1981 | 18/11 | Wembley *WCQ* | | W | 1–0 |
| 1983 | 27/4 | Wembley *ECQ* | | W | 2–0 |
| 1983 | 12/10 | Budapest *ECQ* | | W | 3–0 |
| 1988 | 27/4 | Budapest | | D | 0–0 |
| 1990 | 12/9 | Wembley | | W | 1–0 |
| 1992 | 12/5 | Budapest | | W | 1–0 |
| 1996 | 18/5 | Wembley | | W | 3–0 |

**P19 W13 D1 L5 F50 A27**

### v Iceland

| 1982 | 2/6 | Reykjavik | | D | 1–1 |
|---|---|---|---|---|---|

**P1 W0 D1 L0 F1 A1**

### v Ireland

| 1882 | 18/2 | Belfast | | W | 13–0 |
|---|---|---|---|---|---|

*\* aet Eng lost 4–3 on penalties    † aet Eng lost 6–5 on penalties*

| | | | | | |
|---|---|---|---|---|---|
| 1883 24/2 | Liverpool | | W | 7–0 | |
| 1884 23/2 | Belfast | | W | 8–1 | |
| 1885 28/2 | Manchester | | W | 4–0 | |
| 1886 13/3 | Belfast | | W | 6–1 | |
| 1887 5/2 | Sheffield | | W | 7–0 | |
| 1888 31/3 | Belfast | | W | 5–1 | |
| 1889 2/3 | Everton | | W | 6–1 | |
| 1890 15/3 | Belfast | | W | 9–1 | |
| 1891 7/3 | Wolverhampton | | W | 6–1 | |
| 1892 5/3 | Belfast | | W | 2–0 | |
| 1893 25/2 | Birmingham | | W | 6–1 | |
| 1894 3/3 | Belfast | | D | 2–2 | |
| 1895 9/3 | Derby | | W | 9–0 | |
| 1896 7/3 | Belfast | | W | 2–0 | |
| 1897 20/2 | Nottingham | | W | 6–0 | |
| 1898 5/3 | Belfast | | W | 3–2 | |
| 1899 18/2 | Sunderland | | W | 13–2 | |
| 1900 17/3 | Dublin | | W | 2–0 | |
| 1901 9/3 | Southampton | | W | 3–0 | |
| 1902 22/3 | Belfast | | W | 1–0 | |
| 1903 14/2 | Wolverhampton | | W | 4–0 | |
| 1904 12/3 | Belfast | | W | 3–1 | |
| 1905 25/2 | Middlesbrough | | D | 1–1 | |
| 1906 17/2 | Belfast | | W | 5–0 | |
| 1907 16/2 | Everton | | W | 1–0 | |
| 1908 15/2 | Belfast | | W | 3–1 | |
| 1909 13/2 | Bradford | | W | 4–0 | |
| 1910 12/2 | Belfast | | D | 1–1 | |
| 1911 11/2 | Derby | | W | 2–1 | |
| 1912 10/2 | Dublin | | W | 6–1 | |
| 1913 15/2 | Belfast | | L | 1–2 | |
| 1914 14/2 | Middlesbrough | | L | 0–3 | |
| 1919 25/10 | Belfast | | D | 1–1 | |
| 1920 23/10 | Sunderland | | W | 2–0 | |
| 1921 22/10 | Belfast | | D | 1–1 | |
| 1922 21/10 | West Bromwich | | W | 2–0 | |
| 1923 20/10 | Belfast | | L | 1–2 | |
| 1924 22/10 | Everton | | W | 3–1 | |
| 1925 24/10 | Belfast | | D | 0–0 | |
| 1926 20/10 | Liverpool | | D | 3–3 | |
| 1927 22/10 | Belfast | | L | 0–2 | |
| 1928 22/10 | Everton | | W | 2–1 | |
| 1929 19/10 | Belfast | | W | 3–0 | |
| 1930 20/10 | Sheffield | | W | 5–1 | |
| 1931 17/10 | Belfast | | W | 6–2 | |
| 1932 17/10 | Blackpool | | W | 1–0 | |
| 1933 14/10 | Belfast | | W | 3–0 | |
| 1935 6/2 | Everton | | W | 2–1 | |
| 1935 19/10 | Belfast | | W | 3–1 | |
| 1936 18/11 | Stoke | | W | 3–1 | |
| 1937 23/10 | Belfast | | W | 5–1 | |
| 1938 16/11 | Manchester | | W | 7–0 | |
| 1946 28/9 | Belfast | | W | 7–2 | |
| 1947 5/11 | Everton | | D | 2–2 | |
| 1948 9/10 | Belfast | | W | 6–2 | |
| 1949 16/11 | Manchester *WCQ* | | W | 9–2 | |
| 1950 7/10 | Belfast | | W | 4–1 | |
| 1951 14/11 | Aston Villa | | W | 2–0 | |
| 1952 4/10 | Belfast | | D | 2–2 | |
| 1953 11/11 | Everton *WCQ* | | W | 3–1 | |
| 1954 2/10 | Belfast | | W | 2–0 | |
| 1955 2/11 | Wembley | | W | 3–0 | |
| 1956 6/10 | Belfast | | D | 1–1 | |
| 1957 6/11 | Wembley | | L | 2–3 | |
| 1958 4/10 | Belfast | | D | 3–3 | |
| 1959 18/11 | Wembley | | W | 2–1 | |
| 1960 8/10 | Belfast | | W | 5–2 | |
| 1961 22/11 | Wembley | | D | 1–1 | |
| 1962 20/10 | Belfast | | W | 3–1 | |
| 1963 20/11 | Wembley | | W | 8–3 | |
| 1964 3/10 | Belfast | | W | 4–3 | |
| 1965 10/11 | Wembley | | W | 2–1 | |
| 1966 20/10 | Belfast *ECQ* | | W | 2–0 | |
| 1967 22/11 | Wembley *ECQ* | | W | 2–0 | |
| 1969 3/5 | Belfast | | W | 3–1 | |
| 1970 21/4 | Wembley | | W | 3–1 | |
| 1971 15/5 | Belfast | | W | 1–0 | |
| 1972 23/5 | Wembley | | L | 0–1 | |
| 1973 12/5 | Everton | | W | 2–1 | |
| 1974 15/5 | Wembley | | W | 1–0 | |
| 1975 17/5 | Belfast | | D | 0–0 | |
| 1976 11/5 | Wembley | | W | 4–0 | |
| 1977 28/5 | Belfast | | W | 2–1 | |
| 1978 16/5 | Wembley | | W | 1–0 | |
| 1979 7/2 | Wembley *ECQ* | | W | 4–0 | |
| 1979 19/5 | Belfast | | W | 2–0 | |
| 1979 17/10 | Belfast *ECQ* | | W | 5–1 | |
| 1980 20/5 | Wembley | | D | 1–1 | |
| 1982 23/2 | Wembley | | W | 4–0 | |
| 1983 28/5 | Belfast | | D | 0–0 | |
| 1984 4/4 | Wembley | | W | 1–0 | |
| 1985 27/2 | Belfast *WCQ* | | W | 1–0 | |
| 1985 13/11 | Wembley *WCQ* | | D | 0–0 | |
| 1986 15/10 | Wembley *ECQ* | | W | 3–0 | |
| 1987 1/4 | Belfast *ECQ* | | W | 2–0 | |

**P96 W74 D16 L6 F319 A80**

**v Israel**

| | | | | |
|---|---|---|---|---|
| 1986 26/2 | Tel Aviv | W | 2–1 | |
| 1988 17/2 | Tel Aviv | D | 0–0 | |

**P2 W1 D1 L0 F2 A1**

**v Italy**

| | | | | |
|---|---|---|---|---|
| 1933 13/5 | Rome | D | 1–1 | |
| 1934 14/11 | Arsenal | W | 3–2 | |
| 1939 13/5 | Milan | D | 2–2 | |
| 1948 16/5 | Turin | W | 4–0 | |
| 1949 30/11 | Tottenham | W | 2–0 | |
| 1952 18/5 | Florence | D | 1–1 | |
| 1959 6/5 | Wembley | D | 2–2 | |
| 1961 24/5 | Rome | W | 3–2 | |
| 1973 14/6 | Turin | L | 0–2 | |
| 1973 14/11 | Wembley | L | 0–1 | |
| 1976 28/5 | New York | W | 3–2 | |
| 1976 17/11 | Rome *WCQ* | L | 0–2 | |
| 1977 16/11 | Wembley *WCQ* | W | 2–0 | |
| 1980 15/6 | Turin *ECF* | L | 0–1 | |
| 1985 6/6 | Mexico City | L | 1–2 | |
| 1989 15/11 | Wembley | D | 0–0 | |
| 1990 7/7 | Bari *WCF* | L | 1–2 | |
| 1997 12/2 | Wembley | L | 0–1 | |

**P18 W6 D5 L7 F25 A23**

**v Japan**

| | | | |
|---|---|---|---|
| 1995 3/6 | Wembley | W | 2–1 |

P1 W1 D0 L0 F2 A1

**v Kuwait**

| | | | |
|---|---|---|---|
| 1982 25/6 | Bilbao *WCF* | W | 1–0 |

P1 W1 D0 L0 F1 A0

**v Luxembourg**

| | | | |
|---|---|---|---|
| 1927 21/5 | Luxembourg | W | 5–2 |
| 1960 19/10 | Luxembourg *WCQ* | W | 9–0 |
| 1961 28/9 | Arsenal *WCQ* | W | 4–1 |
| 1977 30/3 | Wembley *WCQ* | W | 5–0 |
| 1977 12/10 | Luxembourg *WCQ* | W | 2–0 |
| 1982 15/12 | Wembley *ECQ* | W | 9–0 |
| 1983 16/11 | Luxembourg *ECQ* | W | 4–0 |

P7 W7 D0 L0 F38 A3

**v Malaysia**

| | | | |
|---|---|---|---|
| 1991 12/6 | Kuala Lumpur | W | 4–2 |

P1 W1 D0 L0 F4 A2

**v Malta**

| | | | |
|---|---|---|---|
| 1971 3/2 | Valletta *ECQ* | W | 1–0 |
| 1971 12/5 | Wembley *ECQ* | W | 5–0 |

P W2 D0 L0 F6 A0

**v Mexico**

| | | | |
|---|---|---|---|
| 1959 24/5 | Mexico City | L | 1–2 |
| 1961 10/5 | Wembley | W | 8–0 |
| 1966 16/7 | Wembley *WCF* | W | 2–0 |
| 1969 1/6 | Mexico City | D | 0–0 |
| 1985 9/6 | Mexico City | L | 0–1 |
| 1986 17/5 | Los Angeles | W | 3–0 |
| 1997 29/3 | Wembley | W | 2–0 |

P7 W4 D1 L2 F16 A3

**v Moldova**

| | | | |
|---|---|---|---|
| 1996 1/9 | Chisinau *WCQ* | W | 3–0 |

P1 W1 D0 L0 F3 A0

**v Morocco**

| | | | |
|---|---|---|---|
| 1986 6/6 | Monterrey *WCF* | D | 0–0 |

P1 W0 D1 L0 F0 A0

**v New Zealand**

| | | | |
|---|---|---|---|
| 1991 3/6 | Auckland | W | 1–0 |
| 1991 8/6 | Wellington | W | 2–0 |

P2 W2 D0 L0 F3 A0

**v Nigeria**

| | | | |
|---|---|---|---|
| 1994 16/11 | Wembley | W | 1–0 |

P1 W1 D0 L0 F1 A0

**v Northern Ireland** (*see Ireland*)

**v Norway**

| | | | |
|---|---|---|---|
| 1937 14/5 | Oslo | W | 6–0 |
| 1938 9/11 | Newcastle | W | 4–0 |
| 1949 18/5 | Oslo | W | 4–1 |
| 1966 29/6 | Oslo | W | 6–1 |
| 1980 10/9 | Wembley *WCQ* | W | 4–0 |
| 1981 9/9 | Oslo *WCQ* | L | 1–2 |
| 1992 14/10 | Wembley *WCQ* | D | 1–1 |
| 1993 2/6 | Oslo *WCQ* | L | 0–2 |
| 1994 22/5 | Wembley | D | 0–0 |
| 1995 11/10 | Oslo | D | 0–0 |

P10 W5 D3 L2 F26 A7

**v Paraguay**

| | | | |
|---|---|---|---|
| 1986 18/6 | Mexico City *WCF* | W | 3–0 |

P1 W1 D0 L0 F3 A0

**v Peru**

| | | | |
|---|---|---|---|
| 1959 17/5 | Lima | L | 1–4 |
| 1962 20/5 | Lima | W | 4–0 |

P2 W1 D0 L1 F5 A4

**v Poland**

| | | | |
|---|---|---|---|
| 1966 5/1 | Everton | D | 1–1 |
| 1966 5/7 | Katowice | W | 1–0 |
| 1973 6/6 | Katowice *WCQ* | L | 0–2 |
| 1973 17/10 | Wembley *WCQ* | D | 1–1 |
| 1986 11/6 | Monterrey *WCF* | W | 3–0 |
| 1989 3/6 | Wembley *WCQ* | W | 3–0 |
| 1989 11/10 | Katowice *WCQ* | D | 0–0 |
| 1990 17/10 | Wembley *ECQ* | W | 2–0 |
| 1991 13/11 | Poznan *ECQ* | D | 1–1 |
| 1993 29/5 | Katowice *WCQ* | D | 1–1 |
| 1993 8/9 | Wembley *WCQ* | W | 3–0 |
| 1996 9/10 | Wembley *WCQ* | W | 2–1 |
| 1996 31/5 | Katowice *WCQ* | W | 2–0 |

P13 W7 D5 L1 F20 A7

**v Portugal**

| | | | |
|---|---|---|---|
| 1947 25/5 | Lisbon | W | 10–0 |
| 1950 14/5 | Lisbon | W | 5–3 |
| 1951 19/5 | Everton | W | 5–2 |
| 1955 22/5 | Oporto | L | 1–3 |
| 1958 7/5 | Wembley | W | 2–1 |
| 1961 21/5 | Lisbon *WCQ* | D | 1–1 |
| 1961 25/10 | Wembley *WCQ* | W | 2–0 |
| 1964 17/5 | Lisbon | W | 4–3 |
| 1964 4/6 | São Paolo | D | 1–1 |
| 1966 26/7 | Wembley *WCF* | W | 2–1 |
| 1969 10/12 | Wembley | W | 1–0 |
| 1974 3/4 | Lisbon | D | 0–0 |
| 1974 20/11 | Wembley *ECQ* | D | 0–0 |
| 1975 19/11 | Lisbon *ECQ* | D | 1–1 |
| 1986 3/6 | Monterrey *WCF* | L | 0–1 |
| 1995 12/12 | Wembley | D | 1–1 |

P16 W8 D6 L2 F36 A18

**v Republic of Ireland**

| | | | |
|---|---|---|---|
| 1946 30/9 | Dublin | W | 1–0 |
| 1949 21/9 | Everton | L | 0–2 |
| 1957 8/5 | Wembley *WCQ* | W | 5–1 |
| 1957 19/5 | Dublin *WCQ* | D | 1–1 |
| 1964 24/5 | Dublin | W | 3–1 |
| 1976 8/9 | Wembley | D | 1–1 |
| 1978 25/10 | Dublin *ECQ* | D | 1–1 |
| 1980 6/2 | Wembley *ECQ* | W | 2–0 |
| 1985 26/3 | Wembley | W | 2–1 |
| 1988 12/6 | Stuttgart *ECF* | L | 0–1 |

| | | | | |
|---|---|---|---|---|
| 1990 11/6 | Cagliari *WCF* | D | 1–1 | |
| 1990 14/11 | Dublin *ECQ* | D | 1–1 | |
| 1991 27/3 | Wembley *ECQ* | D | 1–1 | |

**P13 W5 D6 L2 F19 A12**

**v Romania**

| | | | |
|---|---|---|---|
| 1939 24/5 | Bucharest | W | 2–0 |
| 1968 6/11 | Bucharest | D | 0–0 |
| 1969 15/1 | Wembley | D | 1–1 |
| 1970 2/6 | Guadalajara *WCF* | W | 1–0 |
| 1980 15/10 | Bucharest *WCQ* | L | 1–2 |
| 1981 29/4 | Wembley *WCQ* | D | 0–0 |
| 1985 1/5 | Bucharest *WCQ* | D | 0–0 |
| 1985 11/9 | Wembley *WCQ* | D | 1–1 |
| 1994 12/10 | Wembley | D | 1–1 |

**P9 W2 D6 L1 F7 A5**

**v San Marino**

| | | | |
|---|---|---|---|
| 1993 17/2 | Wembley *WCQ* | W | 6–0 |
| 1993 17/11 | Bologna *WCQ* | W | 7–1 |

**P2 W2 D0 L0 F13 A1**

**v Saudi Arabia**

| | | | |
|---|---|---|---|
| 1988 16/11 | Riyadh | D | 1–1 |

**P1 W0 D1 L0 F1 A1**

**v Scotland**

| | | | |
|---|---|---|---|
| 1872 30/11 | Glasgow | D | 0–0 |
| 1873 8/3 | Kennington | W | 4–2 |
| 1874 7/3 | Glasgow | L | 1–2 |
| 1875 6/3 | Kennington | D | 2–2 |
| 1876 4/3 | Glasgow | L | 0–3 |
| 1877 3/3 | Kennington | L | 1–3 |
| 1878 2/3 | Glasgow | L | 2–7 |
| 1879 5/4 | Kennington | W | 5–4 |
| 1880 13/3 | Glasgow | L | 4–5 |
| 1881 12/3 | Kennington | L | 1–6 |
| 1882 11/3 | Glasgow | L | 1–5 |
| 1883 10/3 | Sheffield | L | 2–3 |
| 1884 15/3 | Glasgow | L | 0–1 |
| 1885 21/3 | Kennington | D | 1–1 |
| 1886 31/3 | Glasgow | D | 1–1 |
| 1887 19/3 | Blackburn | L | 2–3 |
| 1888 17/3 | Glasgow | W | 5–0 |
| 1889 13/3 | Kennington | L | 2–3 |
| 1890 5/4 | Glasgow | D | 1–1 |
| 1891 6/4 | Blackburn | W | 2–1 |
| 1892 2/4 | Glasgow | W | 4–1 |
| 1893 1/4 | Richmond | W | 5–2 |
| 1894 7/4 | Glasgow | D | 2–2 |
| 1895 6/4 | Everton | W | 3–0 |
| 1896 4/4 | Glasgow | L | 1–2 |
| 1897 3/4 | Crystal Palace | L | 1–2 |
| 1898 2/4 | Glasgow | W | 3–1 |
| 1899 8/4 | Birmingham | W | 2–1 |
| 1900 7/4 | Glasgow | L | 1–4 |
| 1901 30/3 | Crystal Palace | D | 2–2 |
| 1902 3/3 | Birmingham | D | 2–2 |
| 1903 4/4 | Sheffield | L | 1–2 |
| 1904 9/4 | Glasgow | W | 1–0 |
| 1905 1/4 | Crystal Palace | W | 1–0 |
| 1906 7/4 | Glasgow | L | 1–2 |

| | | | |
|---|---|---|---|
| 1907 6/4 | Newcastle | D | 1–1 |
| 1908 4/4 | Glasgow | D | 1–1 |
| 1909 3/4 | Crystal Palace | W | 2–0 |
| 1910 2/4 | Glasgow | L | 0–2 |
| 1911 1/4 | Everton | D | 1–1 |
| 1912 23/3 | Glasgow | D | 1–1 |
| 1913 5/4 | Chelsea | W | 1–0 |
| 1914 14/4 | Glasgow | L | 1–3 |
| 1920 10/4 | Sheffield | W | 5–4 |
| 1921 9/4 | Glasgow | L | 0–3 |
| 1922 8/4 | Aston Villa | L | 0–1 |
| 1923 14/4 | Glasgow | D | 2–2 |
| 1924 12/4 | Wembley | D | 1–1 |
| 1925 4/4 | Glasgow | L | 0–2 |
| 1926 17/4 | Manchester | L | 0–1 |
| 1927 2/4 | Glasgow | W | 2–1 |
| 1928 31/3 | Wembley | L | 1–5 |
| 1929 13/4 | Glasgow | L | 0–1 |
| 1930 5/4 | Wembley | W | 5–2 |
| 1931 28/ | Glasgow | L | 0–2 |
| 1932 9/4 | Wembley | W | 3–0 |
| 1933 1/4 | Glasgow | L | 1–2 |
| 1934 14/4 | Wembley | W | 3–0 |
| 1935 6/4 | Glasgow | L | 0–2 |
| 1936 4/4 | Wembley | D | 1–1 |
| 1937 17/4 | Glasgow | L | 1–3 |
| 1938 9/4 | Wembley | L | 0–1 |
| 1939 15/4 | Glasgow | W | 2–1 |
| 1947 12/4 | Wembley | D | 1–1 |
| 1948 10/4 | Glasgow | W | 2–0 |
| 1949 9/4 | Wembley | L | 1–3 |
| 1950 15/4 | Glasgow *WCQ* | W | 1–0 |
| 1951 14/4 | Wembley | L | 2–3 |
| 1952 5/4 | Glasgow | W | 2–1 |
| 1953 18/4 | Wembley | D | 2–2 |
| 1954 3/4 | Glasgow *WCQ* | W | 4–2 |
| 1955 2/4 | Wembley | W | 7–2 |
| 1956 14/4 | Glasgow | D | 1–1 |
| 1957 16/4 | Wembley | W | 2–1 |
| 1958 19/4 | Glasgow | W | 4–0 |
| 1959 11/4 | Wembley | W | 1–0 |
| 1960 19/4 | Glasgow | D | 1–1 |
| 1961 15/4 | Wembley | W | 9–3 |
| 1962 14/4 | Glasgow | L | 0–2 |
| 1963 6/4 | Wembley | L | 1–2 |
| 1964 11/4 | Glasgow | L | 0–1 |
| 1965 10/4 | Wembley | D | 2–2 |
| 1966 2/4 | Glasgow | W | 4–3 |
| 1967 15/4 | Wembley *ECQ* | L | 2–3 |
| 1968 24/2 | Glasgow *ECQ* | D | 1–1 |
| 1969 10/5 | Wembley | W | 4–1 |
| 1970 25/4 | Glasgow | D | 0–0 |
| 1971 22/5 | Wembley | W | 3–1 |
| 1972 27/5 | Glasgow | W | 1–0 |
| 1973 14/2 | Glasgow | W | 5–0 |
| 1973 19/5 | Wembley | W | 1–0 |
| 1974 18/5 | Glasgow | L | 0–2 |
| 1975 24/5 | Wembley | W | 5–1 |
| 1976 15/5 | Glasgow | L | 1–2 |
| 1977 4/6 | Wembley | L | 1–2 |
| 1978 20/5 | Glasgow | W | 1–0 |
| 1979 26/5 | Wembley | W | 3–1 |

| | | | | |
|---|---|---|---|---|
| 1980 24/5 | Glasgow | W | 2–0 |
| 1981 23/5 | Wembley | L | 0–1 |
| 1982 29/5 | Glasgow | W | 1–0 |
| 1983 1/6 | Wembley | W | 2–0 |
| 1984 26/5 | Glasgow | D | 1–1 |
| 1985 25/5 | Glasgow | L | 0–1 |
| 1986 23/4 | Wembley | W | 2–1 |
| 1987 23/5 | Glasgow | D | 0–0 |
| 1988 21/5 | Wembley | W | 1–0 |
| 1989 27/5 | Glasgow | W | 2–0 |
| 1996 15/6 | Wembley *ECF* | W | 2–0 |

**P108 W44 D24 L40 F190 A168**

### v South Africa

| | | | |
|---|---|---|---|
| 1997 24/5 | Old Trafford | W | 2–1 |

**P1 W1 D0 L0 F2 A1**

### v Spain

| | | | |
|---|---|---|---|
| 1929 15/5 | Madrid | L | 3–4 |
| 1931 9/12 | Arsenal | W | 7–1 |
| 1950 2/7 | Rio De Janeiro *WCF* | L | 0–1 |
| 1955 18/5 | Madrid | D | 1–1 |
| 1955 30/11 | Wembley | W | 4–1 |
| 1960 15/5 | Madrid | L | 0–3 |
| 1960 26/10 | Wembley | W | 4–2 |
| 1965 8/12 | Madrid | W | 2–0 |
| 1967 24/5 | Wembley | W | 2–0 |
| 1968 3/4 | Wembley *ECQ* | W | 1–0 |
| 1968 8/5 | Madrid *ECQ* | W | 2–1 |
| 1980 26/3 | Barcelona | W | 2–0 |
| 1980 18/6 | Naples *ECF* | W | 2–1 |
| 1981 25/3 | Wembley | L | 1–2 |
| 1982 5/7 | Madrid *WCF* | D | 0–0 |
| 1987 18/2 | Madrid | W | 4–2 |
| 1992 9/9 | Santander | L | 0–1 |
| 1996 22/6 | Wembley *ECF* | †D | 0–0 |

**P18 W10 D3 L5 F35 A20**

### v Sweden

| | | | |
|---|---|---|---|
| 1923 21/5 | Stockholm | W | 4–2 |
| 1923 24/5 | Stockholm | W | 3–1 |
| 1937 17/5 | Stockholm | W | 4–0 |
| 1947 19/11 | Arsenal | W | 4–2 |
| 1949 13/5 | Stockholm | L | 1–3 |
| 1956 16/5 | Stockholm | D | 0–0 |
| 1959 28/10 | Wembley | L | 2–3 |
| 1965 16/5 | Gothenburg | W | 2–1 |
| 1968 22/5 | Wembley | W | 3–1 |
| 1979 10/6 | Stockholm | D | 0–0 |
| 1986 10/9 | Stockholm | L | 0–1 |
| 1988 19/10 | Wembley *WCQ* | D | 0–0 |
| 1989 6/9 | Stockholm *WCQ* | D | 0–0 |
| 1992 17/6 | Stockholm *ECF* | L | 1–2 |
| 1995 8/6 | Leeds | D | 3–3 |

**P15 W6 D5 L4 F27 A19**

### v Switzerland

| | | | |
|---|---|---|---|
| 1933 29/5 | Berne | W | 4–0 |
| 1938 21/5 | Zurich | L | 1–2 |
| 1947 18/5 | Zurich | L | 0–1 |
| 1948 2/12 | Arsenal | W | 6–0 |
| 1952 28/5 | Zurich | W | 3–0 |
| 1954 20/6 | Berne *WCF* | W | 2–0 |
| 1962 9/5 | Wembley | W | 3–1 |
| 1963 5/6 | Basle | W | 8–1 |
| 1971 13/10 | Basle *ECQ* | W | 3–2 |
| 1971 10/11 | Wembley *ECQ* | D | 1–1 |
| 1975 3/9 | Basle | W | 2–1 |
| 1977 7/9 | Wembley | D | 0–0 |
| 1980 19/11 | Wembley *WCQ* | W | 2–1 |
| 1981 30/5 | Basle *WCQ* | L | 1–2 |
| 1988 28/5 | Lausanne | W | 1–0 |
| 1995 15/11 | Wembley | W | 3–1 |
| 1996 8/6 | Wembley *ECF* | D | 1–1 |

**P17 W11 D3 L3 F41 A14**

### v Tunisia

| | | | |
|---|---|---|---|
| 1990 2/6 | Tunis | D | 1–1 |

**P1 W0 D1 L0 F1 A1**

### v Turkey

| | | | |
|---|---|---|---|
| 1984 14/11 | Istanbul *WCQ* | W | 8–0 |
| 1985 16/10 | Wembley *WCQ* | W | 5–0 |
| 1987 29/4 | Izmir *ECQ* | D | 0–0 |
| 1987 14/10 | Wembley *ECQ* | W | 8–0 |
| 1991 1/5 | Izmir *ECQ* | W | 1–0 |
| 1991 16/10 | Wembley *ECQ* | W | 1–0 |
| 1992 18/11 | Wembley *WCQ* | W | 4–0 |
| 1993 31/3 | Izmir *WCQ* | W | 2–0 |

**P8 W7 D1 L0 F29 A0**

### v USA

| | | | |
|---|---|---|---|
| 1950 29/6 | Belo Horizonte *WCF* | L | 0–1 |
| 1953 8/6 | New York | W | 6–3 |
| 1959 28/5 | Los Angeles | W | 8–1 |
| 1964 27/5 | New York | W | 10–0 |
| 1985 16/6 | Los Angeles | W | 5–0 |
| 1993 9/6 | Boston | L | 0–2 |
| 1994 7/9 | Wembley | W | 2–0 |

**P7 W5 D0 L2 F31 A7**

### v USSR *(see also CIS)*

| | | | |
|---|---|---|---|
| 1958 18/5 | Moscow | D | 1–1 |
| 1958 8/6 | Gothenburg *WCF* | D | 2–2 |
| 1958 17/6 | Gothenburg *WCF* | L | 0–1 |
| 1958 22/10 | Wembley | W | 5–0 |
| 1967 6/12 | Wembley | D | 2–2 |
| 1968 8/6 | Rome *ECF* | W | 2–0 |
| 1973 10/6 | Moscow | W | 2–1 |
| 1984 2/6 | Wembley | L | 0–2 |
| 1986 26/3 | Tbilisi | W | 1–0 |
| 1988 18/6 | Frankfurt *ECF* | L | 1–3 |
| 1991 21/5 | Wembley | W | 3–1 |

**P11 W5 D3 L3 F19 A13**

### v Uruguay

| | | | |
|---|---|---|---|
| 1953 31/5 | Montevideo | L | 1–2 |
| 1954 26/6 | Basle *WCF* | L | 2–4 |
| 1964 6/5 | Wembley | W | 2–1 |
| 1966 11/7 | Wembley *WCF* | D | 0–0 |
| 1969 8/6 | Montevideo | W | 2–1 |
| 1977 15/6 | Montevideo | D | 0–0 |
| 1984 13/6 | Montevideo | L | 0–2 |
| 1990 22/5 | Wembley | L | 1–2 |

† *aet England won 4–2 on penalties*

1995 29/3  Wembley  D  0–0

**P9 W2 D3 L4 F8 A12**

## v Wales

| Year | Date | Venue | | Result |
|---|---|---|---|---|
| 1879 | 18/1 | Kennington | W | 2–1 |
| 1880 | 15/3 | Wrexham | W | 3–2 |
| 1881 | 26/2 | Blackburn | L | 0–1 |
| 1882 | 13/3 | Wrexham | L | 3–5 |
| 1883 | 3/2 | Kennington | W | 5–0 |
| 1884 | 17/3 | Wrexham | W | 4–0 |
| 1885 | 14/3 | Blackburn | D | 1–1 |
| 1886 | 29/3 | Wrexham | W | 3–1 |
| 1887 | 26/2 | Kennington | W | 4–0 |
| 1888 | 4/2 | Crewe | W | 5–1 |
| 1889 | 23/2 | Stoke | W | 4–1 |
| 1890 | 15/3 | Wrexham | W | 3–1 |
| 1891 | 7/5 | Sunderland | W | 4–1 |
| 1892 | 5/3 | Wrexham | W | 2–0 |
| 1893 | 13/3 | Stoke | W | 6–0 |
| 1894 | 12/3 | Wrexham | W | 5–1 |
| 1895 | 18/3 | Kennington | D | 1–1 |
| 1896 | 16/3 | Cardiff | W | 9–1 |
| 1897 | 29/3 | Sheffield | W | 4–0 |
| 1898 | 28/3 | Wrexham | W | 3–0 |
| 1899 | 20/3 | Bristol | W | 4–0 |
| 1900 | 26/3 | Cardiff | D | 1–1 |
| 1901 | 18/3 | Newcastle | W | 6–0 |
| 1902 | 3/3 | Wrexham | D | 0–0 |
| 1903 | 2/3 | Portsmouth | W | 2–0 |
| 1904 | 29/2 | Wrexham | D | 2–2 |
| 1905 | 27/3 | Liverpool | W | 3–1 |
| 1906 | 19/3 | Cardiff | W | 1–0 |
| 1907 | 18/3 | Fulham | D | 1–1 |
| 1908 | 16/3 | Wrexham | W | 7–1 |
| 1909 | 15/3 | Nottingham | W | 2–0 |
| 1910 | 14/3 | Cardiff | W | 1–0 |
| 1911 | 13/3 | Millwall | W | 3–0 |
| 1912 | 11/3 | Wrexham | W | 2–0 |
| 1913 | 17/3 | Bristol | W | 4–3 |
| 1914 | 16/3 | Cardiff | W | 2–0 |
| 1920 | 15/3 | Arsenal | L | 1–2 |
| 1921 | 14/3 | Cardiff | D | 0–0 |
| 1922 | 13/3 | Liverpool | W | 1–0 |
| 1923 | 5/3 | Cardiff | D | 2–2 |
| 1924 | 3/3 | Blackburn | L | 1–2 |
| 1925 | 28/2 | Swansea | W | 2–1 |
| 1926 | 1/3 | Crystal Palace | L | 1–3 |
| 1927 | 12/2 | Wrexham | D | 3–3 |
| 1927 | 28/11 | Burnley | L | 1–2 |
| 1928 | 17/11 | Swansea | W | 3–2 |
| 1929 | 20/11 | Chelsea | W | 6–0 |
| 1930 | 22/11 | Wrexham | W | 4–0 |
| 1931 | 18/11 | Liverpool | W | 3–1 |
| 1932 | 16/11 | Wrexham | D | 0–0 |
| 1933 | 15/11 | Newcastle | L | 1–2 |
| 1934 | 29/9 | Cardiff | W | 4–0 |
| 1936 | 5/2 | Wolverhampton | L | 1–2 |
| 1936 | 17/10 | Cardiff | L | 1–2 |
| 1937 | 17/11 | Middlesbrough | W | 2–1 |
| 1938 | 22/10 | Cardiff | L | 2–4 |
| 1946 | 13/11 | Manchester | W | 3–0 |
| 1947 | 18/10 | Cardiff | W | 3–0 |
| 1948 | 10/11 | Aston Villa | W | 1–0 |
| 1949 | 15/10 | Cardiff *wcq* | W | 4–1 |
| 1950 | 15/11 | Sunderland | W | 4–2 |
| 1951 | 20/10 | Cardiff | D | 1–1 |
| 1952 | 12/11 | Wembley | W | 5–2 |
| 1953 | 10/10 | Cardiff *wcq* | W | 4–1 |
| 1954 | 10/11 | Wembley | W | 3–2 |
| 1955 | 22/10 | Cardiff | L | 1–2 |
| 1956 | 14/11 | Wembley | W | 3–1 |
| 1957 | 19/10 | Cardiff | W | 4–0 |
| 1958 | 26/11 | Aston Villa | D | 2–2 |
| 1959 | 17/10 | Cardiff | D | 1–1 |
| 1960 | 23/11 | Wembley | W | 5–1 |
| 1961 | 14/10 | Cardiff | D | 1–1 |
| 1962 | 21/11 | Wembley | W | 4–0 |
| 1963 | 12/10 | Cardiff | W | 4–0 |
| 1964 | 18/11 | Wembley | W | 2–1 |
| 1965 | 2/10 | Cardiff | D | 0–0 |
| 1966 | 16/11 | Wembley *ECQ* | W | 5–1 |
| 1967 | 21/10 | Cardiff *ECQ* | W | 3–0 |
| 1969 | 7/5 | Wembley | W | 2–1 |
| 1970 | 8/4 | Cardiff | D | 1–1 |
| 1971 | 19/5 | Wembley | D | 0–0 |
| 1972 | 20/5 | Cardiff | W | 3–0 |
| 1972 | 15/11 | Cardiff *wcq* | W | 1–0 |
| 1973 | 24/1 | Wembley *wcq* | D | 1–1 |
| 1973 | 15/5 | Wembley | W | 3–0 |
| 1974 | 11/5 | Cardiff | W | 2–0 |
| 1975 | 21/5 | Wembley | D | 2–2 |
| 1976 | 24/3 | Wrexham | W | 2–1 |
| 1976 | 8/5 | Cardiff | W | 1–0 |
| 1977 | 31/5 | Wembley | L | 0–1 |
| 1978 | 3/5 | Cardiff | W | 3–1 |
| 1979 | 23/5 | Wembley | D | 0–0 |
| 1980 | 17/5 | Wrexham | L | 1–4 |
| 1981 | 20/5 | Wembley | D | 0–0 |
| 1982 | 27/4 | Cardiff | W | 1–0 |
| 1983 | 23/2 | Wembley | W | 2–1 |
| 1984 | 2/5 | Wrexham | L | 0–1 |

**P97 W62 D21 L14 F239 A90**

## v Yugoslavia

| Year | Date | Venue | | Result |
|---|---|---|---|---|
| 1939 | 18/5 | Belgrade | L | 1–2 |
| 1950 | 22/11 | Highbury | D | 2–2 |
| 1954 | 16/5 | Belgrade | L | 0–1 |
| 1956 | 28/11 | Wembley | W | 3–0 |
| 1958 | 11/5 | Belgrade | L | 0–5 |
| 1960 | 11/5 | Wembley | D | 3–3 |
| 1965 | 9/5 | Belgrade | D | 1–1 |
| 1966 | 4/5 | Wembley | W | 2–0 |
| 1968 | 5/6 | Florence *ECF* | L | 0–1 |
| 1972 | 11/10 | Wembley | D | 1–1 |
| 1974 | 5/6 | Belgrade | D | 2–2 |
| 1986 | 12/11 | Wembley *ECQ* | W | 2–0 |
| 1987 | 11/11 | Belgrade *ECQ* | W | 4–1 |
| 1989 | 13/12 | Wembley | W | 2–1 |

**P14 W5 D5 L4 F23 A20**

# INDEX

Bold entries indicate main profile. italic entires indicate picture